America's
First
Woman
Lawyer

America's First Woman Lawyer

The Biography of Myra Bradwell

Jane M. Friedman

Prometheus Books • Buffalo, New York

Published 1993 by Prometheus Books

97 96 95 94 93   5 4 3 2 1

Library of Congress Cataloging-in-Publication Data

Friedman, Jane M.
    America's first woman lawyer : the biography of Myra Bradwell / by Jane M.
Friedman.
        p.   cm   .
    Includes bibliographical references and index.
    ISBN 0-87975-809-0 (cloth : acid-free paper)
    1. Bradwell, Myra, 1831–1894. 2. Women lawyers—Illinois—Biography.
3. Women's rights—United States—History. I. Title.
KF368.B712F75   1993
349.73′092—dc20
[B]
[347.30092]
[B]   92-9206
                                                                                          CIP

Printed in the United States of America on acid-free paper.

Dedication

This book is dedicated to the memory of my family:

My father, Harry Goldbarg
My mother, Pearl Goldbarg
My brother, Edward Goldbarg

Contents

8   CONTENTS

Acknowledgments

This book has been in process for several years. When I first explored the possibility of writing Myra Bradwell's biography, Eileen Kerr, then a law student at Wayne State University, helped me pore through all thirteen hundred issues of the *Chicago Legal News*. It was no small feat, and one which served as the catalyst for my decision to complete this work. After I completed the first few chapters, Professor Sandra VanBurkleo of the Wayne State University history department critiqued them. Her comments were of inestimable value. My thanks also to Mary Eilers, who typed a large portion of this manuscript, and to Professor Beth Eisler, my "dresser."

More recently, I received assistance from two Wayne State librarians, M. Christine Chamness, who prepared the book's index, and Heather Simmons, whose back-up support was invaluable. Also, Phyllis Baker, who was then a student assistant at the Wayne State Law Library, helped me put my endnotes "in shape," again no small accomplishment given the time constraints under which we were working. And, of course, my thanks to my editor at Prometheus Books, Mary Read, who made many helpful suggestions and who labored arduously to ensure that the book went to press as scheduled.

Moreover, during the six months before this book appeared in print, I received a great deal of personal encouragement from friends too numerous to list. I would, however, like to name a few. Three are professional colleagues at Wayne State: Professors Mae Kuykendall, Stephen Schulman, and Robert Sedler. In addition, I received much support and succor from persons in Ann Arbor, Michigan, where I reside, most notably, Adrienne Kaplan and Dr. Alan Krohn. To those at Wayne State and to those in Ann Arbor, I will remain eternally grateful.

Prologue

"Myra Who?"

Their responses were inevitable and almost uniform. "Myra who?" queried my friends and many of my colleagues whenever I mentioned that I was writing this biography. Unfortunately, the name of Myra Bradwell is recognized by virtually no one, except for historians of women and some teachers and students of constitutional law. However, during Myra Bradwell's lifetime (1831–94), her fame was widespread. Upon her death, one legal commentator characterized her as "one of the most remarkable women of her generation and one who had no small share in making that generation what it is."[1]

As America's "first" woman lawyer[2] and also as publisher and editor-in-chief of an extremely prestigious and widely circulated legal newspaper, Myra Bradwell did more to create rights for women and other legally handicapped persons than did any other woman of her day, or perhaps any day. Yet the names of many of her female contemporaries are known to all, while Myra Bradwell has, sadly, been consigned to obscurity.

I first learned of Myra Bradwell two decades ago. I was teaching a course in constitutional law at Wayne State University and decided to expand the unit on gender-based discrimination to include materials not then covered in the textbook. A colleague, Edward Wise, handed me the United States Supreme Court's opinion in *Bradwell* v. *Illinois* (1873), the case in which the Court upheld the right of the state of Illinois to exclude Bradwell from the practice of law solely because she was a woman. In a sonorous voice, I read to my class from Justice Bradley's concurring opinion:

The natural and proper timidity and delicacy which belongs to the female sex evidently unfits it for many of the occupations of civil life. The constitution of the family organization which is founded in the *divine ordinances* as well

11

as in the nature of things indicates the domestic sphere as that which properly belongs to the domain and functions of womanhood. The harmony, not to say identity of interests and views which belongs, or should belong, to the family institution is repugnant to the idea of a woman adopting a distinct and independent career from that of her husband. . . . The paramount destiny and mission of woman are to fulfill the noble and benign offices of wife and mother. *This is the Law of the Creator.*[3]

I repeated my theatrical presentation for several years, and a good laugh was usually had by all. Eventually I began pursuing other interests and dropped the constitutional law course from my teaching curriculum. But I couldn't drop the matter of Myra Bradwell from my mind. What had become of her? Did she ever become a lawyer, or did she simply shrivel up and go back to the kitchen?

My initial investigation of the matter was frustrating. A check of the card catalogues at university libraries, law libraries, public libraries, and even the Library of Congress revealed nothing relating to Myra Bradwell. Biographical dictionaries yielded little that was noteworthy, except that she had been the editor of a newspaper called the *Chicago Legal News*, a fact that I glossed over much too lightly. I surmised that Justice Bradley had had the last word and that Myra Bradwell must have, in large measure, resigned herself to "fulfilling the paramount destiny and mission of woman." Believing that further pursuit of the elusive Myra Bradwell would be futile, I abandoned the project.

Several years later, while browsing in a law library, I stumbled upon a complete set of the bound volumes of the *Chicago Legal News*. I picked up the dusty volume, expecting to find merely synopses of court opinions and news of happenings in the Chicago legal community during the latter part of the nineteenth century. To my great surprise and pleasure, I found much more! The *Chicago Legal News* was Myra Bradwell's alter ego. In her capacity as both publisher and editor-in-chief of that weekly journal for twenty-five years, she advocated, drafted, and secured the enactment of myriad legal reforms in the areas of women's rights, child custody, improvement of the legal system, and treatment of persons alleged to be "insane." In all, she edited thirteen hundred issues of the newspaper, and each of those issues was replete with her personal opinions on countless legal and social subjects, as well as her frequent exhortations to the legislature, judiciary, governor, and members of the bar. Her influence was felt far beyond the boundaries of Illinois. Indeed, for at least two decades, the *Chicago Legal News* was the most widely circulated legal newspaper in the country. Many of Bradwell's proposals, after being enacted by the Illinois legislature, served as prototypes for legislation in other jurisdictions.

After reading the thirteen hundred issues of the *Chicago Legal News,* I became convinced that Myra Bradwell had to be resurrected from oblivion.

I believed that, even if no other Bradwell materials existed, someone needed to tell the story of this remarkable lawyer and legal journalist who changed the course of nineteenth-century legal and social history. But I was also quite certain that there were other Bradwell documents in existence. Anyone as facile with a pen as Bradwell, I reasoned, must have corresponded with other luminaries of the day. For example, I knew (from reading the *Chicago Legal News*) that Myra was a prominent figure in the "woman suffrage"[4] movement and was well-acquainted with Susan B. Anthony. I concluded that there must have been correspondence between them. Moreover, because the *Chicago Legal News* contained many references to Mary Todd Lincoln, I subsequently read several biographies of Mrs. Lincoln. From those, I learned that Bradwell had secured the release of Mrs. Lincoln from an insane asylum. Had the two women corresponded?

I pored through various bibliographies of manuscript collections and found virtually nothing. A telephone call to the Myra Bradwell public elementary school in Chicago revealed that that institution had no materials relating to the school's namesake. "In fact," said the librarian, "I don't even know who Myra Bradwell was." My calls to the Chicago Historical Society and the Illinois State Historical Library were also disappointing. At both institutions, courteous but discouraging librarians told me that there simply was no substantial body of Myra Bradwell papers available anywhere, only a few documents, and nothing of any significance. I was also informed that several historians and at least one journalist had previously explored the possibility of writing a biography of Bradwell. All had abandoned their efforts after concluding, erroneously, that there was no collection of materials upon which to base such a book.

The librarian from the Chicago Historical Society did send me the few Bradwell materials which he possessed. Indeed, it was a scant collection. There was, however, one item that rekindled my hope: a handwritten letter dated July 1931, from Bradwell's granddaughter, Myra Bradwell Helmer Pritchard, to Herma Clark of the Chicago Historical Society. In it the granddaughter stated: "[Myra Bradwell was] a firm believer in woman suffrage and received many letters from Susan B. Anthony and Mary Livermore which I have." Myra Pritchard also spoke of her grandmother's friendship with Mary Todd Lincoln and stated that she (the granddaughter) was in possession of a "wealth of valuable letters, documents, Lincoln relics, etc."

"Eureka!" I cried. "Myra Bradwell materials do exist, or at least they existed in 1931. But how does one go about finding them?" The only clue, and a slim one at that, was in a sentence in a postscript to the granddaughter's letter: "I moved away from Chicago in 1915 when I married Dr. Stuart Pritchard who is the Medical Director of the W. K. Kellogg Foundation [in Battle Creek, Michigan]."

The Kellogg Foundation, then, was my only remaining hope. I realized that Bradwell's granddaughter and her husband must have died several decades ago; but perhaps they left descendants, and (hope springs eternal) perhaps those descendants possessed the missing Bradwell documents.

I called the Kellogg Foundation and spoke with a person in the public relations department. When I explained that I needed some information about their former medical director, Dr. Stuart Pritchard, I was informed that he had died in the 1940s. "Are there any surviving relatives?" I asked, crossing my fingers and toes simultaneously. "As a matter of fact," the man replied, "we had a black-tie dinner here last year, honoring the memory of Dr. Pritchard, and a man showed up who said that he was Dr. Pritchard's cousin. His name is James Gordon, and he lives in Middleville, Michigan."

I thanked the man from the Kellogg Foundation profusely and immediately called Mr. Gordon. When I explained to him that I was writing a biography of Myra Bradwell, his response, predictably, was "Myra who?" But when I mentioned the name of Bradwell's granddaughter, Myra Pritchard, Mr. Gordon's voice telegraphed immediate recognition. He explained that Myra Pritchard and her husband, Dr. Stuart Pritchard, had not had children and that he (Mr. Gordon), although a distant cousin of Dr. Pritchard, was the ultimate beneficiary of the estates of both Dr. and Myra Pritchard. He was aware that Myra Pritchard had had a famous grandmother, but he didn't think that he possessed any of the grandmother's documents. "But I'm a history buff," he said, closing our conversation, "so I'll check all my files, including tons of Kellogg Foundation files, and see if I can find anything. In any event, I'll get back to you."

A month passed, and then another. Not wanting to be a pest, but clinging tenaciously to the hope that the missing documents had devolved to Mr. Gordon, I called him once again. His tone was apologetic. "There doesn't seem to be anything relating to Myra Bradwell," he lamented. "But if you ever happen to be in Middleville, you are welcome to look through my files." Of course, I knew that I would never simply "happen to be in Middleville." I didn't even know where the place was. In fact, it sounded like a fictitious city in a Sinclair Lewis novel. Nonetheless, I made an appointment to visit Mr. Gordon at his home.

It was a scorching day in late August when my research assistant, Eileen Kerr, and I made the three-hour trip from Ann Arbor, Michigan, to Middleville. "I know that I've taken you through some blind alleys," I said, "but how do you feel about one hundred fifty miles of blind highways?" "I've chased wild geese before," was her only reply.

But the geese were not wild and the highways were not blind. What we discovered at Mr. Gordon's home gave us not only cause to rejoice but also reason to despair that Myra Bradwell's granddaughter had had so little sense of history.

When Myra Bradwell died, her personal papers devolved to her daughter, Bessie Bradwell Helmer, a brilliant woman who had graduated as valedictorian of her class at Northwestern Law School. When Bessie died, those papers were bequeathed to Bessie's daughter, Myra Bradwell Helmer Pritchard. Unfortunately, the granddaughter had stored Myra Bradwell's papers in a manner that rendered them virtually undiscoverable.

When I arrived at Mr. Gordon's home and began combing through his files, I immediately noticed a large number of sealed envelopes. Most were unlabeled and simply bore the return address of the Battle Creek Saddle and Hunt Club. I asked for and obtained Mr. Gordon's permission to open the envelopes. I unsealed the first, and out fell six letters written to Myra Bradwell by Susan B. Anthony. I opened a second, and discovered about twenty documents which, when pieced together, described the contents of the correspondence between Myra Bradwell and Mary Todd Lincoln and explained why and how Bradwell's granddaughter had sold those letters to the attorneys for the estate of Lincoln's son Robert. Those documents, together with several clippings from Chicago newspapers, also explained the ingenious strategy that Myra had employed in securing Mrs. Lincoln's release from an "insane asylum."

Scores of other Bradwell documents, too numerous to list, had also found their way into the sealed envelopes of the Battle Creek Saddle and Hunt Club and were almost lost to posterity.

My personal saga ends here, and the chronicle of Myra Bradwell's tribulations and triumphs begins.

NOTES

1. "Death of Mrs. Myra Bradwell," 28 *American Law Review* 278 (1894).

2. Technically, Myra Bradwell was not the first American woman to pass a state bar examination. That honor belonged to Arabella Mansfield, who passed the Iowa bar exam six weeks before Bradwell passed the examination in Illinois.

Mansfield, however, never practiced law, nor was she ever involved in the legal profession in any way. Her admission to the bar was simply part of a plan devised by Francis Springer, an Iowa judge who was dedicated to the cause of advancing the equality of women. After being admitted to the Iowa bar, Arabella Mansfield continued her previous career of teaching English and history at Ohio Wesleyan and DePauw Universities. *Notable American Women, 1607–1950, A Biographical Dictionary* (Cambridge, Mass.: Belknap Press of Harvard University Press, 1971) (entry on Arabella Mansfield).

3. *Bradwell* v. *Illinois* 16 Wall 130 (1873).

4. During the nineteenth and early twentieth centuries, the struggle for women's suffrage was known as the "woman suffrage" movement. Hence, the term "woman suffrage" will be used throughout the remainder of this book.

1

On Defying the Creator and Becoming a Lawyer

This lady, in pondering the additions made to the Constitution of the United States under the 13th, 14th and 15th Amendments, came to the conclusion . . . [which was] interesting in showing the effect produced by legal study on the female mind. Mrs. Bradwell, having applied to the Supreme Court of Illinois for a license as a practicing lawyer, was refused her petition, on the ground that . . . only men could be lawyers. She immediately appealed her case to the Supreme Court at Washington. . . . It is a rather ludicrous illustration of the character of the woman movement, that a prominent female agitator should have seized the opportunity to prove the fitness of her sex for professional life by taking for her first important case one which she must have known the court would decide against her, unless she either supposed that they were likely to be influenced by personal solicitation and clamor, or else that they were all gone crazy.

—*The Nation* (April 1873)[1]

Her primary goal was to be helpful to her husband at his law office. But seven men decreed that she could not. Because those seven were all members of the Illinois Supreme Court, Myra Bradwell was officially barred from the bar.

During the latter part of the nineteenth century, there were two avenues of entry into the legal profession. One could either take a formal course of study at a law school or serve as an apprentice at the office of a practicing lawyer. Many prospective lawyers chose the latter alternative. Among them was Myra Bradwell.

17

Myra's training began informally in 1852, the year of her marriage to James Bradwell, a struggling young law student who was financing his legal apprenticeship by working as a manual laborer. Given the absorptive qualities of Myra's mind, it is probable that much of her early learning took place through the process of osmosis. A few years later, however, after James had been admitted to the practice of law in both Tennessee and Illinois, Myra began a more intensive apprenticeship with her husband. It was then that she became "determined to read [law] in good earnest" so that she and James could "work side by side and think side by side."[2] Her studies, however, were interrupted by several events: the birth of four children (two of whom died in early childhood) and countless civic activities organized all over the North to aid the sick and wounded soldiers of the Civil War.

Finally, on August 2, 1869, Myra Bradwell at the age of thirty-eight, amid predictions that she would "wreck [her] family and break [her] hearthstone to smithereens,"[3] passed the Illinois bar exam with high honors and made a formal application to practice law in Illinois. That she chose this moment to do so was probably due to a confluence of three factors.

First, her two surviving children, aged thirteen and eleven no longer needed constant attention. Second, her husband had decided not to run for reelection as judge. He was returning to a busy practice and was in need of her assistance in doing research and preparing briefs. Third, prior to the summer of 1869, there was little hope that a woman would be permitted to practice law anywhere in the United States. However, on June 15 of that year, six weeks before Bradwell passed the bar exam in Illinois, another midwestern state, Iowa, quietly opened the gates of the legal profession to a young married woman, Arabella Mansfield. Mansfield was a teacher of English and history who had no intention of practicing law and who had no subsequent contact with the legal profession. Her admission to the bar was simply part of a plan devised by an Iowa judge, Francis Springer, who was dedicated to promoting the equality of women.[4]

While Mansfield's admission to the Iowa bar met with some adverse reaction in Canada,[5] it went virtually unnoticed in the United States. Thus, Myra might have reasoned, if there were no gender-based obstacles to Mansfield's admission in Iowa, there should be none to Bradwell's in Illinois.

Myra, however, must have realized that others did not see it that way, for her application was accompanied not only by a document certifying that she had passed the bar examination, but also by a brief in which she stated: "The only question involved in this case is—Does being a woman disqualify [me] under the law of Illinois from receiving a license to practice law?"[6]

The Illinois Supreme Court promptly denied her petition, a decision that probably came as no surprise to either Myra or other interested observers. What jolted many were the grounds upon which the court's denial rested. Myra Bradwell was rejected from the legal profession *not* on the grounds that she was a woman, but because she was a *married* woman. Exactly two months after her stellar performance on the bar examination, she received the following communication from the reporter for the Illinois Supreme Court:

> Madam: The court instructs me to inform you that they are compelled to deny your application for a license to practice as an attorney-at-law in the courts of this State, upon the ground that you would not be bound by the [contractual] obligations necessary to be assumed where the relation of attorney and client shall exist, by reason of the DISABILITY IMPOSED BY YOUR MARRIED CONDITION—it being assumed that you are a married woman. . . . Until such DISABILITY shall be removed by legislation, the court regards itself as powerless to grant your application.[7]

The court's "marital disability" rationale was probably, in part, a pretext—a subterfuge by which the court could mask its antipathy tinged with anxiety over the notion of allowing any woman to mix and compete with the men of the bar. It is unclear whether this fear was premised on the belief that a female attorney would constantly wilt and thereby lose her cases by virtual default; or on the contrary, that she would win her cases either by verbal castration of her opponents or by unconscious seduction of the judges and all-male juries. Perhaps those two fears were undifferentiated in the minds of most; but the latter was explicitly expressed by contemporary male commentators. For example, one such man, writing in 1869, complained:

> But really, it is hardly fair to the rest of the profession . . . to permit a charming fair one to pit herself against a learned brother in argument before a jury of twelve men. The latter [i.e., the male attorney] would simply have no chance at all.[8]

On the other hand, the Illinois court's ruling that Myra could not practice law because of the "disability imposed by [her] married condition" was grounded at least in part on an ancient precedent, still somewhat viable in the nineteenth century—the law of "coverture." Coverture was simply a principle under which:

> by marriage the husband and wife are one person in law: that is, the very being or legal existence of the woman is suspended during the marriage, or at least is incorporated and consolidated into that of the husband; under whose wing, protection, and *cover,* she performs every thing; . . . her condition during her marriage is called coverture. . . . And therefore all deeds executed, and acts done by her, during her coverture are void; . . . .[9]

Thus, the doctrine of coverture, if still alive in Illinois in 1869, could have been a valid basis for the court's refusal to permit Myra to practice law. If that principle were applicable, Myra would not have been legally able to enter into contracts with or on behalf of her clients, a sine qua non for any legal practitioner.

Myra believed, however, that the principle of coverture was no longer viable; or, at the very least, that it had been so greatly whittled away by the courts that it no longer served as a bar to a woman's entry into the legal profession. She quickly filed a counterassault. In a detailed and scholarly brief, she cited countless Illinois statutes and cases under which married women's legal disabilities had been removed. In addition to statutory and judicial precedents, she included reports of recent admissions of women to both law schools and medical schools. She also cited the state of Iowa's granting a license to practice law to Arabella Mansfield; and she discussed the recent opening to women of other trades and occupations from which they had previously been barred.

She concluded her brief with the following exhortation:

> This honorable court can send me from its bar and prevent me from practicing
> as an attorney, and it is of small consequence; but if in so doing, [you base
> your decision on] . . . the disability imposed by [my] married condition, you,
> in my judgment in striking *me* down, strike a blow at the right of every
> married woman in the great State of Illinois who is dependent on her labor
> for support, and say to her, you can not enter the smallest contract in relation
> to your earnings or separate property, that can be enforced against you in
> a court of law.[10]

The Illinois Supreme Court was not obligated to respond to Myra's arguments. It had already rejected her application once, and had communicated its rejection and its ostensible rationale to her. The high court could simply have remained silent, or it could have formally ratified its previous denial by the use of just four words: "petition for reconsideration denied."

The Illinois Supreme Court must have known that it had been bested because it quickly issued a second opinion, once again unanimously denying her application for admission.[11] This time, however, the court gave a different reason: the obstacle to Myra Bradwell's admission to the bar was not that she was a *married* woman, but simply that she was a woman.

The court began by noting that its previous holding, which had been based on married women's disabilities, had been "earnestly and ably" contested by Myra. Moreover, "of the qualifications of the applicant we have no doubt. . . ." But, explained the court,

> After further consultation in regard to this application, we find ourselves
> constrained to hold that the *sex of the applicant,* independently of coverture
> is, as our law now stands, a sufficient reason for not granting this license.[12]

The court then buttressed its decision with a four-pronged rationale. First, the Illinois legislature had been silent on the issue of whether women could enter the profession. Therefore, concluded the court, the legislature must have intended that women should not be permitted to practice law.

The second reason given by the court was one which lawyers often call the "opening of the floodgates." The court reasoned that if it opened the doors of the legal profession to women then "every civil office in this state may be filled by women—that it . . . [would follow] that women should be made governors and sheriffs." The court stood aghast at its own speculation.

Third, the court was concerned that the "hot strifes of the bar" and the "momentous verdicts, the prizes of struggle [would] tend to destroy the deference and delicacy with which it is a matter of pride of our ruder sex to treat [women]. . . ."

Finally, echoing the anxieties of contemporary commentators, the court voiced concern over "what effect the presence of women as barristers in our courts would have upon the administration of justice."

Myra's response to the court's opinion was swift and curt:

> What the decision of the Supreme Court of the United States in the Dred Scott case was to the rights of the negroes as citizens of the U.S., this decision is to the political rights of women in Illinois—*annihilation*.[13] (Emphasis added)

Yet, Myra had the amazing ability to separate her professional and political goals from her relationships with the men who had attempted to "annihilate" those goals. For example, sitting on the Illinois Supreme Court, which had twice ruled unanimously against her, was Justice Sidney Breeze, a friend of Myra's with whom she frequently corresponded and socialized.[14] Even in the wake of Breeze's adverse ruling in Myra's case, their friendship remained unscathed. Moreover, ten years after the Illinois Supreme Court had decided her case, three of the justices who had ruled against her were still on that court and were seeking reelection. Myra endorsed all three of them. In an article in the *Chicago Legal News* (a newspaper that she published and edited)[15] she stated: "There is not a single judge on the Supreme bench who ought not to be re-elected."[16]

Perhaps Myra's continuing friendship with Sidney Breeze and her subsequent endorsement of the other three justices were merely ploys and parts of a strategy to secure the good will of the court while she tenaciously maneuvered to secure legal rights for women and other legally handicapped persons.

Although Myra continued to have cordial relations with members of the highest court of Illinois, she did not hesitate to appeal that court's decision to the United States Supreme Court, retaining as her attorney Senator Matthew H. Carpenter of Wisconsin, one of the country's ablest constitutional lawyers.

Indeed, Justice Miller of the U.S. Supreme Court (who subsequently authored the majority opinion in Myra's case) had declared that Carpenter was the only person of his acquaintance whom he could honestly call a "man of genius."[17] And the *Philadelphia Times* had exclaimed that "no genius so steady, no intellect so sustained" had appeared in American life since Hamilton and Jefferson.[18]

Matthew Carpenter was not only an outstanding constitutional lawyer, he was also a staunch advocate of equal rights for women. In 1870 he had publicly vowed to Elizabeth Cady Stanton that he would fight for women's suffrage in the Senate. Later, in 1874, he pleaded for the remission of a fine that had been slapped on Susan B. Anthony for her audacity in attempting to vote in the presidential election of 1872.[19]

In preparing and arguing Myra's case before the U.S. Supreme Court, Carpenter became intensely involved. Indeed, he seems to have made her cause his own, refusing to accept a fee or even to allow Myra to defray his out-of-pocket expenses.[20]

As Carpenter began to prepare his case, he immediately realized that the greatest *political* obstacle to a favorable judicial decision was the widespread fear that if women were declared constitutionally entitled to practice law, it might follow, as night to day, that they were also constitutionally entitled to vote, even in the absence of a woman's suffrage amendment to the U.S. Constitution.

Carpenter realized that the specter of nationwide woman's suffrage was far more terrifying to the populace than was the threat of women being admitted to the bar. The prospect of women casting the ballot, which was both a symbol and an instrument of independence, was troublesome to every man who feared his wife's (sister's, daughter's, etc.) partial freedom from male control. That idea was terrifying to many nineteenth-century women as well. The prospect of women practicing law, however, was a direct threat to only a select few, the gentlemen of the bar and those few men whose wives or female relatives might wish to enter the profession.

Carpenter thus took great pains to distinguish Myra's constitutional right to practice law from the "establishment of the right of female suffrage, which, it is assumed, would overthrow Christianity, defeat the ends of modern civilization, and upturn the world."[21] He argued with force that women had no constitutional right to vote unless and until a suffrage amendment was passed.[22] This position probably caused him great discomfort, as he had always advocated the cause of woman suffrage. But his first duty was to his client, and he must have believed that the only road to victory was to persuade the Court that a decision favorable to Myra would not, in any way, serve as a precedent requiring the Court to hold that women also had the constitutional right to vote. Not surprisingly, Carpenter's position in Bradwell's case infuriated many suffragists, particularly Susan B. Anthony, who wrote indignantly to Myra:

Carpenter's argument was such a school boy pettifogging speech—wholly without a basic principle—but still the courts are so entirely controlled by prejudice and precedent we have nothing to hope from them but endorsement of dead men's actions.[23]

Susan B. Anthony must have been as furious with Myra as she was with Myra's attorney. After all, it was Myra who had retained Carpenter. Moreover, Myra was both legally trained and politically astute. She obviously understood Carpenter's "school boy pettifogging speech" very well, yet she permitted him to argue in the United States Supreme Court that unless and until a suffrage amendment were passed, women had no constitutional right to vote.

Anthony's letter to Myra presaged a twenty-year relationship of ambivalence between these two feminists, a relationship characterized by both conflict and conciliation. The connection between these two remarkable nineteenth-century women will be explored in chapter 9, which describes Myra's contribution to the woman suffrage movement.

While Anthony's ire was understandable, her assertion that Carpenter's legal argument (relating to women's right to vote) was "wholly without a basic principle" was simply untenable. The major portion of Carpenter's argument was based on the distinction between the political desirability of granting the ballot to women and the constitutional necessity of doing so. His point was that while in the absence of a suffrage amendment the states were not *constitutionally required* to permit women to vote, it would be *socially beneficial* for Congress or the state legislatures to enfranchise the female population. That principle (i.e., that something can be socially desirable but not mandated by the U.S. Constitution) is certainly axiomatic in our American constitutional system.

Carpenter, attempting to accomplish the antithetical goals of winning Myra's case and yet appeasing the suffragists, made the "constitutional necessity–social desirability" distinction very explicitly: "While I do not believe that female suffrage has been secured by the *existing* amendments to the Constitution, neither do I look upon that result as at all to be dreaded." Then in a discourse that was not even tangentially related to the legal issue involved in Myra's case (i.e., the constitutional right of women to practice law), he eloquently implored that society, through Congress or the legislatures, permit women to vote. His argument was that the status that a nation accords to women's rights is an important index of that nation's advance:

It is not, in my opinion, a question of woman's rights merely, but in a far greater degree a question of man's rights. . . . It will everywhere [in the world] be found that, just in proportion to the equality of women with men in the enjoyment of social and civil rights and privileges, both sexes are proportionately advanced in refinement and all that ennobles nature.[24]

He completed his political oration by once again explaining that while it would be desirable for Congress or the state legislatures to grant the ballot to women, they were not, in the absence of a woman suffrage amendment, constitutionally compelled to do so.

The remainder of Carpenter's brief in *Bradwell* v. *Illinois* was based on the argument that the U.S. Constitution *did affirmatively* grant women the legal right to practice law. That assertion was based on the Fourteenth Amendment's "Privileges and Immunities Clause," which provides that "No State shall make or enforce any law which shall abridge the privileges or immunities of citizens of the United States. . . ." Carpenter contended that since Myra was a "citizen of the United States," she had the "privilege" to practice her chosen profession and that that privilege could not be "abridged" by the states. That was the main point to be established, but Carpenter addressed it almost as an afterthought. His argument was based on neither precedent nor logic, and at best can be characterized as a mere assertion:

> I maintain that the Fourteenth Amendment opens to every citizen of the U.S., male or female, black or white, married or single, the honorable professions as well as the servile employments of life; and no citizen can be excluded from any one of them. Intelligence, integrity, and honor are the only qualifications that can be prescribed as conditions.[25]

In responding to the commonly held belief that most men would never retain the services of a female lawyer, Carpenter stated simply that that possibility should be governed by the marketplace, and not by governmental fiat:

> The inequalities of sex will undoubtedly have their influence, and be considered by every client desiring to employ counsel. . . . Of a bar composed of men and women of equal integrity and learning, women might be more or less frequently retained, as the taste or judgment of clients might dictate. But the broad shield of the Constitution is over them all, and protects each in that measure of success which his or her individual merits may secure.[26]

Although Myra exclaimed that Carpenter's argument was "concise and unanswerable,"[27] the State of Illinois did not take the matter the least bit seriously. Indeed, the state did not even deign to send counsel to oppose Carpenter in the Supreme Court.[28]

Moreover, during the pendency of her appeal, Myra was subjected to extreme harassment by her fellow citizens. "Her personal manners [were] outrageously aped; her speech falsely reported—while the idle curious followed her about the streets of Washington as if she were some wild animal from the jungle!"[29]

Not even the nation's highest tribunal was persuaded or even moved by

Myra's poignant plea: "One half of the citizens of the United States are asking—Is the liberty of pursuit of a profession ours, or are we slaves?"[30]

The Supreme Court apparently preferred the slavery option; it dismissed Myra's claim almost unanimously.[31] Justice Samuel F. Miller, speaking for eight members of the Court, wrote the majority opinion. Only Chief Justice Salmon P. Chase (a distant cousin of Myra) dissented.[32]

Justice Miller's majority opinion was straightforward and was not grounded on notions about the proper role of women. Justice Miller merely cited a precedent that the Court had decided only two days earlier by a vote of five to four.

In that decision, known as the *Slaughterhouse Cases,*[33] the state of Louisiana had granted a twenty-five-year monopoly to a corporation to maintain slaughterhouses in large portions of the state. The plaintiffs, butchers not included in the monopoly, claimed that the law deprived them of the right "to exercise their trade" and therefore violated the Fourteenth Amendment by abridging "the Privileges and Immunities of Citizens of the United States."

In the *Slaughterhouse Cases,* the Supreme Court, per Justice Miller, sustained the Louisiana law and held, among other things, that the butchers' exclusion from the state-created monopoly did not violate the Privileges and Immunities Clause of the Fourteenth Amendment. Ironically, the attorney who had argued on behalf of the state of Louisiana, *and against the excluded butchers,* was none other than Matthew Carpenter.

After disposing of the butchers who had been deprived of the right to practice their trade, it was not difficult for Justice Miller and four of his brethren to dispose of Myra. They held only that:

> [T]here are privileges and immunities belonging to citizens of the United States . . . and it is these and these alone which a State is forbidden to abridge. But the right to admission to practice in the courts of a State is not one of them.[34]

But dismissing Myra's claim was not so easy a task for those justices, including Justice Joseph P. Bradley, who had dissented in the *Slaughterhouse Cases,* and who had there pronounced that "among [the privileges and immunities of national citizenship] must be placed the right to pursue a lawful employment in a lawful manner, without other restraint than such as equally affects all persons." Moreover, Justice Bradley had previously declared that "there is no more *sacred right* of citizenship than the right to pursue unmolested a lawful employment in a lawful manner. . . ."[35] How then was Justice Bradley able to deny Myra one of the "sacred rights of citizenship?" The answer is that he did not, for Myra was a woman; therefore (according to the justice), her sacred rights of citizenship were not coextensive with those enjoyed by men. The fallacy underlying Myra's claim, noted Justice Bradley, was that it "assumes that it is one of the privileges and immunities of *women* as citizens to engage in any and every profession, occupation, or employment of civil life." That assumption, he claimed was erroneous.

Bradley then concluded his opinion with an exegesis on the meaning of natural law:

> The civil law, as well as nature herself, has always recognized a wide difference in the respective spheres and destinies of man and woman. Man is, or should be, woman's protector and defender. The natural and proper timidity and delicacy which belongs to the female sex evidently unfits it for many of the occupations of civil life. The constitution of the family organization which is founded in the *divine ordinances* as well as in the nature of things indicates the domestic sphere as that which properly belongs to the domain and functions of womanhood. The harmony, not to say identity of interests and views which belong, or should belong, to the family institution is repugnant to the idea of a woman adopting a distinct and independent career from that of her husband. . . . The paramount destiny and mission of woman are to fulfill the noble and benign offices of wife and mother. *This is the law of the Creator.*[36]

Although Justices Miller and Bradley had both decided the case adversely to Myra, they had reached their results through very different modes of reasoning. Justice Miller had simply construed a provision of the Constitution, and his construction was totally consistent with his earlier decision in which he had dismissed the claim of a group of butchers who had been denied the right to practice their trade. Justice Bradley, on the other hand, had based his concurrence on the distinction between male and female roles, a distinction that he believed was ordained by God and probably handed down at Mount Sinai as part of ecclesiastical law. While Myra was enraged by Justice Bradley's opinion, her reaction to Justice Miller was one of praise. Although she did not agree with the result that he had reached, she took

> great pleasure in saying that the opinion delivered by Justice Miller is confined strictly to the points at issue . . . he does not for a moment lower the dignity of the judge by traveling out of the record to give his individual views upon what we commonly term "women's rights."[37]

In contrast, Myra's contempt for Justice Bradley's concurring opinion was boundless:

> We regard the opinion of Judge Bradley as in conflict with his opinion delivered in what are known as the . . . Slaughterhouse Cases. . . . In that case Judge Bradley said: "*There is no more sacred right of citizenship than the right*

to pursue unmolested a lawful employment in a lawful manner. It is nothing more or less than the sacred right of labor."

. . . How can he, then, and be consistent, deprive an American citizen of the right to follow any calling or profession . . . simply because such citizen is a woman?[38]

The reaction of prominent feminists to the Supreme Court's *Bradwell* opinion was somewhat ambivalent. While they espoused the belief that the Court's opinion was regrettable, they hoped to derive political capital from the Court's nearly unanimous rejection of someone of Myra's stature. For example, shortly after the Court rendered its decision, Myra received the following letter from Susan B. Anthony:

My dear Mrs. Bradwell:

    Like the Frenchman who didn't swear on a certain occasion—so I don't— simply because no swearing could possibly reach the case. I am fired to White heat. Do send me all *you* say in the [*Chicago Legal*] *News* on the decision and do put all *your lawyer's brain* to it. Write me the best letter you possibly can for me to read at our . . . May meeting in New York. Don't fail—I pray you. . . . Just don't fail to send me everything. Our convention will pour hot shot into that old Court.

                               Susan B. Anthony[39]

Although Miss Anthony and other feminists may have wished to "pour hot shot into that old Court," most nineteenth-century commentators were simply amused. Although lawyers and journalists alike had great respect for "our Myra's remarkable attainments,"[40] her earnest and tenacious attempt to become a lawyer was commonly treated as whimsical.[41] For example, the *New York World,* in listing the "follies" that were currently seeking protection under the Fourteenth Amendment, included the "preposterous" claim of a Chicago "she-attorney" that the amendment granted her the right to practice law.[42] Likewise, the *Nation* called Myra's constitutional claim "ridiculous" and "interesting as showing the effect produced by legal study on the female mind." It concluded by surmising that Myra "must have known the Court would decide against her, unless she either supposed that they were likely to be influenced by personal solicitation and clamor, or else that they were all gone crazy."[43]

Among the news media, the *Rockford Register* and the *St. Louis Republican* seem to have stood virtually alone in condemning the state of Illinois and the U.S. Supreme Court for their combined rejection of Myra's application. The St. Louis newspaper lamented:

It seems very hard for some of the Republican States to learn a simple lesson in that liberality which they pretend to teach to others. . . . The Republicans of Illinois appear to have the same horror of a woman that an old-fashioned Democrat once had of a negro.[44]

Similarly, the *Rockford Register,* after referring to the Illinois Supreme Court's rejection of "Mrs. Myra Bradwell, the gifted and accomplished editress of the *Chicago Legal News,*" bemoaned:

So it seems there may be brothers, but not sisters in law. . . . Whatever may be thought otherwise, the spirit and movements of the age are for a rational equality, and nothing—not even the Supreme Courts—can stay the progress or prevent the triumph of just and liberal sentiments. . . .[45]

Those words were prophetic, for neither the Illinois Supreme Court nor the U.S. Supreme Court was, in fact, able to "stay the progress or prevent the triumph" of Myra and a few other female pioneers of the law. Indeed, in 1872, one year prior to the U.S. Supreme Court's *Bradwell* decision, the Illinois legislature had passed a law providing that "No person shall be precluded or debarred from any occupation, profession, or employment (except military) on account of sex."[46] The statute had been codrafted by Myra and Alta M. Hulett,[47] a young woman of remarkable ability, whose application to practice law had been rejected by the Illinois Supreme Court in 1871. Buttressed by Myra's tutelage and encouragement, and granted permission by the newly enacted Illinois statute, Miss Hulett was subsequently admitted to the Illinois bar in 1873, at the age of nineteen. Even though mandated by statute, Miss Hulett's admission was accompanied by a scolding from one of the justices who admitted her: "If you were my daughter, I would disinherit you!"[48]

Technically, then, the U.S. Supreme Court's 1873 *Bradwell* decision was somewhat moot as to Myra Bradwell. She could have successfully reapplied for admission in 1872 when Illinois no longer had any gender-based barriers to entry into the profession. But what Myra had sought by her appeal to the U.S. Supreme Court was not merely a ruling that would have permitted *her* to practice law, but rather a Supreme Court fiat to the effect that nowhere in the nation could any woman be barred from practicing the profession of her choice.

Thus, Myra lost her Supreme Court battle; but she had already won the war for legislative creation of new professional opportunities for women. As she remarked a few weeks after her "defeat" in the high Court:

Although we have not succeeded in obtaining an opinion as we hoped, which should affect the rights of women throughout the nation, we are more than compensated for all our trouble in seeing, as the result of the agitation, statutes passed in several States, including our own, admitting women upon the same terms as men. Women have since been admitted in Wyoming, Utah, the District of Columbia, Iowa, Missouri, Ohio and several other States.[49]

Myra never again sought entry into the legal profession, although if she had her admission would almost certainly have been a mere formality. But she was a proud woman and she might have believed that it was beneath her dignity to reapply for a license.[50] Moreover, by 1873, the year in which the Supreme Court delivered the *Bradwell* opinion, Myra had already achieved extraordinary success as a legal journalist. As she later explained to a reporter for the *Chicago Tribune:*

> My business had acquired such dimensions by the time the barriers to my admittance to the Bar were removed that I had no time to give to law practice, and I didn't care to be admitted just for the privilege of putting "Attorney" after my name.[51]

The "business" to which she was referring was the *Chicago Legal News,* which Myra founded in 1868, and which for at least two decades was the most widely circulated legal newspaper in the nation. For the remaining twenty-six years of Myra's life, the *Chicago Legal News* was, in essence, her alter ego. She served not only as the journal's publisher and business manager, but also, and more importantly, as its editor-in-chief. In the masthead of the weekly newspaper, Myra inserted the motto Lex Vincit ("Law Conquers") and announced her intention "to do all we can to make it a paper that every lawyer and business man in the Northwest ought to take."[52] The paper was an instant success, not only in the Northwest, but throughout the entire country.

The *Chicago Legal News* was, in part, a conventional legal newspaper, offering synopses of important judicial opinions and news of happenings in the Chicago legal community. But its more important function was to serve as the medium through which Myra advocated and obtained the enactment of a vast number of legal reforms. Among those was the Illinois statute which prohibited the state from denying any woman the right to practice any profession or occupation solely on the basis of her gender.[53] She also drafted and was instrumental in obtaining the passage of legislation granting many other legal rights for women.[54] However, she did not confine her energies strictly to the cause of feminism. Many significant nineteenth-century innovations, including those involving the reform of the legal system[55] and the treatment of the "insane"[56] are directly traceable to Myra's advocacy.

It was through her columns in the *Chicago Legal News*—which also contained frequent exhortations to the bar and judiciary—that Myra achieved her reputation as the country's first and leading woman lawyer.[57] Myra was, indeed, practicing law, albeit without a license. Her daily tasks were those of an extremely productive and influential attorney: the drafting not only of social legislation but also of editorial pleas to various courts throughout the country. The latter writings bore a striking resemblance to legal briefs.

In 1890 the *Chicago Legal News* proudly announced to its readers:

> We are pleased to say that last week, upon the original record, every member of the Supreme Court of Illinois, cordially acquiesced in granting, on the court's own motion, a license as an attorney and counselor at law to Mrs. Bradwell.[58]

In 1892 the United States Supreme Court followed suit. On the motion of William Henry Harrison Miller, Attorney General of the United States, Myra Bradwell was admitted to practice before the nation's highest tribunal.[59] Both licenses were granted *nunc pro tunc* ("now for then") as of the date of her original application in 1869, rendering Myra Bradwell the first woman lawyer in the state of Illinois and arguably—depending on how one defines "lawyer"— the first in the United States.

Prior commentators have referred to the actions of these two courts as "noble acts of justice."[60] However, recently discovered correspondence between Myra's husband, James, and the chief justice of the Illinois Supreme Court[61] reveals that Myra's belated admission was carefully orchestrated (without Myra's knowledge) by James. At the time, Myra was terminally ill with cancer; and her devoted husband wanted his dying wife to know that while it may not always be true that "the law conquers," Myra Bradwell had at last conquered the law.

Upon Myra's death in 1894, one of her eulogists proclaimed:

> Discussion of the Myra Bradwell case had the inevitable effect of letting sunlight through many cobwebbed windows. It is not so much by abstract reasoning as by visible examples that reformations come, and Mrs. Bradwell offered herself as a living example of the injustices of the law. [Myra Bradwell] was forbidden by law to practice law, [and that] was too much for the public conscience, tough as that conscience is.[62]

NOTES

1. "The Supreme Court Righting Itself," *The Nation* 16 (April 24, 1873): 280 (unsigned article).

2. Interview with Myra Bradwell, *Chicago Tribune* (May 12, 1889): 26, col. 1–2. See generally, Herman Kogan, "Myra Bradwell: Crusader at Law," *Chicago History* 3, no. 3 (Winter 1974–5): 132–40.

3. Interview with Myra Bradwell, *Chicago Tribune* (May 12, 1889): 26, col. 1–2.

4. See Prologue, endnote 2.

5. See, e.g., anonymous letter to *Canada Law Journal,* signed only "B.B.," reprinted in *Chicago Legal News* 2 (December 25, 1869): 100, col. 3–4. [The *Chicago Legal News* will hereafter be cited as *CLN.*]

6. Bradwell's application to the Illinois Supreme Court for a license to practice law. Reprinted in *CLN* 2 (February 5, 1870): 145, col. 1 .

7. Communication from N. L. Freeman, reporter for the Illinois Supreme Court (October 1869). Reprinted in *CLN* 2 (February 5, 1870): 145, col. 3.

8. Anonymous letter to *Canada Law Journal,* see note 5.

9. Sir William Blackstone, *Commentaries on the Law of England,* vol 1. (Oxford: Clarendon Press, 1765–1769; reprint: New York: Oceana, 1966), pp. 442–45. See also Norma Basch, *In the Eyes of the Law* (Ithaca, N.Y.: Cornell University Press, 1982).

10. Bradwell's "additional brief to the Illinois Supreme Court" reprinted in *CLN* 2 (February 5, 1870): 145, col. 3.

11. In re Bradwell, 55 Ill. 535 (1869).

12. Ibid.

13. *CLN* 2 (February 5, 1870): 146, col. 4.

14. Correspondence between Justice Sidney Breeze and Myra Bradwell, on file in Chicago Historical Library.

15. See text accompanying footnotes 52 through 57 *infra,* and also chapter 5.

16. *CLN* 11 (April 26, 1879): 259, col. 2. The three justices were Pinkney H. Walder, John M. Scott, and Benjamin R. Sheldon.

17. Charles Fairman, *Mr. Justice Miller and the Supreme Court 1862–1890* (Cambridge, Mass.: Harvard University Press, 1939), p. 116.

18. Edwin Bruce Thompson, *Matthew Hale Carpenter: Webster of the West* (Madison: State Historical Society of Wisconsin, 1954), p. 102.

19. Ibid., p. 292, footnote 39.

20. Interview with Myra Bradwell, *Chicago Tribune* (May 12, 1889): 26, col. 1–2.

21. Carpenter's brief in U.S. Supreme Court reprinted in full in *CLN* 4 (January 20, 1872): 108, col. 4–110, col. 1.

22. The gist of Carpenter's distinction was that the right to vote was covered by Section 2 of the Fourteenth Constitutional Amendment, which reduced the number of representatives apportioned to those states that denied blacks the right to vote. That provision contained three references to "male inhabitants" or "male citizens." By the framers' repetitious use of the word "male," deduced Carpenter, "the right of female suffrage is inferentially denied by the [constitutional] provision."

He continued by pointing out that Myra's claim—that the state could not constitutionally prohibit a woman from practicing the profession of her choice—was a derivation from a different portion of the Fourteenth Amendment, Section 1. The pertinent part of that section provides: "No state shall make or enforce any law which shall abridge the privileges or immunities of citizens of the United States." Since that provision, unlike the section relating to voting, did not mention "male" citizens, it was obvious (according to Carpenter) that females were not intended to be excluded from its coverage. Therefore, reasoned Myra's attorney, because the right to pursue one's profession and the right to vote were derived from two very differently-worded portions of the Fourteenth Amendment, it followed that if the Court were to hold that Myra had the constitutional right to practice law, such a ruling would in no way be a step toward the judicial creation of nationwide women's suffrage.

23. See recently discovered letter from Susan B. Anthony to Myra Bradwell, dated July 30, 1873 (in author's possession).

24. This argument by Carpenter seems to be an adaptation of a famous statement made many years earlier by Charles Fourier. See *Women, the Family, and Freedom: The Debate in Documents* 1 (1750–1880) edited by Susan G. Bell and Karen M. Offen (Stanford, Calif.: Stanford University Press, 1983), p. 41.

25. Carpenter's brief in U.S. Supreme Court, reprinted in full in *CLN* 4 (January 20, 1872): 108, col. 4–110, col. 1.

26. Ibid.

27. *CLN* 4 (January 20, 1872): 108, col. 1.

28. Charles Fairman, *Reconstruction and Reunion, 1864–88,* History of the Supreme Court of the United States/The Oliver Wendell Holmes Devise Series, vol. 6 (New York: Macmillan, 1971), p. 1365. The reason for the states' inaction, however, may have been that by the time Carpenter argued the case, the matter was almost moot in Illinois. A few months after the case was heard by the Supreme Court, the Illinois legislature passed a law providing that "no person shall be precluded from any profession on account of sex." See text accompanying notes 46 through 48 *infra*.

29. Eleanor Gridley, "Presentation of Bronze Bust of Mrs. Myra Bradwell, First Woman Lawyer in Illinois," *Transactions of the Illinois Historical Society* 38 (1931).

30. *CLN* 7 (January 20, 1872): 108, col. 1.

31. *Bradwell* v. *Illinois,* 16 Wall 130 (1873).

32. *CLN* 26 (May 12, 1894): 296, col. 2. Chief Justice Chase filed no opinion.

33. 16 Wall 36 (1873).

34. *Bradwell* v. *Illinois,* 16 Wall 130 (1873).

35. This was Bradley's opinion in the lower court hearing on the Slaughterhouse Cases. Bradley, although a Supreme Court justice, was then sitting as a circuit court judge, and he authored the lower court opinion that had sustained the claim of the excluded butchers.

36. 16 Wall 130 (1873). "Divine ordinance" is a term that was used in several subsequent state court decisions upholding laws establishing classifications based on sex. See e.g., *State* v. *Heitman* 105 Kan. 39, 46–47 (1919); *State* v. *Bearcub,* 1 Or. App. 579, 580, 465 P2d. 252, 253 (1970).

37. *CLN* 5 (May 10, 1873): 390, col. 1. A year after the *Bradwell* decision, the Supreme Court, in *Minor* v. *Happersett* 88 U.S. (21 Wall) 162, 22 L. Ed. 627 (1874) held that the right to vote was not one of the "privileges and immunities of United States citizenship." Therefore, states were not forbidden by the Constitution from according "that important trust to men alone."

38. Ibid.

39. Recently discovered letter from Susan B. Anthony to Myra Bradwell, dated April 28, 1873.

40. Fairman, *Reconstruction and Reunion, 1864–88,* p. 1365.

41. The *Boston Daily Advertiser,* April 16, 1873, reported "Judge Bradley's opinion seemed to cause no little amusement upon the Bench and Bar." Cited in Warren, *The Supreme Court in United States History,* vol. 2 (Boston: Little, Brown and Company, 1937), p. 550, f.n. 1.

42. Thompson, *Matthew Hale Carpenter: Webster of the West,* p. 102.

43. "The Supreme Court Righting Itself," *The Nation* 16 (April 24, 1873): 280 (unsigned article).

44. Reported in *CLN* 5 (June 14, 1873): 454, col. 1.

45. Reported in *CLN* 4 (November 18, 1871): 37, col. 1.

46. Harvey B. Hurd (comp. and ed.), *The Revised Statutes of the State of Illinois, 1874* (Springfield: Illinois Journal Co., 1874), p. 169.

47. Alfred Theodore Andreas, *History of Chicago, From the Earliest Period to the Present Time,* vol. 2 (Chicago: A. T. Andreas, 1884–86).

48. *CLN* 5 (April 19, 1873): 453, col. 4.

49. *CLN* 5 (June 14, 1873): 354, col. 2.

50. In a letter dated July 30, 1872, to William K. McAllister, chief justice of the Illinois Supreme Court, Myra's husband James beseeched the court to grant Myra a license on its own motion so that she would not have to reapply for admission (letter in author's possession).

51. Interview with Myra Bradwell, *Chicago Tribune* (May 12, 1889): 26, col. 1–2.

52. *CLN* 1 (1868): 1.

53. See text accompanying footnotes 46–48 *supra*.

54. See chapter 10 *infra*.

55. See chapter 6 *infra*.

56. See chapter 10 *infra*.

57. George Gale, "Myra Bradwell: The First Woman Lawyer," *ABA Journal* 39 (December 1953): 180. See also Kogan, "Myra Bradwell: Crusader at Law," footnote 2 *supra* at 132–40.

58. *CLN* 22 (April 5, 1890): 265, col. 4.

59. Robert M. Spector, "Women Against the Law: Myra Bradwell's Struggle for Admission to the Illinois Bar." *Journal of the Illinois Historical Society* 228 (June 1975): 241.

60. "Chicago Women's Club, Memorial to Myra Bradwell," *CLN* 26 (May 12, 1894): 296, col. 4.

61. Correspondence between James B. Bradwell and Simeon P. Shope, Chief Justice of Illinois Supreme Court. James Bradwell's letter to Chief Justice Shope is dated August 21, 1889, and Justice Shope's letter to James Bradwell is dated March 29, 1890 (in author's possession).

62. "Chicago Women's Club, Memorial to Myra Bradwell."

2

"The Cult of True Womanhood"
Bradwell's Formative Years

Myra Colby Bradwell was a New Englander by birth and ancestry; yet from
the time of her adolescence until the day of her death, she considered Illinois
to be her home. That dual background is reflected in her writings, which
frequently contained a somewhat curious mixture of colonial puritanism on
the one hand and rugged midwestern pioneerism on the other.

Myra was born in Manchester, Vermont, on February 12, 1831,[1] the
youngest of the five children of Eben Colby and Abigail Willey Colby, both
of whom were descended from pioneer settlers of Boston. Several of Myra's
maternal ancestors, the Willeys, had fought in the American Revolution, and
two of them had been acclaimed for their participation in the Battle of Bunker
Hill. Myra's paternal grandfather was a Baptist minister, and she was raised
in that religion. Shortly after Myra's birth, the family moved to Portage, New
York, where they remained until 1843. During that year, when she was twelve
years old, she moved with her family and her father's family to the town of
Schaumberg, which was located in Cook County, Illinois, near Elgin.

Very little is known about Myra's childhood. One fact, however, seems
significant. Both of her parents were prominent in the antislavery movement
and both were close friends of the family of Elijah Lovejoy, a newspaper publisher and staunch abolitionist who was murdered in Illinois in 1837 by a
proslavery mob. The story of Lovejoy's role in the abolitionist struggle, frequently told to Myra during her childhood by her friend Owen Lovejoy, Elijah's
brother, undoubtedly made a deep impression on her. Indeed, it may have
provided the psychological origin of her subsequent devotion to the freeing
of women from many of the conditions of their own enslavement.

35

At some point during Myra's adolescense, she moved to Kenosha, Wisconsin, to attend finishing school while living with a married sister. It may seem curious that one who had been endowed with Myra's intellectual abilities would choose to attend a finishing school; however, it was not a choice. Finishing schools and "female seminaries" were the only forms of education available to American women during the mid-nineteenth century. Indeed, in the 1840s all of the colleges in the United States, except Oberlin, steadfastly refused to open their doors to women. And even at Oberlin women were allowed only to be seen, not heard. Thus, when the prominent feminist Lucy Stone was appointed to write the commencement address for the Oberlin class of 1847, she was told that one of her male professors would read it at the graduation ceremony as it was unseemly for young ladies to read aloud in public. Miss Stone refused to write the address.[2]

Myra returned to Illinois at the age of twenty for one final year of education, this time at the Elgin Female Seminary where she later became a teacher.[3] That institution opened its doors in the spring of 1851,[4] and Myra was a member of its first entering class. Established "for the education of young ladies,"[5] the seminary was first housed in the basement of the local Congregational church and later in the former Elgin House, the town's leading hotel.[6]

While nothing is known about the specific curricula that Myra studied at either the finishing school in Kenosha or the Female Seminary at Elgin,[7] much has been written about the educational and social functions that those two types of institutions served. Finishing schools and female seminaries both had dual purposes. The first was to provide women with a broad liberal education in literature and the arts. The second, and probably of greater importance, was to inculcate "young ladies" in the ideology of "separate spheres," the prevailing nineteenth-century view that both God and nature had relegated women to the private sphere of home and family and men to the public sphere of politics and business.[8] An integral part of the "separate spheres" doctrine was the ethos of "true womanhood," a phrase used to denote the ideal woman of the mid-nineteenth century. As historian Barbara Welter has noted:

> Authors who addressed themselves to the subject of women in the mid-nineteenth century used this phrase ["True Womanhood"] as frequently as writers on religion mentioned God. Neither group felt it necessary to define their favorite terms; they simply assumed—with some justification—that readers would intuitively understand exactly what they meant. Frequently what people of one era take for granted is most striking and revealing to the student from another.[9]

After conducting an extensive survey of the catalogues of female seminaries, as well as women's magazines and mid-nineteenth century medical and sociological literature pertaining to women, Welter concluded that:

The attributes of True Womanhood, by which a woman judged herself and was judged by her husband, her neighbors and society could be divided into four cardinal virtues—piety, purity, submissiveness and domesticity. Put them all together and they spelled mother, daughter, sister, wife—woman. Without them, no matter whether there was fame, achievement or wealth, all was ashes.[10]

Considering Myra's struggles and achievements on behalf of the ideal of gender equality, one might speculate that she had simply rejected the mid-nineteenth-century ethos of "true womanhood." But in fact the contrary seems to be true. By first examining the meanings of each of the four cardinal virtues of "true womanhood," and then reflecting on many of Myra's writings and activities, one can only conclude with the paradox that Myra Bradwell was very much a product of the era in which she was raised and educated.

The first cardinal virtue, piety, was the linchpin on which the other three virtues depended. That is, religion was of paramount importance because the name of God could be invoked to reinforce the values of female submissiveness, domesticity, and purity.

Female piety, moreover, was viewed not only as a social necessity but also as a scientific and medical fact. For example, in a speech entitled *Lecture on Some of the Distinctive Characteristics of the Female,* delivered to the 1842 graduating class of all-male medical students at the Jefferson Medical College of Philadelphia, Dr. Charles Meigs explained why women were inherently religious: "Hers is a pious mind. Her confiding nature leads her more readily than men to accept the proffered grace of Gospel."[11]

One of the primary purposes of the female seminaries was to reinforce the notion of female piety. After examining the catalogues of a number of such institutions, Barbara Welter noted:

Mt. Holyoke's catalogue promised to make female education "a handmaid to the Gospel and an efficient auxiliary in the great task of renovating the world." . . . In Keene, New Hampshire, the Seminary tried . . . to qualify [its students] . . . for "the enjoyment of Celestial Happiness in the life to come." And . . . [the] Principal of Oakland Female Seminary in Hillsborough, Ohio, believed that "female education should be preeminently religious."[12]

Myra, too, was imbued with the spirit of piety. Her writings in the *Chicago Legal News* contained frequent references to God and religion, even though those references were usually not relevant to any matter that she was discussing. For example, in one edition of the *News,* at the bottom of the page, set off by itself and pertinent to absolutely nothing at all, she stated: "A Chicago judge asks 'who can penetrate the life beyond and say that there is no purgatory?' "[13]

By putting her words about purgatory into the mouth of "a Chicago judge," whether real or hypothetical, Myra made it clear that religion was a part not only of the medical realm but of the legal one as well.

The second cardinal virtue of "true womanhood," submissiveness, was deemed to be ordained by God and also venerated by men. As one male commentator noted:

> So long as she is nervous, fickle, capricious, delicate, diffident, and dependent, men will worship and adore her. *Her weakness is her strength, and her true art is to cultivate and improve that weakness.*[14] (Emphasis added)

In addition, female submissiveness was a matter of medical and scientific "fact" since it was premised on the "knowledge" that women had small brains and therefore needed men to take care of them and to dominate them. Dr. Charles Meigs explained this to an all-male class of medical students by contrasting the anatomy of the Apollo of Belvedere (an example of male bodily structure) with that of the Venus de Medici (an example of female bodily anatomy). The physician concluded that "woman has a head almost too small for intellect and just big enough for love."[15]

Most female commentators agreed. For example, Mrs. John Sanford in her book on the sociology and psychology of women emphasized that: "A really sensible woman feels her dependence. She does what she can but is conscious of inferiority, and therefore grateful for support."[16]

Even women of great talent were expected to use their gifts for the purpose of furthering their husbands' careers. For example, in an article entitled "The Sculptor's Assistant: Ann Flaxman," the author expressed her admiration for Ann Flaxman, a very talented sculptress, because "she devoted herself to sustain her husband's genius and aid him in his arduous career."[17]

Lest one believe that Myra's attempts to become a member of the Illinois bar indicate that she had rejected the ethos of submissiveness, one need only recall that Myra originally pursued the study of law *not* because she wished to become an independent practitioner, but rather because she wanted to help James at the office. As she later explained to a reporter for the *Chicago Tribune:*

> I acquired the idea [of studying law] from helping my husband in his office. I was always with him, helping in whatever way I could. Thus, I picked up a considerable smattering of law and about five years after our marriage I determined to read [law] in good earnest. You see [explained Mrs. Bradwell as she glanced at the big husband who was looking at her as she talked], I believe that married people should share the same toil and the same interests and be separated in no way. It is the separation of interests and labor that develops people in opposite directions and makes them grow apart. If they

worked side by side and thought side by side we would need no divorce courts.[18]

The above interview was given in 1889 after Myra in her capacity as publisher and editor of the *Chicago Legal News* had been thinking and acting independently of James for at least twenty-one years. It is clear, however, that much like the sculptress Ann Flaxman, Myra had originally planned to "devote herself to sustain her husband's genius and aid him in his arduous career." It was only after she was rebuffed by both the Illinois Supreme Court and the United States Supreme Court that she threw all of her energies into her legal newspaper and her concomitant law reform activities.

The female seminaries of the nineteenth century also sought to foster the third cardinal virtue of "true womanhood," domesticity. For example, the catalogue of the Mt. Holyoke Female Seminary admonished that both God and nature "enjoin[ed] these [domestic] duties on the sex, and she cannot violate them with impunity."[19] Likewise, the catalogue of a female seminary in Monroe City, Michigan, while admitting that few of its students would be likely "to fill the learned professions," declared that they would, instead, be placed in "other scenes of usefulness and honor," primarily that of "the presiding genius of love" in the home.[20]

The ethos of "true womanhood" mandated that literary women, as well as other "women of genius," conform to the same standards of domesticity. As one female author advised, "as for genius, make it a domestic plant. Let its roots strike deep in your house."[21] Likewise, in an essay entitled "Literary Women," the female author found it self-evident "that her home shall be made a loving place of rest and joy and comfort for those who are dear to her will be the first wish of every true woman's heart."[22]

That Myra cherished the virtue of domesticity, even on the part of "women of genius," was made clear not only in her writings but also in her public pronouncements. For example, in discussing the distinguished suffragist, Mary Livermore, Myra first alluded briefly to the fact that Livermore "did efficient work in this state for the Woman suffrage cause" and had achieved "success in the lecture field." Myra then concluded the article by giving a lengthy testimonial to Livermore's domestic accomplishments:

> She is an excellent wife and mother. We will remember her neat and tidy home for years just across the street from ours. She is a model house-keeper. . . . As a woman, wife, mother and housekeeper, Mrs. Livermore is very proud of her daughter, and according to her own confession, finds greater happiness and more congenial society with her grandchildren than she has ever known in her life.[23]

Myra also spoke proudly of her own domestic accomplishments. In an interview with the *Chicago Tribune,* after discussing her professional accomplishments, Myra ended with a rejoinder to "all the wiseacres of the land [who] . . . predicted that [by becoming a lawyer] I'd wreck my family and break my hearthstone to smithereens":

> That was twenty years ago and I do not know of any other family whose integral character is so unbroken as mine. Of our four children two have lived and grown to maturity. Although both are married we are all housed under one roof. . . . I don't believe there is a happier family in the world than [ours]. I often wish all those excellent folk who . . . picture me as a fanatic destroyer of domesticity and *the sweetness of true womanhood* could see my two daughters and our home life. . . . The world, too, has begun to learn the lesson that it is not necessary for a woman to break up all family ties and sacrifice womanly attributes and graces in order to succeed in other trades than the honored one of housewife.[24] (Emphasis added)

The fourth but by no means least important virtue of true womanhood was sexual purity of both mind and deed. Mid-nineteenth-century women were constantly admonished that they must not even think about sex, and that they most certainly must remain chaste until their wedding night. In fact, one male authority counseled his male readers to test the purity of the women in whom they were interested. He advised young men to make sexual suggestions to the woman. If she failed to respond with a "becoming abhorrence," the young man was warned to stay away.[25]

If a woman lost her virginity prior to marriage, the result would be not only degradation, but also possible insanity. As historian Welter has noted:

> The frequency with which derangement follows loss of virtue suggests the exquisite sensibility of woman, and the possibility that, in the women's magazines at least, her intellect was geared to her hymen, not her brain.[26]

It is not known whether Myra adhered to the principles of both mental and physical purity for women; her writings are virtually devoid of any mention of sex. The absence of that subject, however, is probably in and of itself significant. Myra's writings covered a vast expanse of legal subjects, including, of course, criminal law. Yet nowhere did she ever mention the subject of sex crimes: rape, incest, or child molestation, for example. One can only speculate that she simply believed that those were not fit subjects for the female pen. Merely to mention the subject of sex would be evidence that she had thought about it; and, under contemporary standards, the subject was not to be contemplated by the female mind.

Regardless of what Myra believed about the subject of female sexual purity, it is clear that she ostensibly adhered to the other three cardinal virtues of "true womanhood": piety, submissiveness, and domesticity.

While attending the Elgin Female Seminary, Myra was apparently not only the embodiment of "true womanhood" but also the "acknowledged belle of Elgin."[27] Several months after entering the seminary, she met James Bolesworth Bradwell while James was in Elgin on legal business.[28] That point is not entirely clear, however, because at the time òf their meeting James was not yet a member of the Illinois bar.[29]

Theirs was not an easy courtship. The entire Colby family, with the exception of Myra and her sister Abbie, took an immediate and intense dislike to James. The reason for their animosity is not clear, but it was probably related to the fact that James was "the penniless son of English immigrants"[30] while both of Myra's parents had been descended from "good colonial stock."[31] Indeed, James had been forced to finance both his college education and legal studies by doing manual labor and by working as a journeyman at various trades.[32] Such a suitor was undoubtedly unacceptable to most of the Colbys, but not to the only one who mattered.

Several months after their initial meeting, and pursued by Myra's brother Frank who was armed with a shotgun, Myra and James escaped from Elgin and eloped. Their marriage took place in Chicago in 1852.

Soon after their elopement, Myra and James moved to Memphis, Tennessee, where the couple opened, operated, and taught at a highly respected private school. During that period, James continued to read law, and later that year (1852) he was admitted to the Tennessee bar.[33]

Despite the success of their school in Memphis, James and Myra returned permanently to Chicago in 1854, shortly after the birth of their first child, Myra. During the ensuing eight years, the Bradwells had three more children: Thomas in 1856, Bessie in 1858, and James in 1862. As was common during the mid-nineteenth century, two of the four died in childhood: Myra at the age of seven and James at the age of two. Bessie and Thomas, however, survived to adulthood and both became lawyers. In addition, both Bessie and Thomas married, and each had one child. Bessie bore a daughter named Myra, and Thomas had a son named, not surprisingly, James. The family lineage ended with the grandchildren, as neither of them had progeny.

After their return to Chicago in 1854, James continued studying law. Immediately after his admission to the Illinois bar in 1855, he formed a law partnership with his brother-in-law Frank Colby, the same Frank Colby who had only three years earlier chased Myra and James out of Elgin at gunpoint. Apparently the family feud had ended, probably because James was no longer merely "the penniless son of English immigrants." He was now a member of a learned profession, an attorney who had been licensed to practice law in two states.

Immediately after James's admission to the Illinois bar, Myra began to "read [law] in good earnest" so that she and James would be able to "work side by side and [think] side by side."[34] However, her legal studies came to an abrupt halt in 1861 with the onset of the Civil War. For the next several years Myra, ever faithful to the spirit of "true womanhood," became intensely involved in a number of women's philanthropic organizations that had been formed for the purpose of raising money for the Union Army's sick and wounded soldiers and their families.

Chief among Myra's Civil War activities was a mammoth fundraising event in which she collaborated with the well-known suffragist, Mary Livermore. Together they organized and presided over the Northwestern Sanitary Fair, also known as the Ladies' Northwestern Sanitary Fair, which was held in Chicago in 1865.[35]

The Sanitary Fair was packed daily from eight A.M. until ten P.M. by throngs who had come to pay for the privilege of seeing two exhibits. The first of these was held in Chicago's Bryan Hall, later known as the Grand Opera House. It consisted of a vast display of musical instruments, needlework, silverware, glassware, clothing, and other "fancy goods." The second exhibit was located across Clark Street in the court house. Organized by the fair's committee on "Arms, Trophies, and Curiosities," of which Myra was secretary, this latter display was a showcase of Union flags, captured Confederate flags, trophies, and other war curios.

The fair's official publication, *The Voice of the Fair,* praised Myra for being "the leading spirit in producing that artistic and beautiful exhibition in Bryan Hall":

> Mrs. Judge Bradwell, who long before this magnificent structure in which she presides was animated with its grandeur, was devoting all her wonderful energies to its complete success; her attentiveness to everybody and everything have been unceasing, and in the midst of a melange of questions which would have frenzied an ordinary person, her courtesy and kindness have maintained an equable glow. The flattering success of this department must, to a vast extent, be attributed to her connection with it.[36]

During the Civil War period and the two years that followed, Myra also served as president of the Chicago Soldiers' Aid Society, which sponsored the Soldier's Fair of 1863 and the fair of 1867. These fairs were also held "for the benefit of the families of soldiers, [and] had no more active or efficient worker than Mrs. Bradwell."[37]

And so it was that Myra Bradwell remained faithful to the spirit of "true womanhood" not only during her formative years, but also during the Civil War period when she was already in her early and middle thirties.

While researching and writing about her life, this author constantly pondered the following: How could Myra Bradwell possibly have so thoroughly embraced the ethos of "true womanhood," and yet simultaneously have accomplished more than any other nineteenth-century woman to advance both the concept and the reality of gender equality? It is against this seeming paradox that all her achievements must be measured.[38]

With the closing of the fair of 1867, there were apparently no further women's philanthropic activities that could consume the time and energy of someone as resourceful, zestful, and intelligent as Myra.[39] It was during that year and the ones which ensued that she resumed her legal studies, founded the most successful legal publishing empire of the nineteenth century, became the guiding force for a vast number of law reform activities, and almost singlehandedly secured the release of Mary Todd Lincoln from an insane asylum.

NOTES

1. Unless otherwise indicated, the following biographical information was drawn from a lengthy obituary of Myra that appeared in *CLN* 26 (February 17, 1894): 200, et. seq.; *Notable American Women, 1607–1950; A Biographical Dictionary* 1 (Cambridge, Mass.: Belknap Press of Harvard University Press, 1971), p. 223. Edward T. James and Janet Wilson James, *Dictionary of American Biography* (New York: C. Scribners Sons, 1929), p. 580.

2. Frances Elizabeth Willard and Mary A. Livermore, *A Woman of the Century: Biographical Sketches of Leading American Women* (Buffalo, N.Y.: Charles Wells Moulton 1893), p. 693.

3. E. C. Alft, in his book, *Elgin: An American History* (1984), states that Myra taught at the seminary before her marriage to James Bradwell. That, however, seems highly unlikely, as the school opened its doors in the spring of 1851, at which point Myra enrolled as a student. Myra married James one year later, in May 1852.

4. *The Story of Elgin's First Twenty-Five Years, 1835–1860* (Elgin, Ill.: Elgin Area Historical Society, n.d.).

5. Ibid.

6. *The History of Elgin* (Elgin, Ill.: Lord and Bradford, 1875), p. 58. (No authors on title page)

7. On June 23 and 24, 1988, this author spoke with both the reference librarian at the Gail Bordon Public Library of Elgin and a volunteer worker at the Elgin Area Historical Society. Both persons told her that their institutions did not have copies of the catalogue of the Elgin Female Seminary and that it was highly improbable that such a catalogue, if it ever existed, could currently be located anywhere.

On July 6, 1988, this author spoke with E. C. Alft, former mayor of Elgin and author of *Elgin: An American History* (1984). Mr. Alft, considered to be Elgin's leading historian, stated that it was highly unlikely that such a catalogue or a description of the Seminary's curriculum ever existed. Even if such materials once existed, copies are not currently available.

8. Gerda Lerner, "The Lady and the Mill Girl: Changes in the Status of Women in the Age of Jackson," in *The Majority Finds Its Past: Placing Women in History* (New York: Oxford University Press, 1979), pp. 28–29.

9. Barbara Welter, "The Cult of True Womanhood: 1820–1860," *American Quarterly* 18,

no. 2 (Summer 1966): pp. 151–74. Unless otherwise indicated, the following discussion is drawn from this seminal article by Welter as well as from Nancy Cott, *The Bonds of Womanhood: Women's Sphere in New England, 1789–1835* (New Haven: Yale University Press, 1977); Mary P. Ryan, *Cradle of the Middle Class: The Family in Oneida County, New York, 1790–1865* (Cambridge, Eng.; New York: Cambridge University Press, 1981); Carroll Smith-Rosenberg, *Disorderly Conduct: Visions of Gender in Victorian America* (New York: A. A. Knopf, 1985); Gerda Lerner, "The Lady and the Mill Girl: Changes in the Status of Women in the Age of Jackson" in *The Majority Finds Its Past: Placing Women in History* (New York: Oxford University Press, 1979), pp. 28–29; Catherine Clinton, *The Other Civil War: American Women in the Nineteenth Century* (New York: Hill and Wang, 1984); and Kenneth Karst, "Women's Constitution," *Duke Law Journal* (1984): 447, 451 (discussion of Bradwell).

10. Welter, "The Cult of True Womanhood," p. 152.

11. Ibid., pp. 153.

12. Ibid., pp. 153–54.

13. *CLN* 15 (May 12, 1883): 287, col. 4.

14. Clinton, *The Other Civil War,* p. 147.

15. Welter, "The Cult of True Womanhood," pp. 159–60.

16. Mrs. John Sanford, *Woman, in her Social and Domestic Character* (Boston, 1842), p. 15, quoted in Welter, "The Cult of True Womanhood," p. 159.

17. "The Sculptor's Assistant: Ann Flaxman" in *Women of Worth: A Book for Girls* (New York, 1860), p. 263, quoted in Welter, "The Cult of True Womanhood," p. 161.

18. *Chicago Tribune* (May 12, 1889): 26, col. 1–2.

19. *Mt. Holyoke Female Seminary,* p. 13, quoted in Welter, "The Cult of True Womanhood," p. 168.

20. *The Annual Catalogue of the Officers and Pupils of the Young Ladies Seminary and Collegiate Institute* (Monroe City, 1855), pp. 18, 19, quoted in Welter, "The Cult of True Womanhood," p. 168.

21. "Women of Genius," *Ladies' Companion* 11 (1839): 89, quoted in Welter, "The Cult of True Womanhood," p. 167.

22. Helen Irving, "Literary Women," *Ladies' Wreath* 3 (1850), 93, quoted in Welter, p. 167.

23. *CLN* 16 (January 26, 1884): 166, col. 1–2.

24. *Chicago Tribune* (May 12, 1889): 26, col. 1–2.

25. Thomas Branagan, "The Excellence of the Female Character Vindicated," quoted in Clinton, *The Other Civil War,* p. 148.

26. Welter, "The Cult of True Womanhood," p. 156.

27. The source for the quote and for the following story concerning the courtship and elopement of Myra and James Bradwell is the *Elgin Sunday Courier* (December 12, 1920): 9. The clipping from the *Courier* was sent to this author by E. C. Alft. Along with the article from the newspaper, Mr. Alft sent the following note:

> Although not stated, the author [of the article in the *Courier*] was Charles E. Gregory. He was a former newsman who dabbled in local history. . . . [The story was told to Gregory by] lawyer James Coleman, who was one of Elgin's pioneers [and] was well acquainted with the Colby family. . . .
>
> I have two problems with the story: (1) It is second hand, put into print in 1920, but told to the author by a notorious drunk "in the nineties," [and] (2) James Bradwell may have come to Elgin on legal business, but the Elgin City Court of Common Pleas was not established until 1857.
>
> On the other hand, we do know that Frank Colby [Myra's brother] practiced law in Elgin in the "fifties."

28. *Elgin Sunday Courier* (December 12, 1920): 9.

29. American Council of Learned Societies, *Dictionary of American Biography,* vol. 2 (New York: Charles Scribner's Sons, 1929), p. 580 (entry on James Bradwell).

30. James, *Notable American Women,* p. 223.

31. *CLN* 26 (February 17, 1894): 200 et seq.

32. *Dictionary of American Biography,* p. 580.

33. Ibid.

34. *Chicago Tribune* (May 12, 1889): 26.

35. This description of the Northwestern Sanitary Fair was taken from "Mary Livermore and the Great Northwestern Fair," *Chicago History* 4, no. 1 (New Series, Spring 1975); see also obituary, *CLN* 26 (February 17, 1894): 200. Alice Kessler-Harris, in *Women Have Always Worked: A Historical Overview* (Old Westbury, N.Y.: Feminist Press; New York: McGraw-Hill, 1981), p. 108, notes that many nineteenth-century women developed organizational skills by participating in the fair's activities.

36. *The Voice of the Fair* (June 9, 1865), quoted in obituary, *CLN* 26 (February 17, 1894): 200.

37. Ibid.

38. See Martha Minow, "Forming Underneath Everything that Grows: Toward a History of Family Law," *Wisconsin Law Review* (1985): 819, 850—"Myra Bradwell's experience could be discounted because she was an unusual woman who helped create—and yet was caught in the middle of—the transition from patriarchal family law to a regime of individual rights."

39. Although Bradwell devoted the remainder of her life primarily to legal and social reform, she did play a major role in lobbying for Chicago as the site of the 1892 World's Columbian Exposition. By that time, her health had deteriorated so markedly that it was necessary for her to tour the Exposition in a wheelchair. "Myra Bradwell—Crusader for Reform," *Supreme Court Historical Society Quarterly* 4, no. 4 (Fall 1982): 4.

3

"She Is No More Insane Than I Am" Bradwell Secures the Release of Mary Todd Lincoln from Bellevue Place Asylum

[President Lincoln] led [his wife] gently to a window one day and point[ed] toward an asylum for the insane in the distance. "Mother," he told her sorrowfully, "do you see that large white building on the hill yonder: Try and control your grief or it will drive you mad, and we may have to send you there."

—Abraham Lincoln to Mary Todd Lincoln in 1862, shortly after the death of their son, Willie[1]

The president's words were prophetic, but his prophecy was not fulfilled until ten years after his assassination. The man who "sent her there" was her sole surviving son, Robert. And the woman who secured her release was one of her few remaining friends, Myra Bradwell.

On March 12, 1875, Mary Todd Lincoln, who had been living alone in Florida, and who was still prostrate with grief over the deaths of her husband and three of her sons, boarded a train for Chicago.[2] The purpose of the trip was to visit with Robert and his family. Robert, however, was not particularly pleased to see his mother. Indeed, he was extremely upset by her conduct, particularly her compulsive spending. For years Mrs. Lincoln had been engaged in extravagant shopping sprees. She had trunks full of expensive clothing, some of which she had never even worn. While her personal estate was still worth

47

in excess of $100,000, and although she had not spent any of the principal, Robert was afraid that his mother would eventually become his financial charge. This was too much for him to bear. His only way out, he believed, was to have her adjudged insane and confined to an asylum.[3]

In order to gather evidence, Robert employed a Pinkerton detective to follow Mrs. Lincoln during her stay in Chicago. The detective kept track of her activities for three weeks and then reported that Mrs. Lincoln was being visited by "suspicious looking persons" and was "contemplating leaving town for parts unknown." This was evidence enough for Robert, who was convinced that he must immediately initiate insanity proceedings.

Robert, himself an attorney, retained as counsel his long-time friend Leonard Swett. Swett's strategy was to have Robert write letters to six physicians (all of whom had been consulted in advance), asking them for their opinions of Mrs. Lincoln's mental state. The group of six doctors, four of whom had never even met Mrs. Lincoln, joined together and unanimously issued statements declaring Mrs. Lincoln insane and recommending commitment to an asylum. Armed with those statements, Robert filed a petition for an insanity hearing in Cook County Court on May 19, 1875. The trial was held that very day.

Mrs. Lincoln was not notified that a petition had been filed against her until only an hour before the hearing. After being informed by Robert's attorney, Leonard Swett, of the pendency of the trial, she was coerced by that lawyer into accompanying him to the courthouse. Mrs. Lincoln's "defense" was conducted by Isaac N. Arnold, an attorney who believed that Mrs. Lincoln was insane and who had actively collaborated with Robert Lincoln and Swett during their preparation for the "trial."

Upon arriving at the courthouse, Isaac Arnold, who was very much aware of his conflict of interest, began to have severe reservations about the ethics of his "defending" Mrs. Lincoln. When he expressed his doubts to Swett, the latter retorted: "That means you will put into her head, that she can get some mischievous lawyer to make us trouble; go and defend her, and do your duty."[4]

Mrs. Lincoln stood mute as she listened to seventeen witnesses testify as to her insanity. Many of these were merchants and jewelers who simply recited her transactions from which they had profited and concluded their testimony with the pronouncement that she was insane. Four of the witnesses were physicians, none of whom was an expert in mental disease, and two of whom had never met Mrs. Lincoln. Yet all four declared that she was "insane and a fit subject for hospital treatment." But the testimony that was most difficult for her to bear was that of her son, Robert, who recounted his mother's actions—particularly her compulsive spending—during the two months that she had visited in Chicago.

Mrs. Lincoln's "attorney" chose not to place her on the witness stand.

Nor did he garner any witnesses on her behalf. She was unable to procure witnesses on her own, as she had been unaware of the pendency of the trial against her.

Some recent commentators have surmised that Robert and the six consulting physicians truly believed that Mrs. Lincoln was insane.[5] Those authorities and others, however, have emphasized that at the time that Mrs. Lincoln was unanimously diagnosed as insane, the medical profession—virtually all male— was extremely prejudiced against "annoying" females, especially those who refused to heed male advice.[6] A woman's lack of submission to a male authority figure (a husband, a father, or in Mrs. Lincoln's case, an adult son) was deemed by many physicians to create a presumption of insanity.

There is some strong evidence that all six consulting physicians had grave doubts as to whether Mrs. Lincoln was truly a fit subject for commitment to an asylum. Only a few days after Mrs. Lincoln's insanity trial, Leonard Swett wrote:

> Robert was so careful to keep within the truth that the physicians doubted whether we would be able to make out a case sufficiently strong to satisfy the general public, and perhaps not strong enough to secure a verdict.[7]

The all-male jury did not share those doubts. After deliberating for only a few minutes, the twelve-member panel delivered its unanimous verdict: "insane."

Mrs. Lincoln's insanity trial has been the subject of much historical controversy and debate. Two recent scholars, Mark E. Neely and R. Gerald McMurty, have defended the proceedings by pointing out that in Illinois in 1875, the only way to secure an adult's involuntary commitment to an asylum and to take control over that person's property was to secure a verdict of insanity at a public jury trial.[8]

Another recent commentator, Samuel Schreiner, while agreeing with the historical necessity of a public jury trial, has offered the following rejoinder:

> Granted, but *any* trial for *any* reason becomes a farce when the defendant is given only an hour's warning and assigned improper representation. Although it was evident even in the raw newspaper accounts of the trial, the letters in [Mary Todd Lincoln's] insanity file further confirm the fact that the whole operation was a conspiracy, a frame-up, on the part of some of the sharpest legal minds in the country to make certain that they got the verdict that they wanted.
> And *why* did they want it?[9]

After reexamining the evidence, Schreiner arrived at the same conclusion that had been reached by many earlier scholars. Robert was motivated not only by his financial interest but also by the desire to avoid embarrassment.

> Aside from money there was a motive for Robert Lincoln's action that few people have been willing to discuss. . . . Robert Lincoln wanted to be rid of his mother to be rid of an embarrassment and a source of trouble to himself and his wife. . . . His struggle . . . to keep . . . his mother [confined] is spelled out as a worry that she will get herself talked about, and over and over again he complains about the "trouble" she has made for him.[10]

On the evening following her trial, Mrs. Lincoln was coerced by Swett into giving all her money and securities to Arnold until such time as the court appointed an official conservator. Moments after her money was confiscated, Mrs. Lincoln tried to kill herself. While this attempt was viewed by Robert Lincoln and Swett as a further sign of her insanity, some commentators have noted that the suicide attempt *followed* the trial and was probably a response to it. As Samuel Schreiner has speculated:

> . . . in fact, the suicide attempt was clearly *caused* by the trial; it now has to be viewed as a sign of how fully Mrs. Lincoln understood what had been done to her and what the unpleasant consequences would be. With all her tribulations she had never tried such a thing under any other circumstances; nor, as the Turners[11] noted, had she ever revealed the slightest tendency to self-destruction or violence in a lifetime of copious and unrestrained correspondence.[12]

That Mrs. Lincoln exhibited such suicidal tendencies only *after* her betrayal by Robert and *after* the sham "trial" in which she had been declared insane was a fact that has been noted not only by modern scholars but also by the person who had raised her and probably understood her better than anyone else, her older sister Elizabeth Todd Edwards. Mrs. Edwards viewed the suicide attempt not only as evidence that Mrs. Lincoln was sane and had fully comprehended what had happened to her but also as an effort by a betrayed mother to thwart the will of both her son and the court.[13]

On the morning following her trial, Mrs. Lincoln was taken to Bellevue Place in Batavia, Illinois. That establishment, run by Dr. Richard Patterson, was a private, "exclusive" insane asylum. Admission was confined to "a select class of lady patients of quiet, unexceptionable habits."[14] During the period of Mrs. Lincoln's four-month stay, twenty such "lady patients" were present.

During Mrs. Lincoln's confinement, Robert Lincoln, who not surprisingly had been appointed conservator of her assets, visited his mother weekly. No other person was allowed to see her without Robert's permission, which was consistently withheld during her first two months in the asylum. Moreover, she was not allowed to write to or receive mail from family or friends unless her son gave his consent.

Mrs. Lincoln, a virtual prisoner, repeatedly requested to be released so that she could go to Springfield to reside with her sister, Mrs. Elizabeth Edwards. It was, she said, "the most natural thing in the world to wish to live with my sister. She raised me, and I regard her as sort of a mother."[15] Finally, in late July, after a visit with his mother, Robert told Dr. Patterson that he consented to his mother's being allowed to mail a letter to her sister.

As soon as Robert departed, Mrs. Lincoln took a carriage to the post office so that she could deposit the letter personally. However, she deposited not one letter but, deviously, five. In addition to her sister, she wrote to General Farnsworth, to two other influential public men, and to her very close friends, Myra and James Bradwell.

The precise date upon which the Bradwells became acquainted with the Lincolns is unknown. But it is known that Myra and James had a "long and intimate acquaintance with both Abraham and Mary Todd Lincoln before and after Lincoln became president of the United States."[16] Indeed, immediately after the president's assassination, Myra and James secured a temporary home in Chicago for Mrs. Lincoln, and subsequently, a permanent residence on the same street as their own, West Washington Boulevard. Moreover, James had on many occasions served as Mrs. Lincoln's attorney and was the draftsman of her will.[17] It was not surprising that (as Mrs. Lincoln later wrote):

> When all others, among them my husband's supposed friends, failed me in the most bitter hours of my life, these loyal hearts, Myra and James Bradwell, came to my assistance and rescued me under great difficulty from confinement in an insane asylum.[18]

The precise wording of Mrs. Lincoln's first clandestine plea to the Bradwells has been lost. Indeed, all the correspondence between Myra and Mary Todd Lincoln was destroyed in 1928 as part of a plot that was recently uncovered by this author. That scheme was orchestrated after Robert Lincoln's death by the attorneys for Robert's family and involved Myra's granddaughter's sale of Mrs. Lincoln's letters to the Robert Lincoln estate. The events surrounding the sale and ultimate destruction of that correspondence will be described in the chapter that follows.

Although Myra's granddaughter sold the actual letters, she did preserve the substance of a few of them. In Mrs. Lincoln's first surreptitiously posted letter to Myra and James, she begged them to secure her release from confinement:

[She was] extremely vindictive against her son, Robert Lincoln, who had placed her there. In no uncertain terms she berated him, calling him profligate and dishonest and making some startling assertions.[19]

Myra responded immediately by boarding a train for the insane asylum at Batavia. When she arrived at her destination, Dr. Patterson told her that she could not see or even write to Mrs. Lincoln unless she first secured Robert Lincoln's consent. Myra was incensed! She retaliated with her favorite weapon, journalistic exposé. The very next day the following article appeared in an Illinois newspaper, the *Bloomington Courier:*

MRS. LINCOLN

Is the Widow of President Lincoln a Prisoner?

No One Allowed to See Her Except by Order of Her Son

An Account of a Remarkable Interview With
Her Jailer and Physician

The following communication has been reluctantly furnished us, after the most earnest solicitation, by a lady of this city, who had, for many years, been an intimate friend of Mrs. Lincoln. The writer did not think of such a thing as publishing the result of her visit to Batavia, and from this fact together with the high social position she occupies, great weight will certainly be accorded the statements made, and Mrs. Lincoln's friends be induced to have her case reopened.[20]

It is doubtful that the *Courier* solicited Myra's "communication," for how would the editor have known of her visit to the insane asylum unless she told him? And why would she have told him unless she wanted her communication published? And how could the *Courier's* "solicitation" and Myra's response all have occurred within a twenty-four-hour period? A more likely explanation is that Myra authored her exposé while returning by train from Batavia and hand-delivered it to the staff of the *Courier.* In any event, her published account of her fruitless visit reads as follows:

Anything which concerns the widow of our late lamented President is of interest to your readers. I have concluded, therefore, to give you an account of the visit I paid to Batavia yesterday. But first let me say, that I had no object in view in making this visit except to satisfy myself in regard to Mrs. Lincoln's insanity, of which so many have of late expressed doubts. The morning was a beautiful one. In passing over the country on my way to Batavia I was delighted with its loveliness. Nature did indeed have on her most regal robes.

In due season I arrived at my place of destination, took a carriage to the hotel, and after a good dinner, inquired of mine host the way to the insane retreat. The building, where Mrs. Lincoln is confined is a large stone building with nothing to detract from its general appearance, except the bars at the windows, which, though diamond-shape, are none the less bars. The grounds around the house are beautiful, and are laid out quite artistically. I looked anxiously around, hoping I might possibly see my friend, Mrs. L., for I had learned she could walk in the grounds at her own pleasure, and I knew well how fond she was of such strolls. But not a person did I see anywhere around.

I ascended the steps of the house and rang the bell. Almost immediately the door was opened by a portly, fine-looking gentleman. I said, "Is this Dr. Patterson?" He said, "It is." I then introduced myself, and was courteously invited into his office. I said, "Doctor, I have called to see Mrs. Lincoln; she is a dear friend of mine and I thought I would like to see her a few moments, with your permission." I had no sooner spoken Mrs. Lincoln's name than a cloud passed over the doctor's face, and an expression, which I can best describe as flinty, took the place of what before was agreeable.

"Madam," said he, "have you a line from her son, Mr. Robert Lincoln?"

"No, sir," I replied, "I didn't suppose that was necessary."

"Where are you from, madam?" was his next question.

"From Chicago."

"Well, madam," said he, "you cannot see her unless you have such a paper."

"Couldn't I see her, doctor, in the presence of her attendant, my only object in coming is to see her?"

"Well, madam," said he, "she may be out in a few days and you can see her to your heart's content." I said, "Do you consider her worse Doctor? I understood from your letters to the public that she was allowed to see her friends." "Well, madam, she is no better—for meddlesome people come here to see her, calling themselves her friends, when in reality they come out of self-interest only." I said, "Doctor, please, don't attribute such a motive to me. I assure you my visit is only out of pure kindness to Mrs. Lincoln." He replied, "I did not refer to you, madam." "Well, doctor, as you are not willing for me to see her, will you allow me to leave a note for her?" "No, madam, there is no necessity for that; it would only disturb her mind, and while she is under my care, I shall not permit her to be disturbed either by visitors or letters."

"If she is only permitted to see such persons as you choose, and is not permitted to receive letters except from such, *she is virtually a prisoner, is she not?*"

"Madam, she is no more so than other patients I have under my care."

While this conversation was going on, he kept looking at his watch, a gentle hint, probably, that I was trespassing on his time. "Doctor, it is some little time until my train leaves. If agreeable, I will sit here till then, as it is not very pleasant sitting in the depot."

He hesitated a moment, and getting up, said, very graciously: "You can sit in here," and ushered me into what was, I suppose, the parlor of the establishment, leaving me there and for the time I staid I did not see him again, or any one else. It struck me as being rather strange, inasmuch as I had heard his patients had the freedom of the house, but this, clearly, must be an erroneous impression of a good-natured public. I have no hesitation in saying that, if it should be my fortune to be placed in such asylum, with the feeling within me that my friends placed me there with the desire to be rid of the trouble or care of me, or for some other end in view, or if I really believed they placed me there fully thinking me insane, and I saw no way out, and that speedily, it would take but a few days to make a raving maniac of me. Surrounded by those whose reason is dethroned, kept a prisoner to all intents and purposes, having no voice as to who shall see me or call on me, being left to one particular party, and that party's interest perhaps antagonistic to mine; knowing that I was constantly watched and every move known; soon, very soon, would all interest in life cease, and if death did not end the darkness that moved over me, the seal of insanity would surely be written upon my brain, and all that remained of life would go out in that hour.

I must add that Mrs. Lincoln recently said she would gladly surrender her bonds for her liberty, as money would not replace that nor give back to her the affection of those for whom she would be glad to live and for whom she would gladly lay down her life.[21]

Having been publicly discredited, Dr. Patterson relented temporarily. During the ensuing several weeks, Myra was permitted frequent visits with Mrs. Lincoln. The two women also wrote to each other almost on a daily basis. Finally, on Friday, August 6, 1875, Myra was permitted to spend the night with Mrs. Lincoln at Bellevue Place.

Myra's choice of a Friday night for her overnight visit was undoubtedly not pure happenstance, for it was well-known that Dr. Patterson spent every Saturday away from the premises. That fact enabled Myra to orchestrate a second journalistic exposé, this time with the *Chicago Times*.

Early on the morning of Saturday, August 7, Myra quietly left the asylum. A few hours later she returned, accompanied by "a Mr. Wilkie of Chicago." Mrs. Lincoln greeted her guests and invited them to her room where the three of them visited for two hours. After promising Mrs. Lincoln that she would visit again soon, Myra and "Mr. Wilkie" returned to Chicago. What Myra had failed to disclose not only to the hospital staff but to Mrs. Lincoln as well was that "Mr. Wilkie of Chicago" was Franc B. Wilkie, the editor of the *Chicago Times*.

Upon returning to Batavia and learning of Franc Wilkie's visit, Dr. Patterson was enraged. He immediately wrote Myra a letter in which he voiced his vehement objections to Myra's bringing strangers to see Mrs. Lincoln, especially in his absence and without the approval of Robert Lincoln. He concluded:

> In making future visits, if any should be made . . . I will thank you to select some other day than Saturday, the day when it is well known I am absent from the home.
> . . . I will thank you to call [Robert Lincoln's] attention to the propriety of conveying any letters that Mrs. Lincoln may write [which are] unknown to him or to me.[22]

At that juncture Dr. Patterson was apparently unaware that "Mr. Wilkie" was the editor of a widely circulated newspaper, and that the damage had already been done. Seventeen days later, on August 24, 1875, Franc Wilkie published his account of his visit with Mrs. Lincoln.[23]

The sequence of events that occurred during the seventeen-day interim indicates that Myra was saving Wilkie's story until she needed yet another journalistic bullet to fire at both Dr. Patterson and Robert Lincoln.

On August 7, Robert, vehemently opposed to the release of his mother, wrote a letter to his mother's sister, Mrs. Edwards, in which he warned that Myra Bradwell was "a high priestess in a gang of Spiritualists and from what I have heard *it is to their interest that my mother should be at liberty to control herself and her property.*"[24] Robert, who believed that his mother often consulted with "spiritualists,"[25] was obviously trying to frighten his aunt into believing that Myra and her alleged "gang" were intending to steal (or obtain in some other deceptive manner) Mrs. Lincoln's money.

On August 9, the same day on which Dr. Patterson wrote to Myra "protesting against her bringing strangers to see Mrs. Lincoln," the doctor also dispatched another letter. That one was to Robert Lincoln, indignantly informing him that Myra Bradwell had surreptitiously brought a stranger, "Mr. Wilkie," to visit with Mrs. Lincoln. Although Dr. Patterson was apparently unaware of the fact that Wilkie was a newspaper editor, the doctor nevertheless seemed to believe that Mrs. Lincoln's continued sojourn at Bellevue Place would bring him too much adverse publicity. He may have also sincerely believed that Mrs. Lincoln's confinement was no longer necessary. Regardless of his motive, Dr. Patterson did conclude his letter with a somewhat guarded but favorable prognosis:

> I am happy to say that both mentally and physically, Mrs. Lincoln is greatly improved, and as she has expressed a desire to live with her sister, Mrs. Edwards, I see no reason medically why she may not do so unless her condition should change for the worse.[26]

On August 10, after receiving not only Dr. Patterson's letter but also a visit from Myra, Robert ostensibly changed his mind about his mother's proposed visit to her sister. Knowing that Dr. Patterson no longer wanted Mrs. Lincoln to remain at Bellevue Place Asylum and certainly *not* wanting his mother to live with his own family, Robert quickly wrote the following letter to his aunt, Mrs. Edwards:

[Mrs. Bradwell called on me] this afternoon and we had a long talk—the result of which was that she thinks my mother is not entirely "right" but that she ought to be at large. The only plan she suggested was her visiting you. I told her that I had no objection to that and would await your letter [an invitation that Mrs. Edwards had already sent to Mrs. Lincoln via Dr. Patterson]. *I said in my [last] letter to you that I understood that Mrs. Bradwell is a spiritualist—[Her language] from today indicates that I was misinformed.*[27]

Robert concluded his letter with an indignant reproval of Myra:

How completely recovered my mother really is is shown by Mrs. B's saying she was to take out to her samples of fine goods she wants to buy. [My mother] has with her seven trunks of clothing and then has stored nine more. I told Mrs. Bradwell that the experiment of putting her entirely at liberty would be interesting to those having no responsibility for the results. They can afterwards dismiss the matter with a shrug of the shoulders.

Affectionately,
RTL

p.s. Please regard this letter as confidential.[28]

Meanwhile, Myra continued to apply every conceivable form of pressure not only on the principals, but also on *anyone else* who might prove useful in her battle with Robert Lincoln and Dr. Patterson. For example, during that period she wrote to Abram Wakeman, an influential New York lawyer who had been a close friend of President Lincoln. Of Mrs. Lincoln, Myra wrote:

She is in an insane asylum at Batavia and is very desirous of seeing you—she is quite well and as I think, not insane. . . . It never seemed necessary for her to be sent there—to me at least. *Yet we must silently acquiesce in the decision for a time at least.* I do hope you will write her or visit her.[29] (Emphasis added)

Myra's use of irony may have been unintentional, but it was irony none-theless. Her continual prodding of both Dr. Patterson and Robert Lincoln, as well as her arranging for the covert visit of Franc Wilkie, were hardly manifestations of "silent acquiescence." Indeed, from the time of the Illinois Supreme Court's denial of her right to practice law in 1869 until the date of her death twenty-five years later, "silent acquiescence" was not a term in Myra Bradwell's behavioral repertoire.

Abram Wakeman, who had already allied himself with Robert Lincoln, refused either to visit or to write to Mrs. Lincoln. In a letter of reply, he gently chided Myra not only for her assessment of Mrs. Lincoln's sanity but also for her clandestine meddling into the affairs of the Lincoln family. Wake-man wrote:

> [When Mrs. Lincoln] came to . . . [New York] to see her wardrobe, her con-duct in reference to me and others was such as to leave a painful impression as to the state of her mind. . . . I cannot, without great difficulty, go to Illi-nois to visit her now. . . . May I ask whether your letter to me is with the approval of her son and friends, and whether it should not be brought to their knowledge?[30]

Myra did not appear to be disheartened. Prior to her correspondence with Wakeman, she had sent a brief note to Dr. Patterson. Showing her disdain for him by addressing him as *Mr.* Patterson, rather than *Dr.* Patterson, she wrote: "Will you do as you agreed—and send me Mrs. Edwards' letter [in which Mrs. Edwards had invited Mrs. Lincoln to stay with her]?"[31]

Dr. Patterson, apparently chafing from Myra's tactics, immediately dashed off the following note to Robert:

> Will you please do me the favor to send Mrs. Edwards' letter to Mrs. Bradwell, without a moment's further delay and thus enable me to do as I agreed? . . . I have written to the *irate lady* explaining and expressing my regrets.[32]

Robert momentarily succumbed. He hastily sent Myra not only Mrs. Edwards's invitation but also a contrite note of apology for his delay:

> Dr. Patterson sent . . . me your note asking for Mrs. Edwards' letter. He had already some days sent the letter to me to be transmitted to you and the delay is caused by my accidental neglect or forgetfulness for which I beg to be excused.[33]

Robert's explanation seems disingenuous at best. It is doubtful that his delay was caused by either "accidental neglect" or "forgetfulness." The matter of his mother's pending departure from the asylum was of paramount importance to him. Indeed, so determined was he that his mother remain incarcerated that he was willing to do *virtually anything* to ensure that she not be released. Two days after apologizing to Myra for his "forgetfulness," he wrote the following letter to his mother:

> I am dreadfully disappointed that Aunt Lizzie writes me that she is not well enough to have you visit just now, but I am going to try to arrange it with her very soon. There is nothing I want so much as to have you with her, for I am sure nothing would do you as much good. . . . You must trust me that I can and will do everything that is for your good, and you must not allow yourself to think otherwise. . . .[34]

Robert was lying not only about "Aunt Lizzie's" health but also about his desire to have his mother released to the care of her sister. Elizabeth Edwards had *never* said that she was "not well enough to have . . . [Mrs. Lincoln] visit just now." On the contrary, although somewhat ambivalent about the matter, Mrs. Edwards had already extended an invitation to Mrs. Lincoln, an invitation that Robert had begrudgingly forwarded to Myra along with an apology for his "forgetfulness." Robert was also lying to his mother when he told her that "there is nothing I want so much as to have you with [your sister]" and that he planned to "arrange it with [Mrs. Edwards] very soon." *It had already been arranged,* and Robert was doing everything in his power to see that those arrangements were not carried out. He continued his efforts until the dawn of Mrs. Lincoln's release.[35]

On the same day that Robert had apologized to Myra for his "forgetfulness," he went to Batavia to see both his mother and Dr. Patterson. Robert protested to Dr. Patterson that "Myra Bradwell was a pest and a nuisance."[36] He characterized her clandestine introduction of Franc Wilkie as an "outrage"[37] and indicated that he was unwilling to arrange for his mother to leave the asylum.

At this juncture, Robert was in the throes of a dilemma. On the one hand, Dr. Patterson, spurred on by Myra and the consequent threat of public exposure, had requested that Robert arrange for Mrs. Lincoln to live with her sister and had virtually forced Robert to convey Mrs. Edwards's note to Myra. On the other hand, Robert, who was motivated by self-interest but probably not by malice, believed that "putting [his mother] entirely at liberty" would result in a great deal of public embarrassment for the Lincoln family. He was absolutely horrified at the specter of Mrs. Lincoln's "making herself talked of by everybody."[38] Moreover, he believed that his mother's release would result in the dwindling of her assets. Robert was conservator of his mother's estate. Her four-month stay at Bellevue Place had cost only $729. In contrast, her subsequent nine-month stay with Mrs. Edwards in Springfield cost $4,600.[39] Obviously, while incarcerated in the asylum, Mrs. Lincoln could not indulge her spending addiction. Freedom from restraint would and did bring with it freedom to spend, and spend, and spend.

On the day following his visit to Batavia Robert wrote Myra yet another letter:

> I visited my mother yesterday and I could not help observing . . . a renewal in degree of same appearances which marred her in May and which I had not noticed in my last four visits. I do not know of any outside causes for this unless it is the constant excitement she has been in since your first visit. . . . In view of what I have seen and which I regard as a distraction of the good accomplished by two months and a half of quiet and freedom from all chance of excitement, I am compelled to request that you visit her less often and not at all with persons with whom I am not acquainted and especially that you do not aid her in corresponding with persons other than her relatives. As to them Dr. Patterson will mail unopened as many letters as she desires to write.[40]

At this point, Dr. Patterson, too, was faced with a dilemma. On the one hand, Mrs. Lincoln's stay at Bellevue was causing him a great deal of annoyance and potential embarrassment. On the other hand, he felt responsible to Robert, who truly desired his mother's continuous confinement despite his pronouncements to the contrary. The only solution, Dr. Patterson believed, was to cut off communication between Mrs. Lincoln and the Bradwells. Only then would he and Robert be in control of the situation. Thus, on August 15, Dr. Patterson wrote a letter to the Bradwells forbidding further oral or written communication between them and Mrs. Lincoln. He stated:

> So much discussion with the patient about going away tends to unsettle her mind and make her more discontented and should be stopped. She should be let alone. She should never have been subjected to this unnecessary excitement. It is now apparent that the frequent visits of Mr. and Mrs. Bradwell and especially the letters of Mrs. Bradwell have tended to stir up discontent and thus do harm.[41]

Myra and James were not exactly souls of compliance. Indeed, upon receiving Dr. Patterson's ultimatum, they became more determined than ever to secure Mrs. Lincoln's release. This time their strategy was threefold. First, Myra would visit Mrs. Edwards in Springfield in order to persuade her that Mrs. Lincoln must be released immediately. Second, James would publicly accuse Dr. Patterson of trying to "drive [Mrs. Lincoln] insane." Third, and most important, Franc Wilkie of the *Chicago Times* would then publish his account of his visit with a "perfectly sound and healthy" Mrs. Lincoln and also his interview with "an extremely reluctant" Myra Bradwell.

On August 17 Myra once again visited Mrs. Edwards in Springfield. Mrs. Edwards's response to Myra's visit was, among other things, a testimonial to Myra's extraordinary powers of persuasion. Only six days earlier, on August 11, Mrs. Edwards had written to Robert that she was suspicious of Myra's motives, that her ostensible cooperation with Myra was simply an act of "courtesy," and that she had "made a mistake in explaining to [Myra] my views on the subject of the treatment I supposed would be most beneficial to your mother."[42] However, on August 17, immediately after talking with Myra, Mrs. Edwards did a complete about-face. Informing Robert that "I write in haste," she dispatched the following letter to him:

> I have just had a call from Mrs. Bradwell, on an errand from your mother. You are the chief person interested in this painful case, and should determine it as you think the best. It may be that a refusal to yield to [your mother's] wishes, at this crisis, will greatly increase her disorder. [Mrs. Bradwell] showed me a letter from your mother which satisfies me that you have misapprehended my intention. While willing to receive [her], I shrank from the responsibility after your statement of her condition.
>
> I now say, that *if you will bring her down, [I am] feeling perfectly willing to make the experiment.* I promise to do all in my power for her comfort and recovery. . . . Further arrangements when I see you.[43]

Upon learning that Mrs. Edwards was unequivocally committed to "receive" Mrs. Lincoln, James Bradwell wrote a threatening letter to Dr. Patterson that "just happened" to be published in a Chicago newspaper. In it James argued that if the doctor truly cared about Mrs. Lincoln's well-being, he would release her to the custody of her sister. He stated that Mrs. Lincoln's continued confinement was "calculated to drive her insane." Moreover, if the doctor refused to act, then James "as Mrs. Lincoln's legal advisor and friend" would seek a writ of habeas corpus to "open the door of Mrs. Lincoln's prison house."[44]

Five days later, on August 24, the *Chicago Times* published Franc Wilkie's account of his talk with "a perfectly sound and healthy" Mrs. Lincoln, and also his interview with "an extremely reluctant" Myra Bradwell. Excerpts from Wilkie's very lengthy narrative of his visit with Mrs. Lincoln read as follows:

REASON RESTORED

Mrs. Lincoln will soon return from Her Brief Visit
to the Insane Asylum.

For Her Physicians Pronounce Her as Sane as
Those Who Sent Her There.

And She is Only Awaiting Robert's Return from the
East to Set Her Free Again.

How She Talked with a "Times" Correspondent
in a Recent Interview.

Her recollection of Past Events and What She
had to Say of Them.

What Mrs. Myra Bradwell Has Been doing in Her Behalf.

The public was somewhat shocked a few months since by the announcement that Mrs. Lincoln, the widow of President Lincoln, was insane; and further pained by the announcement of the fact that she had been confined in a private insane asylum at Batavia, in this state, owned and managed by Dr. Patterson. . . .

Recently a Representative of THE TIMES, in quest of scientific facts by means of personal observation, visited the institution of Dr. Patterson at Batavia, *and while there was introduced to Mrs. Lincoln by a mutual friend who happened to be there at the same time, not as a newspaper man but as a gentleman who knew her history and who took a friendly interest in all that pertained to her welfare.*

[This] gentleman of the press [was determined] to discover the exact condition of her mind so far as he was able to do so, by drawing her into conversation on all possible topics in which he deemed her to have been interested, either pleasantly or painfully during her life. If there were any weak points in her mind, he was determined to find out what they were. . . . There was, however, NOT A SIGN OF WEAKNESS or any abnormal manifestations of mind visible. . . . Concerning Mr. Lincoln, she related anecdotes illustrating his extreme good nature. She conversed about the assassination. No mental weakness, under any possible test, could be discovered. . . . Her health at present, she observed, was superb. She had never been better. When she came to Chicago from Florida she had been suffering somewhat from fever, and her nervous system was somewhat shattered. She was prostrated, and any eccentricities she might have manifested then, if any, she attributed to this fact.

There were some light iron bars over the door, to which she called the attention of the gentleman. She said they seemed to menace her, and they annoyed her with the idea that she was in prison. . . . *The gentleman departed thoroughly convinced that whatever condition of mind Mrs. Lincoln may have been in previously, she is unquestionably compos mentis now, and ought not to be deprived of her liberty.*[45] (Emphasis added)

Nowhere in the first part of his article did Wilkie mention that the "mutual friend" who introduced him to Mrs. Lincoln was Myra Bradwell. Perhaps he thought that fact would detract from the force of the concluding portion of his story, which was a verbatim account of his interview with an "extremely reluctant" Myra Bradwell:

A reporter of THE TIMES last evening called on MRS. MYRA BRADWELL at her residence on Michigan Avenue, and obtained from that lady some interesting particulars concerning Mrs. Lincoln. Mrs. Bradwell has been a warm personal friend of Mrs. Lincoln for some years, and has been in active correspondence with her during the past years. She has been associated with her intimately, and is thoroughly acquainted with her mental condition. During the past few weeks this lady has visited Mrs. Lincoln at Batavia several times, and has conversed with her for hours. She has occupied the same room and the same bed with her, and has received letters from her full of sensibility, affection, and pathos.

"What have you to say concerning Mrs. Lincoln's condition, Mrs. Bradwell?" asked the reporter after disposing of the preliminaries to the subject.

"I am extremely reluctant about saying anything about this matter at the present time," replied the lady, "on account of the unpleasant situation of things."

R.—I am informed that you have visited Mrs. Lincoln several times recently, and have had long conversations with her.

Mrs. B.—So I have. I have always had the tenderest regard and love for Mrs. Lincoln, and during her stay in Florida received many long and beautifully-written letters from her. I was inexpressibly shocked when I learned of her alleged insanity, and of her confinement in an asylum at Batavia. I wondered what could have occurred to unbalance her mind so suddenly. It was a matter of the greatest surprise and astonishment to me.

R.—Do you think Mrs. Lincoln is insane?

Mrs. B.—I will be frank with you in answering that question. I think Mrs. Lincoln has no more cause for being confined behind bolts and bars than any other person whose sanity is not questioned. *She is no more insane than I am.*

R.—What was the object of your visit to Batavia?

Mrs. B.—I felt a deep interest in the welfare of Mrs. Lincoln. I went to see her and conversed with her for two hours. I obtained permission of Dr. Patterson to visit her again. I went again and again.

R.—What did you do upon your return to Chicago, Mrs. Bradwell?

Mrs. B.—Upon my return to Chicago from my first visit I obtained an interview with Mr. Robert Lincoln. I told him what I thought of the condition of his mother, and I referred to my long acquaintance with her. He acknowledged to me that he thought I was acting for what I deemed the best interests of his mother. If Mrs. Edwards, of Springfield, a sister of Mrs. Lincoln, would receive her, he would go himself to Batavia and conduct her there, provided Dr. Patterson would sign a certificate of her recovery.

R.—Has Dr. Patterson signed such a certificate?

Mrs. B.—He has, but it had not yet been delivered to Mrs. Lincoln.

R.—Did you learn whether Mrs. Edwards would receive her sister?

Mrs. B.—I did. I made a visit to Springfield. I had a long conversation with her. She promised to receive her sister and take care of her. Mrs. Edwards is a lady of fine feelings and cultivation. She has a beautiful home, surrounded by lawns and flowers. It is just the place for a sorrow-burdened heart like Mrs. Lincoln's to find repose and peace. On my return here I called to see Mr. Robert Lincoln, but he had gone east. Nothing can be done until his return. *It is this circumstance which causes me to regret the publication of anything concerning this matter at the present time. It is premature and places me in a delicate position. It would have been better to have delayed it.*

R.—Do you think Mrs. Lincoln's release can be attained without an appeal to the law?

Mrs. B.—Unquestionably. I have no reason in the world to doubt Mr. Robert Lincoln's word. I believe he will do as he said he would. He informed me though, that he was very certain Mrs. Edwards would not consent to receiving her.

R.—What did Mrs. Lincoln say about the visit to her sister?

Mrs. B.—She implored me in the tenderest and most pathetic terms to go and see Mrs. Edwards and ask her to receive her.

R.—How did you find her situated?

Mrs. B.—I found her very comfortably cared for. When I first went there, there were bars over her windows and doors and this fact seemed to annoy her. I spoke to Dr. Patterson about it, and the next time I visited her she was in a room without bars. The bolt was not turned on the outside, which afforded her some relief.

The reporter thus concluded his conversation with Mrs. Bradwell, who feels the keenest interest in the welfare of her friend. There seems to be no doubt that Mrs. Lincoln's mind is now sound and that she will be restored to the world in a short time. Mr. Robert Lincoln will return from the east next week, when he will act in the matter. The country will rejoice at the liberation.[46] (Emphasis added)

Myra's statement that she was "extremely reluctant" to say anything about Mrs. Lincoln's plight was, to say the least, disingenuous. She not only had arranged for Wilkie's interviews of both herself and Mrs. Lincoln, but also had strategically delayed the publication date of his story. While Wilkie's meeting with Mrs. Lincoln occurred on August 7—the date on which Myra surreptitiously guided him into Bellevue Place—his account of that meeting, along with his interview with Myra, did not appear in the *Times* until August 24.

The timing of the *Times*'s publication must have been Myra's, not Wilkie's. It is unlikely that a newspaper editor would have delayed such a "hot" story for seventeen days without a very good reason for doing so. One can only speculate that Myra had offered to sneak Wilkie into the asylum in return for Wilkie's promise to allow Myra to control the timing of the publication.

The timing was perfect! In the interview, Myra "reluctantly" announced to the readers of the *Times* that Robert had consented to allow Mrs. Lincoln to live with her sister (not true) and that Dr. Patterson had signed a "certificate of [Mrs. Lincoln's] recovery" (also not true). Candor was never one of Myra's redeeming virtues. Ever the utilitarian, she seemed to believe in all her pursuits that any means (including deceit) were permissible as long as the ends were noble. Results were all that mattered, and results were instantaneously achieved.

The public immediately began to clamor for the release of President Lincoln's widow. Ministers made her plight the subject of their weekly sermons, and newspapers inveighed against the manner in which she had been "incarcerated" by her very own son.[47] For example, one journalist poignantly wrote:

> One of the saddest of all sad incidents connected with the life of Mrs. Abraham Lincoln was the recent proceeding by which her own son secured her incarceration in an Insane Asylum. When a woman spends her own money lavishly and appears a little different from others she ought not to be placed behind iron bars. If this sort of proceeding is to be countenanced, where will the end be? Mrs. Lincoln has had enough trials and troubles to break down any ordinary woman and yet she has borne all and wronged no one. Let her be released.[48]

Dr. Patterson felt constrained to defend himself publicly. On August 28 in a letter to the *Chicago Tribune* he reiterated his belief that Mrs. Lincoln was insane, a rather shocking public disclosure judged by today's norms of doctor-patient confidentiality. Those standards did not govern in the nineteenth century, and Dr. Patterson wrote:

> It has been publicly stated that I have "certified" to the recovery or mental soundness of Mrs. Lincoln. This is not true. . . . I have not at any time regarded her as a person of sound mind. . . . *I believe her to be now insane. . . . [But] I am still unwilling to throw any obstacle in the way of giving her an opportunity to have a home with her sister.* But I am willing to record the opinion that such is the character of her malady she will not be content to do this, and that the experiment, if made, will result only in giving her the coveted opportunity to make extended rambles, to renew the indulgence of her purchasing mania, and other morbid manifestations.[49]

Then, in a parting shot at James and Myra, Dr. Patterson wrote:

> [Mrs. Lincoln] has had until the 16th [of this month] private unrestricted personal intercourse with Judge Bradwell, who, in a threatening and insulting letter to me calls himself "her legal adviser and friend." The wife of Judge Bradwell, until the date above named, has been permitted repeatedly to visit

Mrs. Lincoln, write her numerous letters, bear messages and packages of letters from her and lodge over night with her in her room. . . . Mrs. Lincoln has been placed where she is under the forms of law, and if any have a grievance, the law is open to them.[50]

But Myra and James did not need the "law" to redress their grievance. As soon as Dr. Patterson had publicly stated that Mrs. Lincoln could be released, the matter was a *fait accompli.* Indeed, the newspapers of Chicago and its environs immediately announced that "Mrs. Abraham Lincoln of Bellevue, Illinois, will shortly visit her sister, Mrs. Edwards of Springfield, Illinois."[51]

Even though they had accomplished their objective, Myra and James were not willing to allow Dr. Patterson to have the last public word. A few days after Dr. Patterson's letter appeared in the *Chicago Tribune,* James gave an interview to the *Chicago Post and Mail* in which he told a reporter that:

[Mrs. Lincoln] is no more insane today than you and I are. . . . I am as THOROUGHLY CONVINCED OF IT as of my own existence. I have had several business letters from her since she has been there, and Mrs. Bradwell has had letters of womanly friendship from her repeatedly; and she writes straight and intelligible a business letter as she ever did, and as good, friendly letters as one need ask for. There is NOT THE SLIGHTEST TRACE OF INSANITY or of a weak mind in her writings.[52]

James concluded the interview by noting:

DR. PATTERSON IS A VERY PECULIAR MAN. I know that some of the letters [Mrs. Lincoln] has sent have not been allowed to reach her friends, and some that have been sent her have not reached her. You can't tell what motives may tend to keep her there. Human nature is human nature. But, if she is not soon out, there will be startling developments not to be mentioned now.[53]

There was, however, no need for "startling developments" because Mrs. Lincoln was "soon out" in less than two weeks. Robert did, however, make one last-ditch effort to effect the continued confinement of his mother. On September 4, six days before Mrs. Lincoln's release, Robert wrote to Dr. Andrew McFarland, the former president of the Association of Medical Superintendents of American Institutions for the Insane, an organization that was, in some respects, the predecessor of the American Psychiatric Association. Requesting that Dr. McFarland interview Mrs. Lincoln, Robert continued:

As a guest of her sister, I do not think it possible that the same restraint could be exercised over the possible irrational acts should they occur as if she remained under the care of Dr. Patterson.[54]

Dr. McFarland responded by immediately interviewing Mrs. Lincoln "in the strictest secrecy."[55] On September 8, he wrote to Robert that he could "see no good results likely to follow [from Mrs. Lincoln's impending visit to Springfield] beyond gratifying an ardent desire to go."[56] He believed that if released from the asylum, "a desire for further adventure will take possession of her mind . . . that may be attended with hazard if gratified."[57]

Robert did not use McFarland's letter. Two days later, on September 10, 1875, Mrs. Lincoln, escorted by a very begrudging Robert, departed from Bellevue Place to the home of her sister in Springfield.

Mary Todd Lincoln was never again confined to an asylum. After living with the Edwardses in Springfield for nine months, she was summarily declared "sane" by the Cook County Court. She then exiled herself to France for several years until her physical health declined. Returning to the Edwardses' home in Springfield, she died in 1882 at the age of sixty-four.

In their recent book, *The Insanity File: The Case of Mary Todd Lincoln,*[58] Mark E. Neely, Jr., and R. Gerald McMurty conclude that the reason that Robert did not use the letter of the eminent Dr. McFarland was that Robert truly loved his mother and therefore chose, in the end, to defer to her wishes. In the words of Neely and McMurty, "the heart of the son [had] conquered the head of the lawyerly conservator."[59] Or, in other words, Robert Lincoln had finally resolved his Oedipus complex.

This author, however, believes that the real reason that Robert did not use Dr. McFarland's letter was that the letter was simply a matter of too little and too late. Indeed, on the day before he received Dr. McFarland's letter, Robert also received one from Dr. Patterson, who wrote: "Now that so much is said about Mrs. Lincoln's removal to Springfield, I think it would be well if she could go at once."[60]

Even Neely and McMurty, both admirers of Robert Lincoln, concede that:

To date, Robert had used . . . letters [such as McFarland's] . . . to buttress his opposition to the Springfield scheme, *even while he told his mother and Mrs. Bradwell that he was hoping it could be worked out.* His course to this point had been almost perversely legalistic if not downright obstructionist.[61] (Emphasis added)

Robert Lincoln's "course," however, was more than "downright obstructionist." It was also downright duplicitous. Of course, Myra Bradwell also was guilty of duplicity. The fight over Mrs. Lincoln's fate had been a battle between two formidable adversaries. Each was legally trained, and each was willing to use *any* means, including deceit, to accomplish the result which he or she desired. But Robert Lincoln, the much-admired son of the late revered president, never stood a chance.

From the outset of the contest until its denouement, Robert Lincoln had been bested by Myra Bradwell, a woman who had been denied the right to practice law by the Supreme Court of Illinois and also by the Supreme Court of the United States. Myra Bradwell had written her own two versions of the Emancipation Proclamation: one for herself, the other for Mary Todd Lincoln.

NOTES

1. Ishbel Ross, *The President's Wife: Mary Todd Lincoln* (New York: G. P. Putman's Sons, 1973), p. 173.

2. Except where otherwise indicated, this account of Mary Todd Lincoln's commitment was taken from the following sources: Ruth Painter Randall, *Mary Lincoln: Biography of a Marriage* (Boston: Little, Brown and Company, 1953); W. A. Evans, *Mrs. Abraham Lincoln: A Study of Her Personality and Her Influence on Lincoln* (New York: Alfred A. Knopf, 1932); Homer Croy, *The Trial of Mrs. Abraham Lincoln* (New York: Van Rees Press, 1962); Rodney A. Ross, "Mary Todd Lincoln, Patient at Bellevue Place, Batavia," *Journal of the Illinois Historical Society* (Spring 1970): 5–35; Ishbel Ross, *The President's Wife: Mary Todd Lincoln;* Jean H. Baker, *Mary Todd Lincoln: A Biography* (New York: W. W. Norton and Company, 1987).

3. In 1975, Robert's grandson, Robert Todd Lincoln Beckwith, and Beckwith's friend, James Hickey, then the curator of the Lincoln Collection of the Illinois State Historical Library, discovered more than forty books containing copies of Robert Lincoln's correspondence [hereafter cited as RTL Letterbooks]. They also found a separate bundle of papers, tied up in pink ribbon, which Robert had marked "MTL [Mary Todd Lincoln] Insanity File."

Robert's grandson eventually turned both the RTL Letterbooks and the MTL Insanity File over to two Lincoln scholars, Mark E. Neely, director of the Louis A. Warren Lincoln Library and Museum in Fort Wayne, Indiana, and R. Gerald McMurty, former director of the Lincoln National Life Foundation. Those two scholars subsequently published a book entitled *The Insanity File: The Case of Mary Todd Lincoln* (Carbondale, Ill.: Southern Illinois University Press, 1986). This book will hereinafter be cited as Neely and McMurty.

After the original RTL Letterbooks and MTL Insanity File were made public, this author traveled to Fort Wayne and made copies of all the documents concerning Mary Todd Lincoln's relationship to Myra Bradwell. When the actual documents are referred to, the citations will be to "RTL Letterbooks" and "MTL Insanity File," in contradistinction to the citation to Neely and McMurty's book, which will be cited as Neely and McMurty.

4. Leonard Swett to David Davis, May 24, 1875, David Davis Family Papers, quoted in Neely and McMurty, p. 17.

5. See, e.g., Neely and McMurty.

6. See, e.g., Samuel A. Schreiner, *The Trials of Mrs. Lincoln* (New York: Donald I. Fine, 1987), pp. 321–23:

Robert and his advisers . . . had at last found a way to deal with an annoying "hysterical" female who, as Robert said, "never heeds my advice." . . . Neely and McMurty are to be credited with pioneering in establishing the prevailing prejudice against women among physicians at the time when Mrs. Lincoln was so unanimously diagnosed as insane, even though it tends to undermine their own conclusion.

7. Letter from attorney Leonard Swett to Illinois Supreme Court Justice David Davis, May 24, 1875, David Davis Papers, Illinois State Historical Library, Springfield, Illinois.

8. Neely and McMurty, pp. 21–22.

9. Schreiner, *The Trials of Mrs. Lincoln,* p. 321.

10. Ibid., pp. 324–26.

11. J. G. Turner and L. L. Turner, *Mary Todd Lincoln: Her Life and Her Letters* (New York: Alfred A. Knopf, 1972).

12. Schreiner, *The Trials of Mrs. Lincoln,* p. 322.

13. Ibid., pp. 134–35.

14. Letter from Dr. Richard J. Patterson to John S. Winter, August 8, 1876, quoted in Ross, "Mary Todd Lincoln."

15. Quoted in Bellevue Place's "Patient Progress Reports Relating to Mrs. Lincoln," set forth in full in appendix to Rodney Ross's article, "Mary Todd Lincoln" (hereafter cited as "Patient Progress Reports Relating to Mrs. Lincoln").

16. Affidavit of Myra Bradwell's friend, Eleanor Gridley, dated 1929 (in author's possession).

17. See "Statement Regarding the Disposal of Mary Lincoln Letters," signed by Myra's granddaughter, Myra Bradwell Helmer Pritchard, March 1, 1928 (in author's possession).

18. Quoted in Eleanor Gridley, "Presentation of Bronze Bust of Mrs. Myra Bradwell, First Woman Lawyer in Illinois," *Transactions of the Illinois State Historical Society* 38 (1931).

19. Pritchard, "Statement Regarding the Disposal of Mary Lincoln Letters."

20. Undated article in Bloomington, Illinois, *Courier,* in author's possession. Although the article on file is undated, it is clear from the text that it was published one day after Myra's visit to Batavia. In the article, Myra spoke of the visit "I paid to Batavia yesterday."

21. Ibid.

22. Dr. Patterson to Myra Bradwell, August 9, 1875, MTL Insanity File.

23. *Chicago Times* (August 24, 1875): 5.

24. Schreiner, *The Trials of Mrs. Lincoln,* p. 159.

25. See Neely and McMurty, pp. 79–80: "[Robert] scoffed . . . at his aunt's belief in Mary [Todd Lincoln's] indifference to spiritualism. 'She hardly thinks of anything else,' Robert insisted, 'and almost her only companions are spiritualists.' "

26. Dr. Patterson to Robert Lincoln, August 9, 1875, MTL Insanity File.

27. Robert Todd Lincoln to Elizabeth Todd Edwards, August 10, 1875, MTL Insanity File.

28. Ibid.

29. Myra Bradwell to Abram Wakeman, August 12, 1875, MTL Insanity File.

30. Abram Wakeman to Myra Bradwell, August 17, 1875, MTL Insanity File.

31. Myra Bradwell to Dr. Patterson, August 11, 1875, MTL Insanity File.

32. Dr. Patterson to Robert Lincoln, August 12, 1875, MTL Insanity File.

33. Robert Todd Lincoln to Myra Bradwell, August 13, 1875, MTL Insanity File.

34. Robert Lincoln to Mary Todd Lincoln, August 15, 1875, RTL Letterbooks.

35. See text accompanying notes 54 through 57 *infra.*

36. "Patient Progress Reports Relating to Mrs. Lincoln," August 13, 1875.

37. Ibid.

38. Neely and McMurty, p. 71.

39. Ross, "Mary Todd Lincoln," p. 20.

40. Robert Todd Lincoln to Myra Bradwell, August 14, 1875, MTL Insanity File.

41. Dr. Patterson to the Bradwells, August 15, 1875, MTL Insanity File.

42. Elizabeth Edwards to Robert Lincoln, August 11, 1875, MTL Insanity File.

43. Elizabeth Edwards to Robert Lincoln, August 17, 1875, MTL Insanity File.

44. Unidentified newspaper clipping of letter from James Bradwell to Dr. Patterson, dated August 19, 1875 (in author's possession).

45. *Chicago Times* (August 24, 1875): 5.

46. Ibid.

47. Homer Croy, *The Trial of Mrs. Lincoln* (New York: Van Rees Press, 1902).

48. Unidentified newspaper clipping in possession of author. See also *Springfield Journal,* August 25, 1875, which, while referring to the Bradwells as "busybodies," stated that "there will be universal satisfaction to know that Mrs. Lincoln has been restored to her reason and her friends."

49. *Chicago Tribune,* August 28, 1875, letter to editor from Dr. R. J. Patterson (in possession of author).

50. Ibid.

51. See, e.g., *Aurora Beacon* (August 29, 1875): 3, col. 4.

52. Clipping from *Chicago Post and Mail* (in possession of author).

53. Ibid.

54. Robert Lincoln to Dr. Andrew McFarland, Jacksonville, Illinois, September 4, 1875, RTL Letterbooks.

55. Andrew McFarland to Robert Lincoln, September 8, 1875, MTL Insanity File. Dr. McFarland was the same physician who participated in the incarceration of Elizabeth Packard. See chapter 10, *infra,* text accompanying endnotes 38 through 43.

56. Ibid.

57. Ibid.

58. Neely and McMurty, p. 72.

59. Ibid.

60. Dr. Patterson to Robert Lincoln, September 7, 1875, MTL Insanity File.

61. Neely and McMurty, p. 72.

4

"These Letters Could Not Be Published" Bradwell's Granddaughter Disposes of the Bradwell-Lincoln Correspondence

Before departing for France, Mrs. Lincoln showered the Bradwells not only with gratitude and praise, but also with many gifts, remembrances of herself and President Lincoln. Among these were the pen used by the president in signing the Emancipation Proclamation, his "Definition of Democracy" in his own handwriting, a bloodstone seal presented to President Lincoln by the Sultan of Turkey, an oil painting that had hung in the Lincoln home at Springfield, and one of Mrs. Lincoln's most prized and valuable personal possessions, a gold chain bracelet set with pearl that had been a birthday present to Mrs. Lincoln from her husband.[1] Thus, Mrs. Lincoln's generosity extended not only to herself but also to the two people who had been willing to spend their time, effort, and considerable abilities to secure her freedom.

The praise and gratitude that Mrs. Lincoln bestowed upon the Bradwells were in marked contrast to the rancor that she expressed toward her son. On June 19, 1876, four days after she was summarily declared sane, she wrote Robert an extraordinarily bitter and accusatory letter, which began curtly "Robert T. Lincoln." After demanding the return of all her goods, she continued:

> I am now in constant receipt of letters from my friends denouncing you in the bitterest terms . . . six letters from prominent respectable Chicago people such as you do not associate with. . . . Send me all that I have written for you have tried your game of robbery long enough.[2]

And robbery it was, at least with respect to the correspondence between Mary Todd Lincoln and Myra Bradwell. All of Mrs. Lincoln's biographers have been aware that such correspondence once existed, and all have puzzled over its mysterious disappearance. One biographer has written, "[Mrs. Lincoln's] letters to the Bradwells have vanished"[3]; a second has lamented, "It is to be regretted that we have nothing of the Bradwell correspondence except the tradition";[4] and a third, J. G. Turner, has speculated, "None of Mrs. Lincoln's letters to the Bradwells remains, and there is reason to believe Robert had theirs to her destroyed, so damning were they to him."[5]

While Turner's speculation is undoubtedly correct, it explains only the destruction of the letters that Myra and James wrote *to* Mrs. Lincoln, and which then either devolved to or were confiscated by Robert. Turner's conjecture provides no explanation for the disappearance of the letters that the Bradwells received *from* Mrs. Lincoln. Certainly that correspondence would not have devolved to Robert, nor could it have been stolen by him. Or could it have been? The answer, sadly, is yes, fifty years after it came into existence. Among the Bradwell documents recently discovered by this author[6] were affidavits, contracts, letters, and memoranda, which, when pieced together, explain how Robert—or, rather, the attorneys for his estate—were able to obtain and undoubtedly destroy the letters that Mrs. Lincoln had written to Myra.

As has been previously discussed,[7] when Myra died, her personal papers were bequeathed to her daughter, Bessie Bradwell Helmer, a brilliant young woman who had graduated from Northwestern Law School as valedictorian. When Bessie died, the collection passed to Bessie's daughter, Myra Bradwell Helmer Pritchard (hereafter referred to as Myra Pritchard), "with the stipulation that [Myra Pritchard] should write about [the correspondence between her grandmother and Mrs. Lincoln] but not until both [Bessie] and Robert Lincoln . . . passed on." Bessie was "most anxious that these letters be published because she felt that Mrs. Abraham Lincoln had been maligned and that these letters would explain much of the real Mrs. Lincoln to the world and place her in a more favorable light."[8] Unfortunately, the granddaughter not only filed Myra Bradwell's papers in a manner that made them almost undiscoverable[9] but also allowed herself to be bullied into selling Mary Todd Lincoln's letters to the Robert Lincoln estate, whose attorneys undoubtedly destroyed them. To make matters worse, after the death of Myra Pritchard, her executrix destroyed all the copies that the granddaughter had made of the Bradwell–Lincoln correspondence.

As J. G. Turner has hypothesized, it is almost a certainty that Robert Lincoln destroyed all the letters that Myra and James had written *to* his mother, letters written before, during, and after Mary Todd Lincoln's confinement in the insane asylum. It is not clear whether Robert personally attempted to gain access to and get rid of the letters that the Bradwells received *from* his mother.

But that seems to have been the case, for after Robert's death, his wife and children pursued the matter with great tenacity and ultimately obtained and probably destroyed the last remnants of that correspondence.

Robert Lincoln died in 1926. At that time Myra's granddaughter, Myra Pritchard, was in possession of thirty-seven letters written by Mrs. Lincoln to Myra relating to the former's confinement and release from the insane asylum. Myra Pritchard desired to fulfill the wishes of her mother and grandmother to have Mrs. Lincoln's letters published so that history would, perhaps, record her not as a ranting lunatic, but rather as a much misunderstood woman who had been treated shamefully by her son and subsequently rescued by her friend, Myra Bradwell. In pursuit of that goal, Myra Pritchard entered into a contract with *Liberty Weekly*, a New York periodical, in which Myra Pritchard agreed to write "a serial article concerning the life of Mary Todd Lincoln, the wife of Abraham Lincoln, based upon certain letters passing between Mrs. Lincoln and [James and Myra Bradwell]."[10]

Myra Pritchard did in fact write the manuscript "of some twelve or fifteen chapters setting up in narrative form the contents of numerous Mary Lincoln letters constituting an exchange of correspondence between her and the Bradwell family."[11] That manuscript was never published. On January 30, 1928, *Liberty Weekly* and Myra Pritchard canceled their contract and the publisher "returned to [Myra Pritchard] the manuscript and other material connected therewith."[12] On the very next day, Myra Pritchard sold the letters and the manuscript to the attorneys for Robert Lincoln's family for $22,500. Undoubtedly, those materials were promptly destroyed.

Why, one might ask, would Myra Pritchard have bothered to prepare a manuscript of twelve to fifteen chapters on a matter of great historical significance, secure a publisher, and then nullify the arrangement? Greed may have supplied part of the motivation, but only a small part. The major reason, if one believes her own statement, was that the attorneys for Robert Lincoln's family convinced her that:

> *These letters could not be published* due to an old law which reads that the literary properties in letters belong to those who wrote them and to their succeeding heirs and not to the people who received them. Mrs. Woodrow Wilson created a precedent some years ago when Colonel House wished to publish some of President Wilson's letters to him and refused her consent.[13] (Emphasis added)

Myra Pritchard's sale of Mrs. Lincoln's letters to the attorneys for the Robert Lincoln family was, to put it kindly, very foolish. While it is true that, under the law as it then existed, "the literary properties in the letters belonged to those who wrote them and their succeeding heirs and not the people who received them," that meant only that Myra Pritchard could not have published the letters verbatim. Certainly, she could have written a narrative account of Myra Bradwell's relationship with Mrs. Lincoln and could have drawn heavily on Mrs. Lincoln's letters for documentation. Apparently Myra Pritchard did not even consult with an attorney, although as a woman of financial means she certainly could have afforded to do so. The result is that very important historical documents have been lost to posterity.

One can speculate that the attorneys for the Robert Lincoln family paid off not only Myra Pritchard but also the publishers with whom she had contracted. Those publishers seemed extremely amused at the circumstances surrounding the cancellation of their contract. Shortly after the publication agreement was terminated, the vice president of the publishing company wrote to one of his colleagues:

> As I haven't Mrs. Pritchard's address, I cannot return to her direct this copy of her contract. All I can say is that it sews her up as tight as a drum. In point of fact, I think if she is apprehended reading a book about Lincoln, or mentioning his name or the name of his lady, she is likely to subject herself thereby to imprisonment for life, if indeed not summary execution.[14]

But Myra Pritchard was not "sewn up" nearly as tightly as either the publishers or the lawyers believed. In spite of her contractual promise that she would make "no copies of said letters or of said manuscript,"[15] she, in fact, made typewritten copies of both. She placed the copy of the manuscript in her safety deposit box in an envelope bearing these peculiar instructions: "In case of my death this is to be destroyed immediately."[16] One can only puzzle over her ambivalence. She wanted her manuscript preserved, yet she ordered that it be destroyed. And destroyed it was! A few months after her death in 1947, her sister-in-law, Margreta Pritchard, who was also the executrix of Myra Pritchard's estate, "did . . . after announcing to members of my family my intention, personally burn the contents [of the manuscript] and entirely consumed the same in flames."[17]

But it was only the manuscript that she destroyed, not the copies of Mary Todd Lincoln's letters. Those were retained by the executrix until 1951 when, having been convinced that they were worthless, she burned them also.

The catalyst for this latter action was a man named Oliver Barrett, one of the foremost collectors of Lincoln items in the country. In 1947 Mr. Barrett had on display at the Library of Congress a body of materials that purported to be "the complete collection left by Robert Lincoln." Mr. Barrett believed that if copies of Mary Todd Lincoln's letters to the Bradwells surfaced, this would decrease the value of his Robert Lincoln collection.[18] Thus, in a letter written to Myra Pritchard's executrix by Mr. Barrett's attorneys, they counseled:

Mr. Barrett . . . [thinks] it would be advisable for us to make a detailed search of [Myra Pritchard's] belongings to see if we could obtain these typewritten copies. . . . He then feels that we should take these typewritten copies and tie them together securely and place a screw through the middle of them . . . and . . . have them destroyed. He thinks that this would be doing a great service not only to the Lincolns but also to the Bradwells and [Myra Pritchard]. He stated that the Bradwells have always had a fine name, and that he did not believe that it would be exactly morally right for these copies to be now published in view of the fact that Robert Lincoln had so violently objected to their publication during his life and had gone to the expense of purchasing them so that he could effect their destruction. [Mr. Barrett] stated that these letters would have absolutely no historical value and would be of benefit only to that type of person who desired to read the rantings of an insane person. He also felt that [destruction of the Mary Todd Lincoln letters] would tend to increase the value of the Robert Lincoln collection which was recently opened in the Library of Congress. Evidently *Life* magazine has cast some doubts on the fact as to whether or not the Library of Congress has the complete collection left by Robert Lincoln. *Life*'s question was to the effect: "Where are the letters written by Mrs. Lincoln?" . . . Mr. Barrett feels that we would all be rendering a great service if *we could put the question to rest for once and all by destroying these letters.* . . .[19] (Emphasis added)

One wonders how the executrix could have believed that a question could be "put to rest" by destroying the evidence. But Margreta Pritchard was obviously persuaded. On March 19, 1951, she signed an affidavit stating that she had "personally destroyed by burning every portion of all copies known" of all letters written to the Bradwells by Mary Todd Lincoln as well as those which the Bradwells had received from Robert Lincoln and Dr. Patterson.[20]

While at least some current Lincoln scholars believe that Mrs. Lincoln was insane and was justly treated by Robert,[21] no one will ever know with certainty for the "accused" has not been permitted to testify in the court of history. The ultimate irony is *not* that, during her lifetime, the president's widow was silenced by her son, Robert, but that after her death, Mrs. Lincoln's voice was stilled by the granddaughter of her liberator, Myra Bradwell.

NOTES

1. Letter from Myra Bradwell Helmer Pritchard to Herma Clark dated July 1931, Herma Clark collection, Chicago Historical Society; contract between Myra Bradwell Helmer Pritchard and Chicago Historical Society, October 22, 1932 (in author's possession). See also *Battle Creek News,* October 22, 1932.

2. Quoted in Ruth Painter Randall, *Mary Lincoln: Biography of a Marriage* (Boston: Little Brown and Company, 1953), pp. 433–44.

3. Ibid.

4. W. A. Evans, *Mrs. Abraham Lincoln: A Study of Her Personality and Her Influence on Lincoln* (New York: Alfred A. Knopf, 1932), p. 27.

5. J. G. Turner and L. L. Turner, *Mary Todd Lincoln: Her Life and Her Letters* (New York: Alfred A. Knopf, 1972), p. 612.

6. See Prologue.

7. Ibid.

8. Myra Pritchard, "Statement Regarding the Disposal of Mary Lincoln Letters" (in author's possession).

9. See Prologue.

10. See contract between Myra Helmer Pritchard and *Liberty Weekly* dated January 30, 1928, terminating contract between same two parties dated April 6, 1927 (in author's possession).

11. Affidavit re: Destruction of *Liberty* Magazine Manuscript relative to Mary Lincoln letters, signed by Margreta Pritchard, executrix of the estate of Myra Helmer Pritchard, September 18, 1947 (in author's possession).

12. Contract between Myra Helmer Pritchard and *Liberty Weekly.*

13. "Statement Regarding the Disposal of Mary Lincoln Letters."

14. Letter from Karl E. Harriman to Whitney Payne dated March 21, 1929 (in author's possession).

15. Contract between Myra Helmer Pritchard and Norman Frost and Frederic Towers, attorneys for the family of Robert Lincoln (in author's possession).

16. Affidavit re: Destruction of *Liberty* Magazine Manuscript Relative to Mary Lincoln Letters.

17. Ibid.

18. "Memo re: Myra Pritchard Estate Lincoln Collection" written by W. R. Dillon, attorney for Oliver Barrett, dated September 11, 1947, p. 5 (in author's possession).

19. Ibid.

20. Affidavit re: Destruction of Copies of Mary Lincoln collection signed by Margreta Pritchard, March 19, 1951 (in author's possession).

21. In *The Insanity File: The Case of Mary Todd Lincoln* (Carbondale, Ill.: Southern Illinois University Press, 1986), Mark E. Neely and R. Gerald McNulty argued that Mrs. Lincoln was, in fact, insane and was justly and humanely treated by Robert. But see Samuel A. Schreiner, *The Trials of Mrs. Lincoln* (New York: Donald I. Fine, 1987), p. 321; Jean H. Baker, *Mary Todd Lincoln: A Biography* (New York: W. W. Norton and Company, 1987), pp. 340–50.

5

The *Chicago Legal News*
The Vehicle for Reform

[The *Chicago Legal News*] is the first serious attempt by a woman to share in the labors of the law since the fourteenth century when the fair Novella d'Andrea lectured at the University of Bologna with a "Curtain Drawn before her, Lest, if her charms were seen, the students should let their young eyes wander and quite forget their jurisprudence."

—American Law Review (January 1869)[1]

The *Chicago Legal News* made its commercial debut on October 3, 1868. Naming herself publisher, business manager, and editor-in-chief, Myra's first act was to obtain a special charter from the Illinois legislature under which she could head the business without the legal handicaps that ordinarily encumbered married women. Under that charter, she was allowed to enter into contracts in her own name and was not required to turn over her earnings to her husband.

The legal community expressed wonder that a woman, "Mrs. Judge Bradwell," had founded a legal newspaper. Their consensus was that she would never be able to keep it afloat![2] Within a decade, however, those skeptics had to admit that Myra Bradwell had established the most successful legal publishing empire in the nation.[3] With commercial success came power, the power to influence the course of nineteenth-century legal and social history.

The *Chicago Legal News* bore the motto Lex Vincit (Law Conquers). At its inception, the stated goals of the weekly newspaper were modest. In her brief prospectus, Myra announced only that:

The *News* will be . . . devoted to legal information, general news, the publication of new and important decisions, and of other matters useful to the
practicing lawyer or man of business.

It will give abstracts of points decided in our local courts, comment freely,
but fairly, upon the conduct of our judges, the members of the bar, officers
of courts, members of congress and our state legislature in their administration
of public affairs.

In presenting to the public the *Chicago Legal News,* we offer no apology
and make no promises except to say that we shall do all we can to make
it a paper that every lawyer and business man in the northwest ought to
take.[4]

That Myra's prospectus was silent about her hidden agenda—the advocacy of women's rights and other legal and social innovations—is simply a
manifestation of her business acumen. An early announcement of her true
intentions would almost certainly have alienated many of her readers. Indeed,
the early reviews of the *Chicago Legal News,* almost uniformly laudatory, were
quick to compare favorably Myra's initial "mainstream" approach with that
of other, avowedly feminist, publications. For example, a few months after
Myra began publication, the *Western Jurist,* a legal quarterly, showered her
with accolades and contrasted the *Legal News* with contemporary suffragist
publications, which "exaggerate the conditions and consequences of the proposed change [in the legal status of women]—to make it out, indeed nothing
less than a revolution." The author concluded that it was through the deeds
of "quiet," moderate role-models such as Myra Bradwell that the plight of
women would be remedied:

When women learn to come forward and take possession of opportunities
already open to them with the quiet self-possession of Mrs. Bradwell and
show as she has done their ability to fill places heretofore supposed to belong
to the stronger sex alone, opposition to further advances in the same direction
will disappear.[5]

Likewise, another prestigious periodical, the *Central Law Journal,* after
praising the merits of the *News,* opined that Myra's achievements as a legal
journalist and business woman would do more to advance the goal of women's
equality than would the polemics contained in contemporary feminist tracts:
"In her able conduct of this paper we think that Mrs. Bradwell has, perhaps,
done more for the cause of women than any of her sex."[6]

Such reviews must have served to reinforce Myra's strategy to establish
both a solid commercial base and journalistic reputation first; and then to
inveigh for women's rights and other legal and social reforms.

The means that Myra employed in establishing the *News*'s commercial base were ingenious. She literally made the newspaper indispensable to every lawyer in the state of Illinois, and later in the entire nation.

Her first step was to capitalize on the extraordinary time lag between the passage of laws by the Illinois legislature and the state's publication of those laws. Prior to the advent of the *News,* it had been the practice of the Illinois secretary of state to delay publication of newly enacted statutes for three to five months after their passage.[7] Thus, a lawyer, or even a judge, had no way of knowing of changes in the law unless he traveled to Springfield to read the originals. Never one to miss an opportunity, Myra announced in an early issue that lawyers and judges would no longer have to be ignorant of the law. The *News* had entered into an agreement with the legislature whereby that body would furnish the *News* with copies of all newly passed statutes immediately after the adjournment of each legislative session. Moreover, and more importantly, Myra had obtained from the state legislature a special charter that made all laws printed in the *News* valid as "evidence of the existence and contents of such laws before all courts in Illinois."[8] This meant that no one could dispute the validity or correctness of any law that appeared in her newspaper. In order to ensure that this published "evidence" contained no errors, Myra promised that prior to its publication, she would travel personally to Springfield—a practice that she actually followed for twenty-five years—to compare her galley proofs with the original statutes in the office of the secretary of state.[9] She concluded her announcement by guaranteeing that she would "give to our readers these laws months before they can be obtained from any other source."[10]

Myra wanted to make sure that the practicing bar had not missed the point that no Illinois lawyer could effectively practice law without a copy of the *News* in hand. If he tried to do so, he would lose not only lawsuits but money as well. Thus, six weeks after she began publishing the new statutes, which were "valid as evidence in court," she reported an anecdote under the headline, "$750 Made by Taking Legal News."[11] The incident concerned a Chicago lawyer, Mr. Thompson, who, after winning a case, had asked the court to order the losing party to pay his fee. The judge replied that there was no statutory authority for such an order. A few days later, Mr. Thompson once again appeared before the court. This time he came armed with a copy of the *Legal News* that contained "evidence" of a statute, enacted just three days earlier, which authorized the court to order the losing party to pay the fees of the victorious lawyer. The judge, after carefully reading the new law, reversed his prior decision and awarded Mr. Thompson $750 in fees, exclaiming, "Mr. Thompson, you are indebted to Mrs. Bradwell for this!"

The story may have been true, it may have been apocryphal; but Myra had made her point. She had illustrated it with a subject near and dear to every lawyer's heart: the collection of fees. She concluded her column by reporting:

We are in receipt of many letters from attorneys and parties to suits telling us of gaining this or that important suit by seeing some decision or reading some law published in the *News*. The time, in Illinois at least, has come when a lawyer if he wishes to meet his opponent on equal ground must take the *Legal News*.[12]

In order to underscore the point that no Illinois lawyer could effectively practice law without religiously reading the *News*, she reprinted the following letter from the chief executive official of the Illinois Supreme Court:

Mrs. Myra Bradwell:

Madam—I have been gratified to notice the success which has attended the publication of the *Chicago Legal News* under your able and skillful supervision. *By the prompt and reliable report of recent cases, you have made the* News *not only desirable but necessary to every practicing lawyer.* I trust the coming year may secure to it a still more extended circulation and that your enterprise may receive the ample reward it deserves from your profession.

> Very respectfully, your obedient servant
> N.L. Freeman
> [Illinois Supreme Court Reporter][13]

Thus, within fourteen months after its inception, Myra had established the *News* as the official medium for the state's legislative enactments and the unofficial organ for the reporting of the state's judicial pronouncements.

However, even the very early issues of the *News*—those in which Myra was trying to establish its reputation as a conventional legal newspaper—contained far more than merely the texts of newly enacted statutes, recent judicial opinions, and reports of happenings in the legal community. For example, in the very first issue, she inveighed against the "accumulated filth" in her husband's professional habitat, the Cook County Court House.[14] Two months later she decried conditions in the county poor house, making a suggestion—novel for its time—that the board of supervisors make a surprise visit to that institution in order to dine with the local inmates:

It is the practice in many counties in the state for the board to visit the poor house in a body, and to give notice to the warden of the poor house that on such a day the board will make its usual visit. On the appointed day the board, the county officials, their friends and such politicians as desire to go are conveyed in carriages at the expense of the county, to the poor house, where they find the floors scrubbed, the rooms cleaned up in anticipation of their coming, and a good turkey dinner provided for them at the expense of the county. . . . We protest against such visits.

We believe these visits should be made when the parties in charge of the poor house do not expect the visitors, and in a careful manner, with a view of seeing that the wants of the poor are provided for. Instead of having a turkey dinner let the visitors dine with the inmates of the poor house. "What! you say, eat such food as the paupers eat?" If it is good enough for the paupers the whole year round, it will not harm their visitors to be confined to it for a single meal; besides, they will be better able to vote understandingly upon the question of supplies for the poor house when it comes up in the board of supervisors.[15]

Apparently Myra's strategy was to "test the waters" for her subsequent law reform activities by first urging change in the microcosm of many of her readers, the city of Chicago. She might have believed that if those modest attempts were viewed favorably, and that if she could simultaneously build a readership that was national in scope, she would then have achieved the stature necessary to become a credible protagonist for women's rights and other national social causes.

Myra was also acutely aware of the public perception of most contemporary feminists; they were viewed as strident and dour. Wanting her readers to know that she did not fit such a stereotype, and being naturally endowed with a sense of humor, her columns from the outset were studded with self-composed jokes and jingles designed to expose the folly of various laws or practices of the profession. An early verse, for example, was addressed to the topic of restraint of marriage by will, a practice whereby a husband could provide in his will that his wife would lose her inheritance in the event that she remarried:

> In the name of God, amen;
> My feather bed to my wife, Jen;
> Also, my carpenter's saw and hammer;
> Until she marries, then God damn her![16]

In another column, Myra, who had great disdain for the coddling of criminals, proposed "a new theory for the defense": "It consists in proving the previous *bad* character of the accused in *mitigation* of his crime, and as an explanation why nothing better could have been expected of him."[17]

In yet another early issue of the *News,* Myra expressed her contempt for certain members of the judiciary by relating the following tale, which was probably a figment of her fertile imagination:

A certain pompous judge fined several lawyers $10 each for contempt of court. After they had paid their fines, a steady-going old attorney walked gravely up to the bench and laid down a $10 bill. "What is this for?" inquired the judge. "For contempt, your honor." "Why, I have not fined you for contempt."

"I know that," said the attorney, "but I want you to understand that I cherish a secret contempt for this court all the time, and I'm willing to pay for it."[18]

Beginning with the appearance of the first few issues, the *News* was showered with accolades from its readers. The praise was directed at every aspect of the publication: its completeness, its promptness in reporting new laws and judicial decisions, its readable format, its humor, and its forceful pleas for change in Chicago's legal and social milieu. Those virtues were summed-up by one ranking member of the Chicago bar as "a noble enterprise in new journalism." That lawyer, Thomas Hoyne, a man of great influence and eloquence, after congratulating Myra upon the success that her "enterprise is achieving among the entire circle of the legal brotherhood of Illinois as well as the other states of the northwest," continued:

We have too long been dependent for such an organ upon the trashy pro-ductions of the East. By establishment of your Journal, the way has at last opened to forming a standard of legal literature as well as independent modes of our own. . . . Why should we not encourage independent standards of literary culture—by forming them in accord with the demands of the situation, and thus sustain our own home efforts at such noble enterprises in new journalism as your own?[19]

Even those reviewers who were not entirely laudatory based their negative reactions on only one ground, that Myra Bradwell, the *female* publisher and editor, was expressing too much independence, particularly from her husband. For example, one British editor noted with some chagrin:

We have lately received a legal curiosity in the shape of the opening number of an American legal journal, edited by Mrs. Myra Bradwell, wife of Judge Bradwell. The specimen number in question contains promise of much that is profitable and also a good deal that is amusing. [For example,] Mrs. Bradwell does not hesitate to express her notion of what a judge ought to be or to differ from the judges (including her husband) upon occasion. Thus in an article upon a recent criminal lunatic case, she expressed her decided opinion that the criminal was not insane, adding however, "We know there are many good men, who believe him to have been crazy, among them our own hus-band." *It must be a serious thing for [Judge] Bradwell . . . to have an organ of so independent a spirit conducted by a partner of his own bosom.*[20] (Em-phasis added)

Within a few years, this "organ of so independent a spirit" had become a fixture in every law office in Illinois.[21] The *News* then began to expand its horizons beyond its home base—even beyond the midwest itself—to every state and territory in the country. Myra accomplished this feat in the same manner in which she had previously made the *News* indispensable to attorneys in Illinois. She capitalized on the enormous time lag between the rendering of judicial decisions and the publication and dissemination of those decisions to lawyers in all the states and territories. After entering into special arrangements with the United States Supreme Court and all the lower federal courts across the nation, the *News* was soon able to claim that it printed more federal court decisions, and published them more promptly, than did any other legal newspaper in existence.[22]

Throughout the country, the *News* had achieved unofficial officialdom. While the newspaper was valid as "evidence" only in the courts of Illinois, judges in other state and federal jurisdictions—including those on the Supreme Court of the United States—realized that lawyers throughout the country would first become aware of their decisions by reading them in the *News*. Thus, it was common practice for judges and even Supreme Court justices to communicate directly with Myra about any corrections or changes in their decisions prior to her publication of them.[23] It is not surprising, therefore, that within a decade the *News* became the most widely circulated legal newspaper in the United States,[24] "familiar in nearly every law office in the country."[25]

The publishing of a highly successful weekly periodical was only one of the ventures conducted by the Chicago Legal News Company. Myra was a true entrepreneur; within a few years her company was also carrying on a large-scale printing and bindery business, servicing law firms and courts throughout the country.

The original goals of Myra's printing and bindery business were quite modest. At first she wished to have her own machinery and physical plant only so that the weekly issues of the *News* could be printed on her own presses and then bound into yearly volumes. Having made this capital expenditure, her next project was to publish all recently enacted Illinois statutes in bound pamphlet form. While she had originally published those new laws in the weekly issues of the *News,* the enactments of the legislature eventually became so voluminous that a separate publication comprised solely of new Illinois statutes seemed indispensable to the practicing bar. As she later explained to her readers:

> The Legislature closed its session on the fifteenth of this month. The Governor has signed two hundred and four bills. . . . Within 48 hours, which will be at 12 o'clock Monday night, [t]he Chicago Legal News Company will have all the laws passed at the last session printed in pamphlet form and ready for delivery.
>
> The [current] Legislature has made more changes in the laws than any Legislature for 15 years. It will take the courts of Illinois twenty years to settle the law so as to place it in as good a condition as it was in January

last. The changes have been so sweeping that every judge, lawyer, and business man should make himself familiar with the work of the Legislature.

Although the volume of the laws passed at this session will be larger than that of any session of the Illinois Legislature for 15 years, the price will not be raised.[26]

Myra's printing and bindery business quickly received a nationwide reputation for its efficiency and accuracy. From across the country came pleas from lawyers, judges, and other court personnel, imploring the Chicago Legal News Company to publish the statutes and judicial decisions of their states in addition to the laws of Illinois and the decisions of the federal courts. They expressed despair that without Myra's intervention, the nation's lawyers would continue to be kept in the dark as to the workings of their own legal institutions. For example, when the New Hampshire Supreme Court was six years old, Myra received a poignant letter from the reporter of the court beseeching her to do something about the length of that court's opinions, and, more importantly, about the fact that none of those opinions had yet been published. His letter began:

My Dear Mrs. Bradwell:

This court began its active life on August 14, 1876. It consists of seven judges. It has decided between one and two thousand cases, making several volumes. But no volume has yet been published. . . . The opinions of the court, as you have justly said, were the longest of any court in the Union, and as far as known of any in the world, not excepting even those of the Supreme Court of the U.S.[27]

He concluded with a personal plea to Myra:

As you have had great influence upon the question of condensation, suppose you lend the profession in this State a helping hand by suggesting that the reports be published some time while the present generation are upon earth.[28]

Myra responded with the "divine command" that the court reporter send the manuscripts of the New Hampshire cases to the Chicago Legal News Company, which would promptly publish them:

If the statements made by [the reporter of the New Hampshire Supreme Court] are true, and we do not doubt them, the judges ought to be impeached or removed from office. If the *Legal News* has had any influence in shortening the opinions of this court, we have done the profession some service. Obey the divine command, "Let your light shine!" Publish your opinions within a reasonable time. If you cannot get them out in time, send the manuscript to the *Legal News* and we will return you the bound volume within thirty days.[29]

The printing and bindery component of the Chicago Legal News Company soon became an empire unto itself. From the printing and publication of its initial product—annual volumes of the statutes of Illinois—it had expanded to the printing of statutes and judicial decisions of other states as well. From there it had branched out to the publishing of law books in general. Soon Myra was able to advertise that:

The Chicago Legal News Company, making its own machinery, having its own Printing Office, Stereotype, and Electrotype Foundry and Bindery, is able to make *all kinds of books* as rapidly and at as low rates as any publishing house in the United States. Send for estimates before getting books printed elsewhere.[30]

The Chicago Legal News Company also printed hundreds of different types of legal forms—leases, wills, bankruptcy petitions, etc.—which Myra had composed herself, and which were voraciously consumed by the practicing bar.[31] Finally, again at the request of her fellow attorneys, she began the process of printing and binding briefs that lawyers had prepared for submission to the various courts of the country. With the printing of lawyers' briefs came Myra's first and only problem with a labor union. It involved the practice of featherbedding.

The dispute was not a complicated one. Lawyer's briefs were usually divided into sections, and the sections were often partitioned by the placing of blank pages in between each section. Myra's typesetters demanded to be paid for the "composition" of those blank pages. Myra refused. In a strongly worded editorial, she took an extremely aggressive and unrelenting stance:

We have never since we had a printing office failed to pay our hands every week and have always paid as much for the work as any printing office in the city. We have never charged for BLANK PAGES in brief work and never will. Because we refused to pay our compositors for entire blank pages or in other words, PAY THEM FOR WORK THEY NEVER DID, the Typographical Union of this city ordered our compositors to strike, as it is commonly called, unless we granted this unjust and tyrannical demand, and when we positively and unqualifiedly refused, as we always shall, TO PAY FOR COMPOSITION ON BLANK PAGES WHICH ARE NEVER SET, all our compositors, with two exceptions, left the office. We were left with only two compositors, our foreman, our proof reader, pressman and pressboys. We at once called the *Times* and other non-union offices and were put in communication with non-union printers, and in three hours after the Union men left our office we were again running, AND OUR PAPER IS OUT IN TIME, FOUR PAGES LARGER THAN ITS USUAL SIZE.[32]

She closed with a warning that if she gave in to the demands of the union, the cost would be passed onto the consumers, the lawyers whose briefs were being printed and bound by the Chicago Legal News Company:

Every lawyer, aside from the principle involved in this question, is interested to the extent of one dollar and twenty five cents for each blank page of his brief which lacks a printed page. Of course if our offices have to pay this, it comes out of the lawyers in the end.[33]

One week later, she gleefully announced that the union had backed down:

On last Saturday afternoon . . . the president of the Typographical Union called at our sanctum and informed us that the Union had rescinded the rule as to blank pages and desired that the *Legal News* should be again run as a Union office and said that in that case all our former men would return.[34]

While Myra allowed the strikers to come back to work, she did so with rebuke, warning that "in the future we [will] allow no interference or dictation by the Union in the affairs of our office but [will] run it as we please." In a parting shot, she noted that during the week of the strike—when the business had functioned almost entirely with scab labor—she had expanded not only the volume of her business but her production facilities as well.

We had no difficulty in getting all the compositors we desired and never since we had a printing office have we done as much work in a week as we have during the week just closed. We have had to purchase a large amount of new type and material to meet the increased demand upon our office for printing, and today no office in the State can turn out as many pages of abstracts, briefs, or law books as ours.[35]

Myra's display of bravado was apparently effective, for there is no indication that she was ever again plagued with labor difficulties or any other economic difficulties for that matter.

Even the event that proved cataclysmic for virtually every other business in Chicago—the great fire of 1871—provided financial grist for Myra's flourishing empire. The Chicago Legal News Company seemed invincible even in the wake of history's most devastating conflagration.

"Chicago Is Burning!" announced the *Chicago Evening Journal* of October 9, 1871:

Up to this hour of writing, the best part of the city is already in ashes. An area of between six and seven miles in length and nearly a mile in width, embracing the great business part of the city, has been burned over and now lies a mass of smoldering ruins! . . . It is utterly impossible to estimate the losses. . . . The scene of ruin and devastation is beyond the power of words to describe. Never in the history of the world has such a scene of extended, terrible and complete destruction by conflagration been recorded, and never has a more frightful scene of panic, distress and horror been witnessed among a helpless, sorrowing, suffering population.[36]

The Bradwell family's initial response to the event that reduced Chicago to ashes was recounted more than fifty years later by Myra's daughter, Bessie, in a letter to the Chicago Historical Society. Bessie's account seems significant in two respects. First, it sheds light on Myra's personality and character. Second, it vividly portrays James Bradwell as a bully who could badger his way out of any situation, even the Chicago fire. As Bessie recalled:

My experience on that memorable October 9th was certainly a unique one. We had retired when we were awakened by the fire. I was thirteen years old at the time. . . . My mother, Myra Bradwell, slipped on a wrapper and proceeded to pack a trunk with our most precious possessions. Passing by a closet where my father's Masonic clothes were, she picked up father's Masonic hat (he was a 33rd degree Mason). She put it on her head exclaiming "Masonry will certainly be an aid at a time like this." With her bird cage tightly clasped in her arms and the poor little bird gasping for breath in the smoke, she went down to the Lake at the floor of Washington St. with my brother. . . .

I went down with . . . [my father] to his law office [where] he spent his time picking out [rare] books. After staying there a while I concluded to go back to the Lake. I picked up the subscription book of my mother's law journal, the *Chicago Legal News* [which] contained all the accounts and the list of subscribers and it was very heavy indeed. I said to father "this is a good thing to save and I will take care of it."

After I left, my father [abandoned his] valuable books and ran down Washington Street to the Lake. There he found my mother and brother. His first words were "Where is Bessie?" My mother said, "Why I thought she was with you." My father was sure I was dead. My mother, who was always an optimist said, "No, I'd trust that girl to go to the ends of the earth. She'll come out all right, don't you worry." . . . My father concluded that the fire would sweep all over the park and that the only way to save the trunk [which my mother had packed] was to bury it. He went to a neighbor's house and got a shovel and proceeded to dig a hole in the park to bury the trunk. The park was used as the City's baseball grounds. Up walked a policeman and showed his star. "Sir you are defacing the ball grounds." My father raised his shovel to strike the policeman if he tried to stop him. "You go on or

I'll make you see more stars than you ever saw in your life." Evidently this powerful 6 foot 3 man with a shovel ready to strike was more than the policeman bargained for and he said, "Oh, go on, captain, go on." . . . About ten o'clock Monday morning October 9th father dug up his precious trunk, the only thing which was saved on the Lake front. An expressman appearing on the scene, father said to him, "Will you take us down Michigan Avenue for $50?" "Alright," said the expressman and he put the trunk on the wagon. Then looking down and seeing the clouds of smoke made worse by the blowing up of the buildings, said, "No, I won't," and pulled the trunk off the wagon. Then my desperate father concluded to bluff the expressman à la cave man. He roared at the expressman, "Take your choice of three things: take us as you agreed to do and we may go through in safety or we may die in the attempt or you may stay right here and die now." The bluff worked. Grabbing the trunk and putting it back on the wagon, the expressman said "For God's sake, come on." The poor little bird in mother's lap was gasping for breath as they rode through to safety but its life was spared and it lived to a good old age.

The next night after the fire, my father attended a citizens meeting and spoke of the loss of his little girl. A gentleman with whom I had breakfasted on Monday morning jumped to his feet and said, "Don't worry, Judge Bradwell, your daughter is safe on the west side and she carted the great heavy *Legal News* subscription book for nine hours."

With the full list of her subscribers Myra Bradwell went up to Milwaukee and brought out her *Chicago Legal News* on its regular publication day without missing an issue.[37]

Bessie's story seems implausible in at least two respects. First, she claimed that she had grabbed the subscription book of the *Chicago Legal News* while in the company of her father at his law office. It is highly unlikely, however, that the book would have been in James's office rather than in the offices of the Chicago Legal News Company where Bessie obviously went alone. Indeed, Myra, in her contemporaneous account of the episode, stated that "Bessie [had] rushed into the [*Chicago Legal News*] office, grasped the subscription book . . . and went out into the wild night."[38] Second, Bessie (and later Myra) claimed that the daughter was acting entirely on her own, and not under instructions from her mother. Once again, that seems like an unlikely scenario: Myra Bradwell concerned only with a masonic hat, a bird, and a trunk full of possessions while her thirteen-year-old daughter decides that her first priority is to save Myra's business empire. A more likely explanation is that Myra, busy packing the family's "precious possessions" requested that Bessie salvage the subscription book from the offices of the Chicago Legal News Company. If so, then Myra might have been asking Bessie to risk her life in order to save the business. On that very night, the offices of the *News* were consumed by flames and entirely destroyed.

In most respects, Bessie's version of the story is the same as the one that Myra told her readers a half-century earlier in the edition of the *News,* which was published in Milwaukee five days after the fire. Myra wrote:

> In the late terrible destruction of our beautiful city, the office of the *Legal News* was consumed with its entire contents, including a library of near two thousand volumes. All were destroyed with the exception of our Subscription Book and Ledger. It was near midnight when the fiery fiend took possession of the block in which we were. *Our little daughter Bessie, twelve [sic] years of age, rushed into the office, grasped the Subscription Book* and the portraits of a brother and sister who are in the spirit world, *and went out into the wild night,* and crowded through the surging mass of humanity until finding her burden too great, she was prevailed upon to resign her pictures into the hands of an acquaintance, and pressed forward. She continued to walk the streets until 3 o'clock the next day—first going to the North Side, then back to the South Side—and when found was near Western Avenue—the extreme western portion of the city. In our escape from the burning district, we rushed down Washington Street to the Baseball Grounds and there buried the few articles which alone remained of our household goods and wearing apparel not exceeding one hundred dollars in value.[39] (Emphasis added)

At this juncture, Myra's story, too, seems implausible; for if the "few articles" that the Bradwells buried had a value "not exceeding one hundred dollars," then why had James assaulted a policeman with a shovel and later threatened the life of an expressman (whom he had also paid fifty dollars) to salvage such worthless trinkets?

Myra's account continued:

> We were driven by the flames to the lake, and there, amid smoke and falling cinders and a heat that was almost stifling, remained until two o'clock the next day when we made our escape to the West Side being obliged to go by way of 12th Street, rushing by falling walls and through clouds of smoke. Yet we do not feel like uttering one word of complaint when we compare our hardships with hundreds of others; when we take into consideration the thousands who are today undergoing all that mortals can, and live, mourning the death of loved ones whose ashes they may not be permitted to gather— orphaned children wandering helpless and homeless. The Good Father only knows how they are to be provided for the coming winter.[40]

On the very same page, Myra made it clear why she did "not feel like uttering one word of complaint": the *Chicago Legal News* was in a position to profit immensely from the tragedy that had struck Chicago. She began with an article entitled, "Legal Matters in Chicago," which stated:

The members of the Bar are most of them ruined. Not a single law office remains, either in the North or South Division of the city. The law offices on the West side, which number some five or six are still left, but their libraries are very small. A large number of the members of the bar are without offices—without books—without money—without business, and with no immediate prospect of any. Most of the insurance companies in which they insured their houses, libraries and other property are bankrupt, and the hope they entertained of being able to support themselves and families by the money derived from their insurance, in case they should suffer from the hand of the fire king, has vanished and they find they have been leaning on a broken reed.[41]

After describing the financial ruin of virtually every attorney in Chicago, and lamenting that they were "without offices—without books—without money," it seems that Myra was extraordinarily crass in choosing to conclude the sad tale with the following "Notice to Law Book Publishers":

More law books will be bought in Chicago within the next twelve months than in any city in the world. At least 300 lawyers will commence to renew their libraries. There is no other medium through which law book publishers can reach the members of the profession better than the LEGAL NEWS.[42]

In other words, the *News*'s advertising revenues were about to soar! While one cannot be too critical of Myra for capitalizing on the tragic losses occasioned by the fire, one can certainly find fault with her sense of timing. Stripped of its verbiage, her message was as follows: (1) Virtually every member of the Chicago bar has lost his offices, his books, and his money; (2) each of these victims will have to begin the painful process of rebuilding his library; (3) thus, all law book publishers are in a position to profit, especially if they advertise in the *Chicago Legal News,* the best medium for reaching members of the profession; and (4) consequently, the *Chicago Legal News* will also profit through increased advertising revenues.

Myra also did not hesitate to remind her readers that "The destruction of almost every law library in Chicago will make the *News* doubly valuable . . . [because of] its weekly report of important cases indispensable to the profession here." Moreover, past copies of the *News,* admissible as evidence in the courts, would certainly be invaluable in proving the contents of prior judicial decisions and previously enacted statutes, particularly since most official records of those laws had been destroyed in the fire. Of course, the lawyers who had lost their libraries would have to reorder those back copies from the Chicago Legal News Company. She concluded by urging "our subscribers to remember us by sending in their subscriptions [for current and back copies] in this your trial hour." As for "Subscribers who wanted back numbers without paying," Myra had nothing but disdain. As she wrote a few months after the fire:

Some of our subscribers write to us to send them missing numbers without enclosing the money for the same. And some of the members of the bar in our city, even, come into the office and in a gentlemanly way, ask for one or more numbers, saying, perhaps, some pleasant words about the *News* and go out without handing in their 10 cents. Compliments are well enough in their place, but they will not pay the printer. . . . We . . . treat our responsibility as ended when we carefully mail the *Legal News* and intrust it to Uncle Sam. The price of our paper is known to our subscribers. If they wish back numbers and send the money for them, we send the numbers.[43]

Charity and sensitivity were obviously not Myra's fortes. But her readers and advertisers, having no choice, responded affirmatively. Ten months after the fire, Myra reported that she had rebuilt her entire enterprise (which had probably been well-insured) and was "constantly increasing in strength and circulation."[44]

Myra achieved one final coup in the wake of the fire. She convinced the Illinois legislature to choose the *Chicago Legal News* to be the *official* medium for the publication of all court records, including Land Title Notices, which had been destroyed by the fire, but which were subsequently restored or recreated. The pertinent statute, the "Burnt Records Act," caused a vast expansion in the *News*'s circulation. The *News* was now indispensable not only to attorneys but also to every single person who owned or claimed to own land in Cook County, Illinois. As Myra explained to her readers:

Every person who owns any land in Cook County should at once forward us $2 and become a subscriber to the *Legal News,* as by looking over its Land Title Notices once a week, he will be able to discover if any person has brought a proceeding under the "Burnt Records Act" to affect the title to his real estate. . . . A person at the expense of $3.25 per year—$2.00 for subscription and $1.25 for binding—may have a complete record of all Land Title Notices published in the courts.[45]

Thus, the *Chicago Legal News* flourished, in part, because Chicago had burned. In fact, the event which had impoverished so many residents of the city enabled Myra to purchase a large mansion on the shores of Lake Michigan.[46]

The tale of Myra Bradwell's prosperity, however, is in and of itself of no great import. True, she was one of the few female tycoons during the post-Civil War era. The true significance of the *Chicago Legal News*'s economic and journalistic success, however, is not that it was an end in and of itself, but that it served as a means, the vehicle by which Myra Bradwell waged successful warfare on so many of the legal and social inequities of her day.

NOTES

1. *American Law Review* (January 1869): 362, reprinted in *CLN* 1 (January 30, 1869): 141, col. 3–4.

2. Eleanor Gridley, "Presentation of Bronze Bust of Mrs. Myra Bradwell, First Woman Lawyer in Illinois," *Transactions of the Illinois Historical Society* 38 (1931).

3. *CLN* 11 (September 21, 1878): 5, col. 1.

4. Prospectus, *CLN* 1 (October 3, 1868): 1, col. 1.

5. Article in *Western Jurist*, reprinted in *CLN* 1 (May 15, 1869): 274, col. 4.

6. Editorial in *Central Law Journal*, reprinted in *CLN* 6 (January 31, 1874): 154, col. 3.

7. Illinois Press Association, Memorial to Myra Bradwell, *CLN* 26 (February 17, 1894): 200–202.

8. *CLN* 1 (March 13, 1869): 188, col. 1.

9. Illinois Press Association, Memorial to Myra Bradwell. See also *CLN* 19 (June 18, 1887): 327, col. 3 and *CLN* 19 (June 25, 1887): 335, col. 1.

10. *CLN* 1 (March 13, 1869): 188, col. 1.

11. *CLN* 1 (May 1, 1869): 246, col. 1.

12. Ibid.

13. *CLN* 2 (January 1, 1870): 109, col. 2.

14. *CLN* 1 (October 3, 1868): 4, col. 2.

15. *CLN* 1 (December 5, 1868): 76, col. 1.

16. Quoted in George Gale, "Myra Bradwell: The First Woman Lawyer," *American Bar Association Journal* 39 (December 1953): 1080.

17. *CLN* 9 (August 18, 1877): 400, col. 4.

18. *CLN* 8 (July 15, 1876): 341, col. 3.

19. Letter from Thomas Hoyne to Myra Bradwell, September 8, 1869 (in author's possession).

20. Editorial, *London Solicitors Journal and Reporter*, reprinted in *CLN* 1 (November 14, 1868): 51, col. 4.

21. Article in *Albany Times*, reprinted in *CLN* 14 (April 22, 1882): 254, col. 2–3.

22. *CLN* 1 (March 20, 1869): 196, col. 1.

23. See, e.g., letter from United States Supreme Court Justice John Marshall Harlan to Myra Bradwell, dated April 8, 1885, Chicago Historical Society manuscript collection; letter from Judge William A. Woods (United States District Court, Indiana), February 9, 1885, to Myra Bradwell, Chicago Historical Society manuscript collection.

24. *CLN* 11 (September 21, 1878): 5, col. 1.

25. The quote is from an article in the *Albany Times*, reprinted in *CLN* 14 (April 22, 1882): 254, col. 2–3.

26. *CLN* 19 (June 25, 1887): 335, col. 1.

27. Letter from reporter of the court, New Hampshire Supreme Court, reprinted in *CLN* 15 (October 28, 1882): 62, col. 1–3.

28. Ibid.

29. Ibid.

30. *CLN* 19 (October 16, 1886): 44, col. 4.

31. See, e.g., *CLN* 9: 80.

32. *CLN* 7 (October 5, 1874): 21, col. 1.

33. Ibid.

34. *CLN* 7 (October 12, 1874): 31, col. 1.

35. Ibid.

36. *Chicago Evening Journal* (October 9, 1871): 1, col. 1.

37. Letter from Bessie Bradwell Helmer to Caroline M. MacIlvaine, Chicago Historical Society, October 7, 1926 (in author's possession).

38. *CLN* 4 (October 15, 1871): 2, col. 1.

39. Ibid.

40. Ibid.

41. Ibid. at col. 2.

42. Ibid.

43. *CLN* (April 6, 1872), reprinted in *CLN* 10 (April 20, 1878): 250, col. 4.

44. *CLN* 4 (August 31, 1872): 545, col. 1.

45. *CLN* 4 (July 20, 1872): 360, col. 1.

46. Obituary, *CLN* 26 (February 17, 1894): 200.

6

"Disreputable Shysters Who Now Disgrace the Profession" Reform of the Legal Profession and Judicial Process

By a thorough organization of the bar . . . the standard of professional conduct could be elevated, *and the disreputable shysters who now disgrace the profession could be driven from it.*

—Myra Bradwell (1873)[1]

From the very inception of the *Chicago Legal News,* Myra made it clear that she would use her newspaper to campaign for improvements in everything related to the practice of law in Chicago. Ever class conscious, she advocated that the legal profession be stratified into two tiers. The first would encompass *all* current lawyers as well as all of those who were seeking admission to the bar.

With respect to applicants for admission, Myra insisted on strict standards of both integrity and educational preparation. Once admitted to practice, if an attorney were found to be either incompetent or dishonest, Myra believed that the offender's license should be permanently revoked.

The second tier of the profession, a subset of the first, would consist of the top echelon of those who had been licensed to practice law. Myra believed that this latter group would both define itself and maintain its selectivity by forming a private, nongovernmental organization, the Chicago Bar Association, *into which the more worthy members of the profession would be invited to come—at the same time reserving the power to keep out the unworthy,* and thus make it an association of honorable gentlemen of the legal profession, having the best interests of the profession at heart.[2] (Emphasis added)

With respect to the first tier of the profession—all those who had been licensed or were seeking a license to practice law in Illinois—Myra constantly pushed for standards that would demand both intellectual rigor and a vast breadth of legal knowledge. In an early issue of the *News,* she bemoaned:

The crude and vulgar course of study pursued in law offices has been the means of placing the names of many very poor lawyers upon the roll of the profession who, if they had taken a thorough and well-digested course of reading, might have numbered among its most useful members.[3]

In order to assist prospective lawyers in their preparation for the Illinois bar examination of 1869, Myra published a voluminous recommended reading list that included several volumes of *Blackstone's Commentaries, Paschal's U.S. Constitution in U.S. Jurisprudence,* a vast array of Illinois statutes, and the entire Illinois Constitution of 1848.[4] The proposed reading list would make most contemporary lawyers stand in awe. In particular, one wonders how many modern-day lawyers have read the entire text of their own state constitutions.

As a further aid to candidates for the Illinois bar, Myra published a booklet that contained a full report of the oral bar examination of each of the candidates seeking a license to practice law in Illinois in 1873 and 1874. That publication included all questions asked by those conducting the examination (justices of the Illinois Supreme Court), the answers of the candidates, the remarks and admonitions of the justices, and their decision with respect to each candidate.[5] Apparently Myra was not concerned with the possibility that her publication might cause some of the failing candidates to be publicly humiliated. It was her avowed goal to spare ill-prepared candidates from the indignity of failure. In the preface to the 1874 booklet, she stated:

Our object in publishing these volumes is . . . to give [students] some idea of the amount of legal knowledge they must possess in order to pass safely through the ordeal and prevent . . . them from applying until they possess this knowledge and save them from the mortification of being rejected.[6]

Noting that her report of the 1873 exam had been "received with such favor that the edition has for some time been exhausted," she continued:

The great mass of the Bar heartily sympathize with the Supreme Court in its efforts to elevate the standard for admission to the Bar, over what it was in former years. *It is a satisfaction to us to believe, that in publishing a report of the examination, we have to some extent aided the Court in these efforts, and called the attention of the courts in other States to what the Supreme Court of Illinois is doing to prevent incompetent men from entering the profession.*[7]

While Myra believed that the matter of bar examinations was to be taken very seriously, her writings on that subject, as well as on virtually all others, contained flashes of humor. For example, in discussing the examination of an applicant for admission to the bar in the neighboring state of Indiana, Myra reported that the presiding judge had asked the candidate what the first duty of a lawyer was. The applicant responded, "To secure his fees, sir." Myra commented:

This answer to a question strangely general and indefinite, so apt and unexpected, produced an irrepressible burst of laughter at the judge's expense, who blushing and indignant, cried out to the clerk, "Prepare a license for the applicant. I find him well qualified to practice law in the state of Indiana."[8]

The story might have been true, or it might have been apocryphal; but its inclusion in the *News* served to illustrate that while Myra's primary goals were to inform her readers and to advocate and initiate reform, a secondary purpose was simply to entertain.

Elevation of the profession, Myra believed, involved the weeding out not only of those who were deficient in knowledge and/or intellect, but also, and more importantly, of those who were unethical. During the twenty-five-year period of her editorship of the *News,* much space was devoted to her condemnation of four types of unethical attorney behavior. The first was the bribery of jurors, a practice that was rampant in Chicago during the last quarter of the nineteenth century. Myra believed that this behavior was extremely heinous, and even suggested (in what was undoubtedly a hyperbole) that those offering and accepting jury bribes should be punished by public lynching:

Many . . . [jurors] are now bummers and vagabonds. . . . No punishment can be too severe for a juryman who accepts a bribe *or the [attorney] . . . who bribes them [sic].* They are both outside the law regulating legitimate legal warfare, and were it not for the possibility of mistake should, when caught, *be either shot or hung on the nearest lamppost by an indignant public whose justice they have outraged.*[9] (Emphasis added)

Indeed, Myra considered jury bribery to be such an abomination that she suggested, in an extremely bold editorial, that investigations of that crime should be aimed at the upper strata of the legal profession as well as the lower:

If the [newly formed Chicago Bar] Association would investigate some of these cases of attorneys improperly influencing jurors and deal with offenders without regard to whether they are men of ability, who are celebrated for gaining their points or belong to the shyster class, it would greatly aid the officers who have charge of enforcing the jury law.[10]

Myra probably had reason to believe that some of the offenders came from the ranks of "the honorable gentlemen of the legal profession,"[11] for her editorial represented a marked departure from her usual view, i.e., that professional misconduct was almost exclusively the domain of the "shyster class."

It took two decades for the bar association to respond to Myra's plea for thorough investigations of jury bribery among *all* strata of the legal profession. It was not until the late 1890s that substantial progress was made in eliminating the widespread practice. Unfortunately, Myra's proposal had not come to fruition until a few years after her death.

While jury bribery may have ranked highest on Myra's list of abhorrent practices by attorneys, a close second (both in gravity and in frequency) was the conduct of attorneys who breached their relationship of trust with their clients, either by stealing their clients' funds or by any other abuse of the power with which they had been entrusted. Myra regarded these attorneys as outlaws, the "highwaymen" of the profession:

We hear complaints of the unprofessional conduct of some of the members of the bar of this city—cases where they have collected money [for their clients], used it and refused to pay it over; where they have used the process of the courts for improper purposes; where the papers in cases have been stolen to delay and prevent justice being done. These things are done by a few men who have managed to steal their way into the legal profession, and are now stealing their way through it. *The profession regard these men as the community do highwaymen.* We are glad to know that there is a combined effort being made by the members of the profession in this city to drive these men from the bar.[12]

For the next fifteen years Myra admonished the "respectable member[s]" of the profession to bring charges against these "deadbeats" and "frauds" so that they could be disbarred by the Illinois Supreme Court.[13]

A third category of lawyers whom Myra believed to be unfit were those who drank heavily. Excessive alcohol consumption by the city's one thousand attorneys seemed to reach its zenith in 1871, the year of the great Chicago fire. Myra was saddened by that fact:

We remember quite a number of men who, in their day, were distinguished at the bar, had all the clients they desired and wealth sufficient to make them comfortable for life. We have seen them take to drink, neglect their business, and client after client left them to return no more. Their wealth would, day by day, drop from their nerveless hands, their friends would forsake them and, at last, they would die a miserable death, and be saved from filling a pauper's grave only through the kindness of some surviving friend who would collect enough money to give them a Christian burial.[14]

During the latter part of the nineteenth century, there was an alliance between groups advocating woman suffrage and organizations promoting temperance. It is unclear whether Myra was a proponent of temperance or if she was simply upset by the fact that immoderate drinking had taken such a heavy toll on the practicing bar. Regardless of her motive, she was willing to go to any lengths to weed out heavy drinkers from the ranks of the legal profession. She didn't hesitate to name names or narrate gory details, even though she was undoubtedly aware of (and probably desired) the public humiliation that her narrations would engender. For example, in reporting on the unsuccessful attempt at suicide of a Michigan judge, Myra wrote:

A. H. Giddings of Newago, Michigan, for many years a circuit judge in that state, attempted to commit suicide in this city on Wednesday by jumping into the river off Clark Street bridge. Instead of falling into the water, as was evidently his intention, he fell upon the dock below, broke his right leg and injured his head. He was removed to the county hospital where he now lies in a precarious situation. Judge Giddings was a man of fine natural powers, good education, and an able lawyer, but unfortunately, for several years he has indulged to such an extent in the use of intoxicating drinks as to be almost entirely unfitted for any kind of business. There is no doubt but at the time of this attempt on his life he was insane.[15]

Even death brought no respite to lawyers who drank heavily. For example, when Myra announced the demise of a Chicago attorney, she commented: "Newel Pratt, one of the divorce attorneys of this city, died last week. It was liquor killed him."[16]

Myra's posthumous comment regarding Mr. Pratt was extraordinarily callous, judged not only by today's standards of civility and decency but also by Myra's own espoused standards. Several years earlier, when commenting on the Chicago bar's resolutions regarding its deceased members, Myra admonished:

The Committees appointed [to formulate resolutions regarding recently deceased members of the bar] should carefully avoid saying anything in their resolutions that would injure the character of the dead, or hurt the feelings of his living relatives and friends. They should gather together the good things which the deceased has done and weave them together into a tribute to his memory.[17]

Myra's willingness to deviate from her own standards of decency was undoubtedly inspired not only by Pratt's excessive consumption of alcohol but also by the nature of his law practice. Mr. Pratt was, after all, a divorce attorney, and Myra intensely disliked both divorce and the attorneys who procured them. She believed that, in most instances, a lawyer who merely assisted his client in obtaining a divorce was a "shyster"[18] who deserved disbarment or, at best, only "nominal membership at the Bar."[19]

Only when one becomes aware of the depths of Myra's loathing of divorce can one understand the extent of her animosity toward the lawyers who assisted their clients in obtaining them. Most persons in the nineteenth century believed that marriage was sacred and divorce, therefore, immoral. However, even in light of the mores of the Victorian era, Myra's attitudes on the subject were still incongruous, for her espoused beliefs about marriage and divorce were totally inconsistent with most of the causes to which she had devoted her life. Most revealing is the following portion of an interview that she gave to the *Chicago Tribune* only five years before her death—after many of her labors in the area of women's rights had already come to fruition:

> I believe that married people should share the same toil and the same interests and should be separated in no way. It is the separation of interests and labor that develops people in opposite directions and makes them grow apart. If they worked side by side and thought side by side, we would need no divorce courts.[20]

Coming from the woman who had secured for married women both the right to keep their own earnings and the right to pursue any profession or occupation of their choice, Myra's remarks seem ironic. What her comments reveal, however, is a vehement disdain for divorce, shaped, of course, in part by the ethos of "true womanhood." She was thus willing to relegate divorce attorneys to the cellar of the legal profession.

Myra's proposed remedy for the twin evils of divorce and divorce attorneys was twofold. First, all divorce cases should be tried by juries. The prospect of facing a trial by jury, which meant that one's domestic grievances would be publicly aired, would undoubtedly deter many persons from seeking a divorce.

> Chicago dockets have been burdened for sometime with divorce cases resulting from lawyers successfully advertising to obtain cheap divorces without publicity. [Currently] . . . when both parties are willing or one is absent the case is referred to a Master and upon his report a decree is entered. . . . This could

be prevented by substituting a jury and trial in open court so that the parties and witnesses will have to face the court and jury.[21]

Myra's second line of attack was to endorse a proposal that would have subjected all lawyers who advertised "with intent to procure any divorce" not only to disbarment but also to a mandatory jail sentence of between three months and one year for each offense *and* a mandatory fine of between $100 and $1000.[22] While it is true that during the nineteenth century (and most of the twentieth) *any* type of advertising by attorneys was considered unethical and often illegal, such infractions were generally dealt with merely by the imposition of a fine, particularly in the case of a first offense. A mandatory jail term of at least three months was an unusually harsh sentence, which Myra and many other members of the bar wanted to impose only on the most heinous form of advertising—that aimed at the obtaining of a divorce.

In sum, Myra believed that there were four types of "disreputable shysters who disgrace[d] the profession . . . [and ought to] be driven from it": those who bribed jurors, those who stole their clients' funds, those who drank heavily, and those who assisted their clients in obtaining "easy" divorces. The policing of these "shysters," Myra believed, should be performed by the Chicago Bar Association, a private organization formed in 1874, and for whose creation Myra had zealously campaigned.

Indeed, it may have been an early *News* editorial that sowed the germinal seeds for the formation of the association. In February 1869, four months after the *News*'s inception, Myra published an editorial advocating the creation of a bar association, the purpose of which would be to increase the fees that attorneys could charge and consequently to raise the standard of living of members of the Chicago bar.[23] She noted that Chicago physicians had an association that held monthly meetings to fix and increase their charges and lamented the absence of a similar organization for lawyers:

> How can courts be expected to allow attorneys a higher rate of fees than the bar has fixed in its fee bill [of 1852] for such services?
> As a general rule lawyers are paid less for their services than any other class of men. It is safe to say that not more than one out of fifty members of the bar throughout the United States ever became rich by their practice.[24]

For the next five years Myra "steadfastly trumpeted the need" for a local private bar association.[25] In addition to the setting of attorney's fees and the policing of "disreputable shysters,"[26] Myra believed that the organization should perform a third function—that of exclusivity.

Such an association, to a certain extent must be exclusive, or the objects to be attained would be defeated at the very outset; . . . an organization must be accomplished by someone, *into which the more worthy members of the profession would be invited to come.*[27] (Emphasis added)

As previously noted, some of Myra's criteria for exclusion from the bar association—most notably, unethical behavior and lack of intellect—were explicitly set forth in her writings. Other factors were less discernable and could be gleaned only from her commentaries on other subjects. For example, while Myra never explicitly stated that Jewish attorneys should be denied admission into the Chicago Bar Association, in some early issues of the *News* she made it clear that she had little use for lawyers of the "Hebrew faith."

Her confrontation with the Jewish legal community began in October 1868 with the publication of the very first issue of the *News*. Her first statement on the matter seems relatively innocuous:

Many political communications have been sent to us by members of both parties. We can publish none of them; but take this opportunity of saying that the *Legal News* in religion is *Christian,* in politics *neutral.*[28]

The statement drew a sardonic response from the *Hebrew Leader,* a Jewish newspaper published in New York City:

Were it not ungallant, we should allude with some severity to the averment that "The *Legal News* in religion is *Christian.*" As many of our most eminent lawgivers in Europe and America believe in the faith of our fathers, *and as a large proportion of the bar of the U.S. feel a personal pride in knowing that they are Hebrews,* we feel that the lady's platform might have been broad enough to give place to a body of such importance. . . . We can . . . forgive the gentle Myra's thrusts at armor which grows brighter with advancing years. May the lady live long enough to outgrow her prejudices, and then the modern Madam Methuselah will be the wonder of the Western world.[29]

Myra replied not by denying her prejudices but instead by elaborating on them with great pride:

We embrace this opportunity of saying that if we *should* live to the age of Methuselah, we earnestly believe that we should not "*outgrow*" our veneration for Christians, even though in cherishing this love for the followers of Christ, we should be in danger of losing the esteem of "*a large proportion of the bar of the U.S.*"[30]

The following item is what the gentleman terms our "platform," and *we*

must assure him that we cannot conscientiously add one single plank to accommodate our "gallant" friends of the Hebrew faith:
  "The *Legal News* in religion is *Christian,* in politics neutral."[31]

Judged by today's standards, Myra's contemptuous refusal to "accommodate our 'gallant' friends of the Hebrew faith" seems at best impolitic. Looking at the matter through nineteenth-century eyes, however, Myra's statement was apt to garner many more friends than enemies. Anti-Semitism in the legal profession during the post–Civil War era was rampant. One example, frequently cited by legal historians, is the famous (perhaps infamous) diary entry of George Templeton Strong, a prominent New York lawyer. Writing in 1874 (the same year that Myra was actively involved in the formation of the Chicago Bar Association), Strong supported the following requirement for admission to Columbia Law School:

Either a college diploma or an examination including Latin. This will keep out the little scrubs (*German Jew boys mostly*) whom the school now promotes from the grocery-counters . . . to be "gentlemen of the Bar."[32]

Thus, Myra's anti-Semitic "platform" was probably calculated to stand her in good stead with the more prominent members of the bar in Chicago and elsewhere. It was also undoubtedly a genuine statement of her sentiments. Nevertheless, her statement is both disconcerting and ironic, given that it was penned by the woman who espoused a belief in "perfect equality, admitting no privilege on the one side nor disability on the other."[33]

Myra's refusal to "accommodate our gallant friends of the Hebrew faith" was not accompanied by a refusal to accommodate other minorities. Indeed, when Chicago's first black lawyer, Lloyd G. Wheeler, was admitted to the bar in April 1869, it was Judge James B. Bradwell who vouched for Wheeler's intelligence and fitness. Myra published James's statement of praise for Wheeler in an early edition of the *News:*

Mr. Wheeler is an intelligent and worthy gentleman, an honor to his race and no disgrace to the bar of Illinois. He is the first Negro ever admitted to the bar in this state. We wish him success.[34]

Subsequently, James not only published an extremely laudatory article entitled "The Colored Bar of Chicago,"[35] but also, with Myra's staunch support, periodically recommended various black attorneys for membership in the Chicago Bar Association. The association rejected each of them without comment.[36] The bar association's rejection of blacks and others whom *it* deemed "unworthy" did not escape comment by Myra:

More dissatisfaction exists among the members of the Association and the
bar on account of these rejections than from all other sources, and it is evident[ly]
not without reason.[37]

Myra's expression of dissatisfaction may have been, in part, self-serving,
for it appears that she, too, was "rejected" by the Chicago Bar Association
or, at least, that she was never invited to become a member. That rebuff was
in stark contrast to Myra's acceptance by the Illinois State Bar Association,
the statewide private organization for lawyers, which was formed in January
1877, and which, according to the *Legal News,* "exercised an [immediate]
influence upon the legislation of the State [and] . . . caused many valuable
changes to be made in the laws relating to the practice of the courts."[38]

At the second annual meeting of the Illinois State Bar Association, Myra
was invited to become a member. Upon accepting that invitation, she became
the first woman admitted to membership in any bar association in the United
States.[39] It is somewhat ironic that Myra became a member of the Illinois
State Bar Association twelve years *before* she received a license to practice
law from the state bar itself.

It was not only through the auspices of the Illinois State Bar Association
(of which she was an esteemed member) and the Chicago Bar Association
(of which she was a valuable outsider) that Myra labored to reform the legal
profession and the judicial process. In her never-ending campaign to improve
every facet of the practice of law, Myra often spoke only for herself. And
nowhere did the many different facets of her personality, both positive and
negative, become so manifest as in her comments on the legal profession and
the judicial process. On the positive side were abounding examples of Myra's
sense of humor and her creative use of allegory and metaphor.

Much of Myra's humor was aimed at the various personae involved in
the litigation process: the lawyers, clients, judges, and jurors. Her jokes usually
took the form of anecdotes, many of which were undoubtedly figments of
her fertile imagination. Thus, instead of simply declaring that some lawyers
were fools, Myra gave the following account of a "recent court case":

A Connecticut lawyer at Bridgeport, the other day, took exception to a judge's
ruling that some evidence was inadmissible. He said, "I know that it is proper
evidence. Here I have been practicing at the bar forty years and now I want
to know if I am a fool?" "That," quietly replied the court, "is a question
of fact and not of law, and so I won't pass upon it, but will let the jury
decide."[40]

Similarly, instead of chastising attorneys for making inane arguments, Myra
related the following incident:

Not long ago in the Court of Appeals a certain lawyer of Celtic extraction, while arguing with earnestness his case, stated a point and then proceeded: "And if it plaze [sic] the court, if I am wrong in this, I have another point that is equally conclusive."[41]

Not only attorneys but judges as well frequently made verbal faux pas. As Myra recounted:

Judge _____ . . . was a very blundering speaker. On one occasion when he was trying a case . . . involving the right of property in a lot of hogs, he said, "Gentlemen of the jury, there were just twenty-four hogs in that drove; just twenty-four, gentlemen; exactly twice as many as there are in that jury box."[42]

In another vignette, rather than bemoaning the fact that many "gentlemen" of the jury were often intoxicated during their deliberations, she recalled the following:

"Are the jury agreed?" asked the judge of the bailiff on the steps of the Des Moines court house one morning recently. "Yes," said the bailiff, "they have just agreed to send out for another half gallon."[43]

On at least one occasion, many of the dramatis personae in the litigation process were simultaneously the subject of Myra's contemptuous humor:

"Gentlemen of the jury," charged a western judge, "in this case counsel on both sides are unintelligible, the witnesses on both sides are incredible, and the plaintiff and defendant are both such bad characters that to me it is indifferent which way you give a verdict."[44]

While Myra was capable of joking about corrupt juries and incompetent judges, she also frequently spoke about these matters in earnest, particularly during her later years. Thus, while in an early issue of the *News* she had written facetiously about the matter of jury misconduct and intoxication, two decades later she addressed the matter seriously and with great ire:

We call the special attention of our readers to the report . . . of the action of Judge Brentano in fining nine jurors ten dollars each for contempt of court. It hardly seems possible that nine men could be found on one jury who would . . . send in a request to the judge for cards and liquor while deliberating upon the value of a human life, and after finding by their verdict that the defendants had caused the death of the child to say to the mother . . . that the life of her child was worth only one cent. . . . The power to commit for

contempt of court is arbitrary and should be exercised with great care; but
sometimes its exercise is necessary, not only to maintain the dignity of a court
but its self-respect. The action of Judge Brentano will have a good effect
in letting jurors know that courts can deal with them for misconduct without much ceremony.[45]

Intoxication and lack of seriousness of purpose were not the only vices
exhibited by jurors in nineteenth-century Chicago. Even more egregious, Myra
believed, was the widespread practice of jurors blackmailing the lawyers who
had cases pending before them. Even in her early writings, when she was generally
more prone to humor, Myra realized that blackmail by jurors was no laughing
matter:

> No system of the law needs reform more than the jury system. Litigants often
> know that their rights have been sold by some members of the jury. Some
> men having no business of their own because of their incompetence resort
> to every conceivable means to get on [the jury] and once there make all the
> money they can out of the position, often blackmailing attorneys by demanding
> loans which they never intend to pay back, and the attorney knows unless
> he complies his client will have a determined enemy on the jury.[46]

The system of blackmail was fostered, Myra believed, by the fact that
jurors were compensated for their time in the amount of $1.50 per day:

> [This] is an inducement for men having no business of their own and therefore
> unfit to be trusted with business of other people to foist themselves on the
> community as jurors, but yet the compensation is inadequate for good
> businessmen.[47]

The solution to this problem, Myra wrote, was that the legislature should
consider a proposal whereby jurors would receive *no* compensation other than
traveling expenses, that they would serve only one week at a time unless actually
impaneled in a case lasting longer, and that they would be exempt from jury
duty for two years after serving.[48]

Myra's proposal had several pitfalls that she either did not see or else
consciously chose to ignore. Denying even a small amount of compensation
to jurors for a period of one week (or longer if the case lasted longer) would
obviously exclude very poor persons from juries. Myra, of course, recognized
this and condoned it on the ground that "men having no business of their
own . . . are . . . unfit to be trusted with business of other people." Even if
one accepts her dubious premise, however, it does not demonstrate that "men
having no business [or money] of their own" are more likely to be corrupt
than those of some means. It was, after all, the problem of corruption and

blackmail that she was attempting to solve. Several years later, Myra herself recognized that there was no necessary correlation between poverty and corruption, and thus opposed a plan that would have made ownership of land a prerequisite for eligibility to serve as a juror. She wrote:

> There may be some question whether it would greatly improve our jurors if only freeholders [landowners] were selected. Brains, not land, should qualify a man to be a juror. There are many corrupt and dishonest men who own land.[49]

Thus, Myra's proposal that jurors should receive no compensation bore no rational relationship to the end that she was seeking to achieve: the elimination of jurors who would blackmail the attorneys who had cases pending before them. Myra's plan would not only have excluded men who were poor but honest, but also would have failed to weed out men of some means who were corrupt.

The second problem with Myra's proposal is that it was simply unfair not only to the impoverished persons who would be unable to serve as jurors, but also to a certain class of litigants, i.e., poor persons, who might have an interest in having their cases tried before a jury that contained some members of their own economic class.

The only explanation for Myra's advocacy of a plan that was both unfair and irrational is that her mind was clouded by class bias. While she often expressed sympathy for the poor, and frequently offered proposals for their social betterment, her concern was borne from a typical nineteenth-century attitude of noblesse oblige, not from egalitarianism. She made that patently clear when she wrote that "men having no business of their own [are] therefore unfit to be trusted with business of other people." Consequently, she did not want the poor, for whom she had obvious contempt, to participate fully in the legal process.

Corrupt practices between jurors and attorneys did not always originate with the former. As has been previously discussed, bribery of jurors *by* attorneys was a practice that was epidemic in nineteenth-century Chicago. A closely related corrupt practice was that of jury-packing. Unlike blackmail and bribery, which consist of improper dealings between lawyers and jurors *after* the jury has been chosen, the term jury-packing refers to the practice of using improper means to *select* the jury. Usually this would be accomplished by persuading or bribing the appropriate court personnel to have the jury made up of persons favorably disposed to the client of the attorney who was doing the "packing." Often, jury-packing was done by a middleman. An attorney who was trying a case would employ another attorney who "specialized" in jury-packing to use his "expertise" to ensure that the jury was composed of favorably disposed members.

By the latter part of the 1880s, lawyers who engaged in jury-packing had virtually disappeared from Chicago, a fact that gave Myra cause to rejoice:

> What has become of the jury-packing lawyers? . . . The fact is, Mr. Grinnel [the state's attorney] came very near putting two or three of these jury-packers in the legal car for the penitentiary. They know this and hence have for the time virtually abandoned their profession. *They hope to be able when Mr. Grinnel has retired from the State's attorney's office, and public attention is turned another way, to be able to resume their evil practices.* We mistake the character of . . . [the incoming state's attorney] if he does not look after these gentlemen. We believe he would just like to send two or three of them to Joliet.[50] (Emphasis added)

In the above passage, Myra was taking a certain amount of poetic license. She obviously had no firsthand knowledge that attorneys who had engaged in jury-packing "hope to be able when Mr. Grinnel has retired from the state's attorney's office . . . to resume their evil practices." Certainly, attorneys who wished to engage in such practices would not communicate their intentions to Myra or to anyone else in a position of power or authority. It seems, therefore, that Myra's discussion of the jury-packers' desire to resume their practices was simply an implicit warning to the incoming state's attorney. She was letting him know that she would be ever-vigilant, and that if the jury-packers ever reappeared, she would publicly place the blame for their reappearance on the new state's attorney.

Although Myra devoted much editorial time and space to the subject of corruption among jurors and attorneys, the most frequent objects of her criticism were the members of the state judiciary. Those who sat in judgment on any level—from the lowly justices of the peace to the exalted members of the Illinois Supreme Court—were constantly subjected to Myra's scrutiny, but not her utmost candor.

The justice-of-the-peace "courts" not only constituted the lowest rungs in the Illinois judicial hierarchy but also were the most seriously flawed.[51] Originally established as "poor-mens courts," their jurisdiction extended only to minor criminal cases and civil matters involving small amounts of money.

By provision of the Illinois constitution of 1870, the justices of the peace were appointed by the governor upon recommendation of a board of higher-court judges. More significant than the manner in which they were appointed, however, was the manner in which they were compensated. The justices of the peace received no salary. Instead, they were paid fees and costs by the plaintiffs who filed suits before them. This led to many "unmeritorious" and "harassing" civil cases being decided in favor of plaintiffs, whose attorneys would then be encouraged to file more suits before the same justice of the peace.[52]

A decision in favor of a defendant would generally serve to discourage future suits by attorneys representing plaintiffs, and since only plaintiffs paid fees and costs to the "justices," only those officials possessing extremely high integrity were capable of deciding all their cases evenhandedly.

The "you scratch my back and I'll scratch yours" pacts between many of the justices of the peace and numerous attorneys for plaintiffs were often flagrant. Indeed, in the 1880s and 1890s the Chicago Bar Association assisted several groups of former defendants in bringing civil suits based on the claim that they had been defrauded by such deals.

In an editorial entitled "Reform of the Justice of the Peace System," Myra stated that "[The problem] . . . is mainly the fee system." She then argued that it was simply human nature for judges who were compensated under a fee system to try to schedule as many cases as possible, thereby not allowing themselves the requisite time to deliberate on any given case. She cited as examples two former higher court trial judges who had been compensated under a fee system. She stated that those two "learned jurists" had been both "honest" and "capable," yet they had "run a race with each other to see which could obtain the most fees."[53]

Myra did not allude to the more serious flaw in the fee system: that it encouraged many justices of the peace to decide unmeritorious cases in favor of plaintiffs who were the payers of the fees, and had resulted in actual deals between some "justices" and attorneys representing plaintiffs. Myra obviously did not want to impugn the integrity of the justices or of anyone else who held power.

Many justices of the peace lacked not only integrity but also ability. Not required to have legal training and appointed by a panel of judges who often engaged in political trade-offs dividing the offices between the political parties, the justices of the peace were, in many instances, political hacks of low moral character and even lower intellect.

In an early edition of the *News,* Myra decried the sleazy atmosphere in which many justices of the peace conducted their work. She did so by reprinting an article from an Illinois periodical that read, in part, as follows:

> In an upper room, reached by a rickety pair of stairs, in a slimy, weather-beaten, tumble down frame structure, this dispenser of justice is found, dealing out law, cheap in quality and price. . . . The most ludicrous spectacles are here presented. Usually as many as can gain admittance elbow each other in their efforts to draw attention, thinking their success or defeat depends on their physical exertions to obtain a prominent position in the estimation of the dirty court and its chief centre.[54]

The above sketch, depicting the general absence of decorum displayed in the justice-of-the-peace "courts," was merely impressionistic and did not set forth proposals aimed at remedying the situation. However, Myra used that article as a springboard for several subsequent editorials in which she set forth her suggestions for reform.

Myra's main recommendation was for the abolition of the appointment system under which justices of the peace were recommended to the governor by a panel of judges:

> Every candid person conversant with the facts, whatever his politics, must admit that the system adopted for selecting justices of the peace for Chicago is a failure. While many of the men selected by the [board of] judges for justices this year are capable and well qualified for the position, some are not. . . . The appointing board is too large to work efficiently. . . . The judges of this county are all honest and capable men, and in the selection of Justices have tried to do their duty.[55]

It should be noted that Myra did not assert that the low quality of many of the justices of the peace was due to political trade-offs within the appointing board of judges. Indeed, she praised the appointing judges, calling them "honest and capable men" who had "tried to do their duty." Moreover, she defined the problem as simply being that "the appointing board [of judges] is too large to work efficiently," and let her readers draw their own conclusions. This serves as an example of Myra's political acumen. She consistently refrained from attacking the integrity of any individual judge who was currently sitting on any court in Illinois. She must have believed that she would not be able to achieve her broader goals unless she continued to maintain the good will of those who sat in judgment.

In another editorial, Myra discussed a second negative aspect of the appointment process. Its effect on the appointing judges was both time-consuming and excruciating:

> There are nineteen justices [of the peace] to be appointed, and at least two hundred applicants for the position. . . . To read all these [applications] and come to an intelligent conclusion . . . would require weeks of time to say nothing of the button-holing to which the judges have to submit. This is not properly a judicial duty and the judges ought to be relieved from it. *To ask the judges to appoint the justices is as bad, if not quite, as to ask a prisoner to run an Indian gauntlet.*[56]

Once again, Myra showed great restraint in her treatment of the issue. While she referred to "the button-holing to which the judges have to submit," she did not explicitly state that many of the judges succumbed to those political pressures, and that their capitulation resulted in the appointment of "justices" whose only "virtues" were their persistence and their party affiliation. Instead of focusing on the low quality of their appointments, Myra focused, kindly, on the beleaguered judges themselves.

Myra's proposal for changing the method of selection of justices of the peace had no immediate effect. In 1904, however, ten years after Myra's death, a new amendment to the Illinois constitution abolished justice of the peace courts within the city limits of Chicago and replaced them with one municipal court which was staffed by one chief justice and twenty-seven associate justices, all salaried and all chosen in city-wide elections. The new consolidated court was widely hailed as a vast improvement over the former justice-of-the-peace system.

Finally, in 1964, the Illinois constitution was amended so as to eradicate all justice-of-the-peace courts throughout the state. Myra, no doubt, would have been pleased by the denouement of this sordid chapter in Chicago's "judicial" history.

Myra's pleas for reform of the judicial system were not confined to the justice-of-the-peace courts. She frequently editorialized about the need for change in both the Illinois Supreme Court and the general trial courts. Her criticism of judges, however, was always guarded, and she rarely named names. Moreover, while she was willing to criticize the judicial *opinions* of various judges and to comment on lapses in judicial decorum, she was careful never to impugn the integrity of any Illinois judge. The purported reason for her uncharacteristic restraint was that she believed that there were few, if any, dishonest judges:

> The people expect so much of their judges; the standard of ability and integrity with which they measure their official acts is so high, that to place a citizen on the bench is calculated to make him much more honest as a judge than he was as a citizen. It takes a very bad man to make a dishonest judge. The United States have been blessed by an honest and independent judiciary. Few judges here have ever been dishonest outside of New York City, and the whirlwind of an outraged public opinion drove them as convicted felons from the temple of justice they had disgraced.[57]

The above editorial was probably disingenuous. It is doubtful that Myra, who was so acutely aware of almost everything that was happening in the judicial community, truly believed that "few judges [in the United States] have ever been dishonest." A more likely explanation for her comment is simply that she was politically astute and knew that it was important for her, in her entwined roles as legal journalist and social crusader, to maintain the good will of the state and federal judiciary. Attacks on judicial integrity were, therefore, verboten. Criticism of judicial decorum, on the other hand, was fair game.

Myra believed that one serious breach of judicial etiquette was tardiness. In an early editorial she chastised the Illinois Supreme Court for not always being punctual in opening court at the designated hour. She noted that this often worked great hardship on attorneys who, because the court failed to meet at the appointed hour, missed the train back to their city of residence and were compelled to remain overnight in a distant city. Tardiness by judges was tantamount to theft, she wrote, because an attorney's time was worth at least five dollars an hour:

> A judge has no more right, morally speaking, by his tardiness to take an hour from the time of a lawyer than he has to put his hand in the attorney's pocket and extract five dollars.[58]

The remedy, Myra suggested, was simply to tell the justices how angry the attorneys became when the court failed to open at the scheduled time. Of course, most attorneys would not have the temerity to express their displeasure directly to the justices, so Myra did it for them.

> If the courts could hear the remarks that are made about them by the attorneys, when they fail to open their courts at the appointed time, we are satisfied that punctuality would soon be the rule and not the exception.[59]

Apparently Myra's prophesy was self-fulfilling. By writing the above piece, she ensured that the "courts could hear [i.e., read] the remarks that are made about them." Thus, punctuality, at least in the Illinois Supreme Court, became "the rule and not the exception." Only one year later, Myra praised the Illinois Supreme Court for its recently established habit of punctuality and stated that the justices ought to serve as role models for trial court judges who often came late to court.[60]

An even more serious breach of decorum was the habit of many trial court judges of entering into side conversations with friends or attorneys while simultaneously conducting a trial. Myra scolded:

> We would like to see a court sustain its dignity. While on the bench a judge should allow no person to approach him in a private matter and address him in an undertone. A person approaching the Supreme Court privately would be dealt with in a moment in such a manner that the offense would never be repeated. A court that respects itself and maintains its dignity will always be respected.[61]

Any action of a judge that detracted from a court's dignity was promptly noted and denounced by Myra:

A court, no matter how extensive may be its jurisdiction, to be respected must respect itself and conduct its business in such a manner as not to shock the finer feelings of those appearing before it. How often have we seen judges of fine legal talents, presiding in courts of record with their feet higher than their heads, their mouths full of tobacco, stop in the midst of an argument and enter into conversation with parties not at all connected with the case, and in their rulings use slang and phrases and indulge in low jokes which might be tolerated in a troupe of negro minstrels, but not in a court of justice.[62]

She even held the judges responsible for the bad manners of many of the attorneys who tried cases in their courts:

We have frequently remarked in these columns that if judges did their duty, there would never be an ill-mannered bar. It is a fact that the keeping of the manners of the bar is with the judges. When lawyers so far forget their duty to the court and their clients as to leave their case and abuse each other in court, they should at once be made to feel the power of the court in a mild but firm manner.[63]

She continued that column by praising a New York judge for administering "a merited rebuke to two legal functionaries" who had used the words "shyster," "pettifogger," and "fraud" in the courtroom. The judge had warned that in the future members of the bar who indulged in such impropriety would be disciplined by the court, not only by the imposition of a fine but also by imprisonment.

It is difficult to understand not only the New York judge's ire but also Myra's endorsement of his stern rebuke. After all, Myra herself frequently used the word "shyster," and Susan B. Anthony had once called Myra's attorney a "pettifogg[er]."[64] Perhaps Myra believed that those words were permissible when used journalistically or in private correspondence, but not when uttered in the courtroom.

Whatever her reasons, Myra did voice approval for the New York judge's reprimand and also for his threat to punish further improprieties by imprisonment. It is somewhat surprising, therefore, that when the courts in New Zealand did the very thing that the New York judge had threatened to do, Myra called the New Zealand judges "petty tyrants":

A New Zealand court has recently committed a barrister for one month for alleged contempt of court while acting professionally. There is hardly a month passes in New Zealand but what some lawyer is committed to jail for contempt of court. They must have a very bad Bar, or else a very bad Bench there. *We are inclined to think the judges in New Zealand are a set of petty tyrants.*[65]

The significant difference between the New York judge who threatened to imprison attorneys for contempt and the New Zealand judges who actually did imprison attorneys for contempt was the jurisdiction in which they presided. Myra obviously felt more comfortable aiming harsh words of criticism at a distant judiciary. Such criticism was unlikely to result in a loss of political capital.

Myra's criticism of the judicial system was not confined to disapproval of the actions and demeanor of various judges. Many of her editorials were aimed at improving the conditions under which Illinois judges labored. Three topics were of special importance: judicial salaries, improved courthouse facilities, and the need for one, instead of three, meeting places for the Illinois Supreme Court.

Within a month after the debut of the *Chicago Legal News,* Myra editorialized about the low salaries paid to Illinois judges: $1200 to Supreme Court justices and $1000 to trial court judges.[66] Such low salaries, she argued, caused judges who were not "men of fortune" either to return to the practice of law or "to continue on the bench in poverty—putting up with second or third rate hotels when attending court away from home."

It was undoubtedly no coincidence that five months later Myra announced that "Judge James Bradwell declines reelection for a third term and announces that he will resume his law practice."[67] Apparently James did not wish "to continue on the bench in poverty." Perhaps he would have been willing to do so if he had known that his wife would soon expand her publishing business into an empire and would thus become a woman of great wealth.

Several months after James's resignation, Myra again editorialized about the low salaries paid to judges and recommended that Illinois Supreme Court justices and trial court judges in large cities should receive $5,000 per year.[68] However, when the legislature responded affirmatively and raised the justices' pay to the amount suggested by Myra, she immediately complained that a salary of $5,000 was an "injustice." She predicted that if the salary remained at that level, some judges would resign:

> [They will then] engage in another branch of the profession that will return them a handsome reward for their labor. Will the State allow this, when a fair salary would prevent it? The judges of our Supreme Court are an honor to the State. Let us keep them.[69]

The above editorial appeared in 1871, only two years after the Illinois Supreme Court had denied Myra the right to practice law and after she had responded to that decision by accusing the court of "annihilat[ing] . . . the political rights of women in Illinois." It is somewhat ironic that in 1869 she expressed rage at the court's obliteration of women's rights (and, in particular, *her* rights) and then in 1871 she felt impelled to plead for a raise in the justices' salaries on the grounds that those same men were "an honor to our state." Ironic it was, yet it was also very much in keeping with her desire to appease those seven men who might someday again sit in judgment on an issue that was important to her.

Myra's most plaintive statement regarding judicial poverty concerned not the Illinois Supreme Court, but a former member of the Supreme Court of the United States. Seven years after the death of the Court's esteemed Chief Justice Roger Taney (the author of the infamous Dred Scott decision), Myra reported that his daughters were being forced to support themselves and their aged mother by laboring as copyists (i.e., transcribers of documents). She appealed to all her readers to send five dollars or more to be invested in U.S. bonds for the benefit of Taney's widow and children, concluding that "the daughters and wife of this distinguished jurist [should] be placed beyond the reach of want."[70]

The Illinois judiciary was demeaned, Myra believed, not only by low judicial salaries but also by the substandard conditions in and around the buildings in which the judges labored. In the very first issue of the *News,* Myra railed against the filthy conditions in and near the Cook County Court House:

> The grass upon the square has been trampled out by boys, cows and goats. . . . The hall is covered with the accumulated filth of years, its walls are defaced and decapitated. . . . We notice piles of old furniture in the county court room, and if we were the judge instead of the judge's wife we would order the sheriff to send it to an auction room and supply it with new.[71]

Myra did not have long to fret over the conditions in the courthouse, for in 1871 the building was totally destroyed by the Chicago fire. During the ensuing ten years, the court of Cook County was, in Myra's words, "held in old temporary sheds—for we can call the old wooden buildings erected after the fire, and named 'City Hall,' nothing else."[72]

During the ten-year hiatus between the destruction of the old courthouse and the opening of the new one, Myra constantly pleaded with city and county officials to complete construction of the new building so that the Cook County judges, attorneys, and court personnel would not have to labor in such "miserable quarters."[73]

In 1881 construction of the new court house was completed. Notwithstanding the long delay, Myra seemed absolutely dazzled by the new edifice. She believed that the modern courthouse would bring a new sense of dignity and decorum to the judges of Cook County:

The new court rooms are really elegant and are being finished off in a style that would surprise the early inhabitants of Chicago, who built the old wood court house that used to stand on the corner. The plain, old-fashioned ways of the pioneer judges will hardly be tolerated in this new and magnificent temple of justice. It is expected by some that the judges will appear in holiday attire. We hear it rumored that some of them already purchased a new suit of black in anticipation of being transferred to the new court house.[74]

Myra voiced no complaints about the new Cook County courthouse until her very last edition of the *News,* published four days before her death. In that issue, she complained that the building's poor ventilation system was literally killing the county judges:

Judge Tully has returned from his short vacation in the South, somewhat refreshed and benefitted in health, but it would take many months of the balmy air of the South to restore that health and vigor of which he has been deprived by too constant work in the foul air of the man-killing court house. [Two] . . . judges [are] dead. [Another] is not well, and [another] has had his health seriously undermined by the vile escaping gas in the court house. Judge Kohlsaat has had to fly to the forests of North Carolina in the hope of regaining his health and strength lost by constant work in the poisonous air of the court house. Judge Tulley was in his chambers the past week disposing of some . . . matters, but it is expected that the foul air will soon drive him again to seek health and fresh air in the South. The county authorities have no right to murder our judges. It is their duty to see to it that they are provided with healthy and properly ventilated rooms.[75]

The above, written when Myra was severely ill and when in all likelihood she knew that her death was imminent, was probably more of a metaphoric commentary on the cancer that was invading her body than on the poisonous air that was invading the Cook County courthouse. Nevertheless, it demonstrates that even at a time of great personal agony Myra was still able to turn her thoughts to the improvement of the conditions under which attorneys and judges labored.

Another of those negative conditions, and one which Myra thought both undignified and wasteful of time and money, was the practice of holding proceedings of the Illinois Supreme Court in three cities instead of one. By her forceful use of simile and visual imagery, Myra portrayed the indignity to which the justices were being subjected:

If it is thought best to have the Judges of our Court of last resort travel the circuit like so many Methodist ministers with their carpet-bags under their arms, then by all means let us have a term of Court in [several] district[s].[76]

There were, moreover, additional disadvantages to the system. Holding Supreme Court proceedings in three locations meant that the state had to provide "three libraries, three court houses, three janitors, three clerks, etc."[77] Still another "great evil of the present system is the delay it occasions." She noted that after the Supreme Court decided each case, the task of writing the opinion would be assigned to one of the judges, who might at that time be holding court in a city distant from some of the other judges.

> These opinions were many of them written six weeks ago and could have been announced then had the judges all been living at the capital so they could have met and finally passed upon them. In some of these cases this delay was costly to the litigants, the subject of the litigation becoming worthless.[78]

She concluded by pleading for a consolidated Illinois Supreme Court, noting that had the judges been working together in one city, they could have performed at least twice as much judicial labor during the past year.

There was considerable agreement among members of the Illinois Bar that the justices of the state Supreme Court were overworked. With a view toward relieving the state's highest court of its burdensome caseload, in 1877 the state legislature passed a law that set up an intermediate appellate court system in Illinois. While this new system had the salutary effect of relieving the Illinois Supreme Court of some of its caseload, the justices were still compelled to hold Supreme Court proceedings in three separate cities. Although Myra continued to press for a consolidated Illinois Supreme Court,[79] that goal was not fulfilled during her lifetime.

The problem of compulsory judicial travel also existed at the federal level. Although the U.S. Supreme Court, unlike the Illinois Supreme Court, had only one meeting place, federal law required that the U.S. Supreme Court justices preside also as trial court judges in the federal judicial "circuits" to which they had been assigned. That practice, known as "circuit riding," was extremely time-consuming and made it very difficult for the court to keep up with its ever increasing caseload. During the 1880s, Myra editorialized frequently about this problem. In one such column she noted:

> It is said there are more than one thousand cases on the calendar of the Supreme Court of the U.S.—as much work as the Court could properly dispose of in five years. This fact suggests the absolute necessity of some immediate legislation respecting the court, which may tend to relieve it of some of its work.[80]

During the ensuing years, she reviewed several proposals for reducing the court's case load and concluded that two of them ought to be implemented. First,

It would seem that the best plan to be adopted is the one looking to the establishing of [federal intermediate] appellate courts. The limit of appeals from the appellate to the Supreme Court should be so fixed that the greater portion of the cases could never go beyond the appellate courts.[81]

Second, "the [Supreme Court justices] should be exempted from [riding] circuit."[82]

In 1891 Congress amended the Federal Judiciary Act. Among its many reforms was a provision creating a federal intermediate appellate court system and a concomitant abolition of the odious practice of "circuit riding" by Supreme Court justices.

While Myra's goal of a streamlined *state* judiciary was not entirely accomplished during her lifetime, she did have the pleasure during the last three years of her life of living under a reorganized *federal* court system, one which had been designed to upgrade "the dignity and usefulness of [the U.S. Supreme] Court."[83]

It was not only the judicial system that needed streamlining, Myra believed, but also the jargon used by attorneys and expert witnesses. She continually inveighed—usually with humor and often with the use of metaphor—against bombastic language and pretentious style. In an editorial advocating the use of short and concise legal forms for the pleading of cases and the conveyance of land, she concluded: "We know there are many who cling to every surplus word in the forms of a hundred years ago, as they do to life itself."[84]

When urging medical experts to give their court testimony in "intelligible English" rather than scientific jargon, she remarked:

Scientific evidence . . . should be as unscientific as possible. The longest and most learned scientific word must mean something which is comprehensible to the finite mind. If so, and there is a word for it in English, that is the word you will require; the word which the jury will understand. A doctor could put all the phraseology of his art into intelligible English. I wonder what he called a bruise before "echymosis" was naturalized?[85]

Myra's writings about the legal profession and judicial process manifested not only her virtues—her intelligence, wit, and creativity—but also her vices. Chief among these was her capacity to be intellectually dishonest.

One glaring example of Myra's intellectual dishonesty was the stance that she took in a dispute that pitted the constitutional right of freedom of the press against another right guaranteed by the Constitution: the right of a fair trial for any person accused of a crime. The debate, which still rages today, centered on the extent to which a court can prevent the press from commenting on certain facets of a *pending* criminal case on the ground that inflammatory publicity might poison the minds of the judge and also the jurors or potential jurors.

The controversy in which Myra chose to involve herself arose in 1872 when various members of the Illinois press began to censure the Illinois courts for not hanging criminals quickly enough. Those journalists were particularly critical of certain Illinois Supreme Court judges who, while a criminal trial was in progress, would grant an order temporarily suspending the proceedings until the court had an opportunity to resolve certain legal issues. Occasionally, when a legal irregularity was discovered, the judge would order a new trial for the accused, an act that provided further fuel for the outrage of certain members of the press.

At first, Myra denounced these journalistic criticisms of the courts. In her first editorial on the subject, she wrote:

> We regret that some of the daily press have seen fit to reflect upon the judges of the Supreme Court for granting [orders temporarily suspending judicial proceedings] in capital cases. It is their duty under their official oaths when a record in a criminal case is presented to them, showing error, to [grant such an] order . . . and allow a review of the case. They cannot conscientiously allow the most guilty wretch to be condemned and executed except in accordance with the law of the land.[86]

One month after Myra wrote the foregoing editorial, a man named Chris Rafferty was placed on trial for murder. Rafferty's lawyer quickly applied to the Illinois Supreme Court for a temporary suspension of Rafferty's trial. The higher court granted the attorney's application so that it could resolve some legal issues involved in the case. After Rafferty's trial had been delayed for an unspecified period of time, a Chicago newspaper, the *Evening Journal,* published the following indignant editorial, urging the court to hang Rafferty immediately:

> At the time [the court order] was granted in the case of the murderer, Chris Rafferty, the public was blandly assured that the matter would be examined into by the Supreme Court and decided at once—that possibly the hanging of this notorious butcher would not be delayed for a single day. Time speeds away, however, and we hear of nothing definite being done. . . . We must simplify our mode of procedure in murder trials. *The criminal should be tried at once and when found guilty should be hanged at once, and the quicker the hanging the better.*[87]

Soon thereafter, the Illinois Supreme Court held two officials of the *Evening Journal* in contempt of court for attempting to influence the administration of justice in the pending Rafferty case. One of the men was fined one hundred dollars and the other, two hundred.[88] Myra reacted to the contempt citations with several scathing editorials, arguing that the court's action against the journalists violated the constitutional right of freedom of the press. In one of these she wrote:

> The liberty of the press to comment freely upon the conduct of all of our public servants is one of the greatest bulwarks of American liberty. We have always exercised this right and we always shall, so long as we are able to wield a pen, come imprisonment or death. There is no court so high but that we will freely censure when we think it wrong.[89]

A second editorial was even more searing:

> Since the organization of our State, this court has made no decision that will degrade and lower its dignity as this one. If the Supreme Court is to have arrested and brought before it every newspaper editor who comments about its actions and every lawyer who says it decides its cases wrong, etc. etc., to be punished for contempt, it will have very little time to attend to other business.[90]

Comparing the court's actions to that of "the most despotic of governments of ancient times [where] the will of the sovereign was the law of the land,"[91] she once again decried the serious judicial encroachment on the First Amendment guarantee of freedom of the press.

But Myra was a lawyer as well as a journalist, and she undoubtedly realized that the journalists had been held in contempt *not* for commenting negatively on actions that the court had already taken but, instead, for *commenting in advance of Rafferty's trial, thereby attempting to influence the acts of the judge and jury in a pending criminal case.* Certainly, such journalistic commentary, which urged that Rafferty be "found guilty . . . [and] hanged at once," carried the potential of intimidating both the judge (Illinois judges were elected officials) and the jurors. Thus, the *Evening Journal's* editorial might have interfered with the defendant's right to a fair trial, a right also guaranteed by the Constitution. Had Myra's goal truly been to *inform* her readers, she would have explained that the contempt citations against the journalists presented a very complex issue, i.e., the extent to which *one* constitutional right (the First Amendment guarantee of freedom of the press) should or should not be allowed to have precedence over *another* right also guaranteed by the Constitution (i.e., a defendant's right to a fair trial). Certainly it behooved Myra, who had made repeated editorial promises to present both sides of legal controversies, at least to allude to the fact that there were compelling countervailing arguments in the matter. Yet her only gesture in that direction was to print letters from two readers—one a judge[92] and the other an attorney[93]—supporting the Illinois Supreme Court's contempt decision.

When one reads the opinion of the Illinois Supreme Court,[94] it is clear that the court had confined its contempt powers to cases in which members of the press attempted to "influence and control the administration of justice in a pending case." Thus, Myra's denunciation of the court for empowering itself to "have arrested and brought before it every newspaper editor who comments about its actions" was a *deliberate* obscuring of the issue and a clear manifestation of her intellectual dishonesty. She wanted her readers to believe that the Illinois Supreme Court had declared open season on the press. Her aim was to galvanize public support for legislation that would make it virtually impossible for the court to exert a restraining influence on members of the press even when those persons were jeopardizing the rights of defendants in pending criminal cases.

The lengths to which Myra was willing to go sometimes bordered on the ludicrous. On the same day that the Illinois Supreme Court rendered its contempt decision against the journalists, Myra published an editorial entitled "A Faithful and Dignified Attorney." While the ostensible purpose of the editorial was to commend the behavior of the attorney for Mr. Rafferty, Myra's actual goal was to take yet another jab at what she perceived to be the undignified and vindictive actions of the Illinois Supreme Court. The editorial reads as follows:

A Faithful and Dignified Attorney

The course of Edward A. Small, of our bar, in the Rafferty case, is to be commended. Rafferty is condemned to death. Murders are numerous and our people are excited and exclaim almost with one accord that condemned murderers must be hung. Mr. Small is assailed in the press. He turns neither to the right or left, but attends strictly to the interest of his client; gets an [order temporarily postponing proceedings in Rafferty's case]; obtains a new trial; and *in wasting no time in attempting to get editors punished for contempt who have commented on the case, shows that he possesses a dignity entirely wanting in the Supreme Court.*[95]

Of course, Rafferty's attorney had no power to "get editors punished for contempt who have commented on the case," but that did not matter; Myra had made her point.

Less than three months later, James Bradwell, who was then a member of the state legislature, submitted to the state house of representatives a bill, drafted by Myra, which virtually eliminated the courts' powers to punish members of the press for contempt.[96] Although initially opposed by half the members of the House Judiciary Committee,[97] James successfully maneuvered the bill through the state legislature, and it was soon enacted into law. Myra had won yet another victory. And a sweet victory it was, for it enabled Myra, two decades later, to escape punishment for publishing an editorial that was virtually identical to the one for which the *Evening News* officials had been held in contempt.

In October 1893, four months before her death, Myra published an editorial that commented on the pending murder trial of a Chicago attorney, Patrick Prendergast.[98] Prendergast, whose application for the position of Chicago's corporation counsel had been rejected by Mayor Carter H. Harrison, became enraged and fatally shot the mayor. Criminal proceedings were brought against Prendergast, who entered a plea of not guilty by reason of insanity. While Prendergast's trial was pending, Myra thrust her editorial pen into the case and pronounced Prendergast sane and therefore guilty. She decreed that he should be hanged, perhaps even lynched:

> It would seem from all reports of the case that Prendergast, at the time of the shooting, was in a condition of mind to know right from wrong, and if so, he was responsible for his acts *and ought to be hung with as little delay as possible.* It should take strong evidence to establish insanity in the case of a man who attends to his regular business and is never suspected of insanity by his relatives and friends until after he kills a man. Chicago is the greatest law abiding city in the world. *Had this crime been committed in Mr. Harrison's own state, Kentucky, his murderer would have never reached the jail—and many people would have said "Amen."*[99]

Prendergast was defended by Clarence Darrow and Stephen Strong Gregory, who subsequently became president of the Chicago Bar Association, the Illinois Bar Association, and the American Bar Association. In spite of the eminence of his counsel, Prendergast was found to be sane and was sent to the gallows. Indeed, he was the only one of Darrow's clients who was ever subjected to capital punishment. One wonders if the forceful advocacy of Myra and other contemporary journalists served to sway the judge and jury and bring about a result that even Clarence Darrow could not avert. If so, then Myra had certainly influenced the administration of justice and had been instrumental in depriving the defendant of his constitutional right to a fair trial.

Even if Myra was not, in fact, instrumental in causing the guilty verdict and subsequent hanging of Prendergast, she certainly *attempted* to bring about these results. She could not, however, be punished for such an attempt, for she was protected by the anticontempt legislation that she had drafted, and which her husband had successfully guided through the state legislature.

Myra's journalistic commentaries regarding the *Evening News* case, coupled with her subsequent editorial demanding that defendant Prendergast be convicted and hanged, demonstrate the hollowness of her promise to present both sides of all legal controversies. Myra was probably capable of presenting both sides, but only when she was uninterested in the result. When she was not interested in a result, however, she did not bother to waste editorial time and space on a matter. But, then, how many editors would?

In spite of the occasional flashes of the undesirable facets of her character— her intellectual dishonesty, her anti-Semitism, her unabashed willingness to humiliate others publicly—Myra's writings about the legal and judicial processes generally displayed great intelligence, wit, foresight, and a true spirit of reform. One is saddened, therefore, to read her last editorial on the subject of the legal system. Reflecting on almost three decades of observation of and participation in attempted reforms of the legal profession, she despaired that her profession, unlike all others, had actually retrogressed during the past thirty years:

THE DIFFICULTY

Law, in its practice and administration has deteriorated within the past thirty years. This fact is manifest to every thoughtful lawyer and is fast becoming the conviction of an observant public. . . . *The difficulty is not that lawyers cannot conceive a more perfect system, but that they do not.* The conservatism of which Burke complained a century ago, fetters the profession today; and this conservatism, stupid, blind, and remorseless, is the Gibralter in the pathway of law reform. . . . Lawyers and judges need to be inspired with the spirit of progress which permeates the other professions, if they would secure for jurisprudence the position to which it is entitled.[100]

It is difficult to understand Myra's deep despair and pessimism regarding the profession about which she cared so deeply. It is true that she had not witnessed remarkable advances in the reform of the legal profession comparable to those that she had seen—indeed, helped secure—in other areas of endeavor, particularly women's rights. Certainly, however, there had been *some* progress; it was simply not true that the legal profession was in a state of retrogression. For example, Myra had assisted in the formation of the Chicago Bar Association and had worked closely with both that organization and the Supreme Court of Illinois to "elevate the standard for admission to the Bar over what it was in former years."[101] By her own earlier admission she had:

To some extent aided the Court in these efforts and called the attention of the courts in other states to what the Supreme Court of Illinois is doing to prevent incompetent men from entering the profession.[102]

She had also witnessed the demise of the abominable practice of jury-packing and had publicly warned the state's attorney that she would hold him personally responsible if the jury-packers ever reappeared. Furthermore, her writings undoubtedly had some effect on the improvement in standards of judicial conduct, the increase in judicial salaries, and the construction of adequate courthouse facilities.

Moreover, she had staunchly campaigned for and then witnessed the fruition of the reorganization of both the Illinois court system and the federal judiciary. Those events had many salutary effects, the most important of which was to relieve both the Illinois Supreme Court and the United States Supreme Court of their debilitating caseloads. Finally, there had been Myra's most self-serving "reform"—the enactment of an Illinois law, which she had drafted and which James had successfully guided through the state legislature, that virtually eliminated the courts' powers to punish members of the press for contempt.

Why, then, the pessimistic editorial regarding the status of the legal profession? The answer most likely is that when Myra wrote it she was already severely ill with cancer and probably also severely depressed. The foregoing piece concerning the legal profession was written in late August 1893. Since May of that year, Myra had been so weak that she could sit up for only very short periods and did much of her writing while reclining on her side.[103] In early September 1893, only a week or two after her despairing editorial, "she took to her bed and never left it."[104]

Myra's pessimism, therefore, was probably more of a manifestation of the retrogression of her own health, mental as well as physical, than an objective assessment of the retrogression of the legal profession. It was undoubtedly her illness that rendered her unable to evaluate objectively both the advances in the profession and her own contributions to those advances. Her achievements, however, did not go unnoticed by the members of the bar of the state of Illinois.

Three weeks before Myra's death, the Illinois State Bar Association paid tribute both to the *Chicago Legal News* and to Myra personally, calling her "our sister" and expressing "tender fit words of acknowledgement for favors received."[105]

The *Legal News* has always been in fullest sympathy with the aims and efforts of this Association, and no effort has been wanting and no expense spared if only its best interests could be advanced. Not only has it been the official medium of the Association, but its columns have teemed with Association matters and references. Nor is this all. . . . [Mrs. Bradwell] is a woman of bright intellect, of rare common sense and with all, filling as she has a public place as a business woman, a woman of marked modesty, gentility and refinement.

[We] . . . who have seen the result of her work in the State of Illinois in shaping and helping carry through . . . reformatory measures . . . desire to express [our] appreciation.

. . . *To us, she is the pioneer woman lawyer.*[106]

The bar association had thus recognized that Myra's accomplishments were not limited to the area of woman's rights but actually went to the very core of the legal profession itself.

Almost a century later, Herman Kogan, a Chicago journalist who had recently finished authoring the definitive history of the Chicago Bar Association,[107] wrote a short article about Myra Bradwell's contributions to the law and the legal profession," in which he concluded: "She left a legacy of accomplishment unmatched [sic] by few Chicagoans of her day, or any day."[108]

More than a decade later, Mr. Kogan wrote a letter to this author, which concluded: "I do hope you do [Myra Bradwell's biography]. She was quite a woman! . . . Onward!"[109]

NOTES

1. *CLN* 6 (December 6, 1873): 89, col. 2.
2. Herman Kogan, *The First Century: The Chicago Bar Association, 1874-1974* (Chicago: Rand McNally and Co., 1974), p. 17.
3. Ibid, p. 30.
4. Ibid.
5. Ibid.
6. Myra Bradwell, *Report of the Examination of Law Students for Admission to the Bar, in the Supreme Court of Illinois at the June Term, 1874* (Chicago: Chicago Legal News Company, 1874).
7. Ibid.
8. Kogan, *The First Century*, p. 30.
9. Ibid., p. 44.
10. Ibid., p. 43.
11. Ibid., p. 17.
12. *CLN* 6 (May 23, 1874): 284, col. 1-2.
13. See, e.g., *CLN* 22 (October 5, 1889): 36, col. 4.
14. Kogan, *The First Century*, pp. 31-32.
15. *CLN* 6 (July 11, 1874): 338, col. 3.
16. Kogan, *The First Century*, p. 31.
17. *CLN* 12 (January 24, 1880): 163, col. 3.
18. *CLN* 3 (October 15, 1870): 20, col. 2.
19. *CLN* 9 (June 27, 1887): 151, col. 3-4.
20. *Chicago Tribune* (May 12, 1889): 26, col. 1-2.
21. *CLN* 2 (September 10, 1870): 400, col. 3-4.
22. *CLN* 9 (January 27, 1877): 151, col. 3-4.
23. *CLN* 1 (February 13, 1869): 156, col. 2-3.

24. Ibid.

25. Kogan, *The First Century*, p. 33.

26. *CLN* 6 (December 6, 1873): 89, col. 2.

27. Kogan, *The First Century*, pp. 16–17.

28. *CLN* 1 (October 10, 1868): 4, col. 1.

29. *CLN* 1 (November 7, 1868): 45, col. 2–3.

30. Ibid.

31. Ibid.

32. Lawrence M. Friedman, *A History of American Law* (New York: Simon and Schuster, 1973), p. 553; Henry W. Taft, *A Century and a Half at the New York Bar* (New York: Simon and Schuster, 1938), p. 146.

33. Robert M. Spector, "Women Against the Law: Myra Bradwell's Struggle for Admission to the Illinois Bar," *Journal of the Illinois State Historical Society* 68 (June 1975): 228–42.

34. Kogan, *The First Century*, p. 200.

35. James Bradwell, "The Colored Bar of Chicago." The article appeared originally in the *Chicago Legal News* and was reprinted in the *Michigan Law Journal* 5 (1896): 385.

36. Kogan, *The First Century*, p. 201.

37. *CLN* 6 (May 16, 1874): 273, col. 3.

38. *CLN* 10 (December 15, 1877): 101, col. 2.

39. Proceedings of Illinois State Bar Association, January 24 and 25, 1894, reprinted in part in *CLN* 26 (April 28, 1894): 281, col. 3–4.

40. *CLN* 13 (May 14, 1881): 296, col. 4.

41. *CLN* 6 (December 20, 1873): 107, col. 2.

42. *CLN* 1 (February 27, 1869): 173, col. 4.

43. *CLN* 3 (June 3, 1871): 285, col. 4.

44. *CLN* 3 (February 4, 1871): 149, col. 4.

45. *CLN* 25 (December 24, 1892): 145, col. 1–2.

46. *CLN* 4 (January 27, 1872): 116, col. 2–4.

47. Ibid.

48. Ibid.

49. *CLN* 12 (March 27, 1880): 241, col.4.

50. *CLN* 20 (November 26, 1887): 97, col. 2–3.

51. The sources for this overview of the Illinois justice-of-the-peace system were John Dean Caton, *Early Bench and Bar of Illinois* (Chicago: Fergus Printing Company, 1893); Kogan, *The First Century*, pp. 110–113; Usher F. Linder, *Reminiscences of the Early Bench and Bar of Illinois* (Chicago: The Chicago Legal News Company, 1879).

52. Kogan, *The First Century*, p. 111.

53. The text of Myra's editorial is quoted in Kogan, *The First Century*, pp. 112–13.

54. This article originally appeared in the *General Illinoisan*, was reprinted in the *Chicago Legal News*, and is quoted in Kogan, *The First Century*, p. 32.

55. *CLN* 15 (June 16, 1883): 331, col. 4.

56. *CLN* 11 (February 15, 1879): 179, col. 3.

57. *CLN* 18 (December 19, 1885): 131, col. 2–3.

58. Quoted in Kogan, *The First Century*, p. 32. See also *CLN* 5 (January 11, 1873): 186, col. 2–3.

59. *CLN* 5 (January 11, 1873): 186, col. 2–3.

60. *CLN* 6 (January 31, 1874): 154, col. 2–3.

61. Ibid.

62. *CLN* 7 (June 5, 1875): 303, col. 2.

63. *CLN* 8 (June 24, 1876): 317, col. 2–3.

64. Letter from Susan B. Anthony to Myra Bradwell, dated July 30, 1873 (in author's possession).

65. *CLN* 10 (May 18, 1878): 282, col. 4.

66. *CLN* 1 (November 28, 1868): 68, col. 1–2.

67. *CLN* 1 (April 17, 1869): 228, col. 2–3.

68. *CLN* 2 (November 6, 1869): 44, col. 1–2.

69. *CLN* 3 (May 27, 1871): 276, col. 1–2.

70. *CLN* 3 (January 28, 1871): 140, col. 1.

71. *CLN* 1 (October 3, 1868): 4, col. 2.

72. *CLN* 12 (January 24, 1880): 163, col. 2–3.

73. *CLN* 10 (December 1, 1877): 85, col. 3. See also *CLN* 11 (August 2, 1879): 366, col. 4; *CLN* 12 (January 24, 1880): 163, col. 2–3.

74. *CLN* 13 (May 7, 1881): 281, col. 4.

75. *CLN* 26 (February 10, 1894): 193, col. 4.

76. *CLN* 3 (October 8, 1870): 12, col. 2.

77. *CLN* 6 (January 10, 1874): 129, col. 2.

78. Ibid.

79. *CLN* 21 (February 16, 1889): 207, col. 4.

80. *CLN* 14 (October 29, 1881): 53, col. 4.

81. *CLN* 14 (March 4, 1881): 204, col. 3. See also *CLN* 20 (April 11, 1888): 270, col. 3.

82. *CLN* 16 (February 2, 1884): 174, col. 4.

83. *CLN* 20 (April 1888): 270, col. 3.

84. *CLN* 6 (November 22, 1873): 73, col. 2.

85. *CLN* 19 (May 21, 1887): 297, col. 3–4.

86. *CLN* 5 (September 28, 1872): 4, col. 2.

87. Quoted in *CLN* 5 (October 26, 1872): 54, col. 1.

88. *CLN* 5 (November 9, 1872): 78, col. 1–2.

89. *CLN* 5 (October 26, 1872): 54, col. 1–3.

90. *CLN* 5 (November 9, 1872): 78, col. 1–2.

91. Ibid.

92. *CLN* 5 (November 16, 1872): 90, col. 3 (letter from Judge Lamphere of Galesburg, Illinois).

93. *CLN* 5 (November 23, 1872): 101, col. 3–4 (anonymous letter, signed "A Lawyer").

94. The court's very lengthy opinion is reprinted in *CLN* 5 (November 16, 1872): 85–88.

95. *CLN* 5 (November 16, 1872): 91, col. 4.

96. *CLN* 5 (February 8, 1873): 231, col. 2.

97. *CLN* 5 (March 8, 1873): 282, col. 2.

98. Kogan, *The First Century,* pp. 75–76.

99. Ibid.

100. *CLN* 25 (August 26, 1893): 451, col. 3.

101. Bradwell, *Report of the Examination of Law Students.*

102. Ibid.

103. "Memorial to Myra Bradwell," delivered by the Chicago Women's Club and reprinted in *CLN* 26 (May 12, 1894): 296, cols. 1–4.

104. Herman Kogan, "Myra Bradwell: Crusader at Law," *Chicago History* 3, no. 3 (Winter 1974–5): 132–40.

105. Proceedings of the Illinois State Bar Association, January 24 and 25, 1894, reprinted in part in *CLN* 26 (April 28, 1894): 281, col. 3–4.

106. Ibid.

107. Kogan, *The First Century.*

108. Kogan, "Myra Bradwell: Crusader at Law," pp. 132–40.

109. Letter to Jane Friedman from Herman Kogan, dated March 24, 1986 (in author's possession).

Chicago Legal News.

𝕷ex bincit.

MYRA BRADWELL, Editor.

Published *EVERY SATURDAY by the*

CHICAGO LEGAL NEWS COMPANY

NO. 87 CLARK STREET.

TERMS:

TWO DOLLARS AND TWENTY CENTS per annum, in advance. Single Copies, TEN CENTS.

CHICAGO, SEPTEMBER 10, 1887.

☞ **The Chicago Legal News Office has been removed to No. 87 CLARK St., directly opposite the court house.**

𝕰llinois 𝕷aws 𝕻assed in 1887.

All the laws passed by the Legislature at its recent session, may be had at the CHICAGO LEGAL NEWS office, in law sheep for $2.00; in pamphlet for $1.50.

Masthead of the *Chicago Legal News,* which Myra Bradwell founded in 1868 and edited until her death in 1894. She was succeeded as editor by her daughter, Bessie.

Robert Todd Lincoln (1867) was the only child of the assassinated president to live to adulthood. Courtesy of the Lincoln Museum, Fort Wayne, Indiana, a part of Lincoln National Corporation.

Mary Todd Lincoln in 1863, mourning for her son Willie, who died in 1862. Courtesy of the Lincoln Museum, Fort Wayne, Indiana, a part of Lincoln National Corporation.

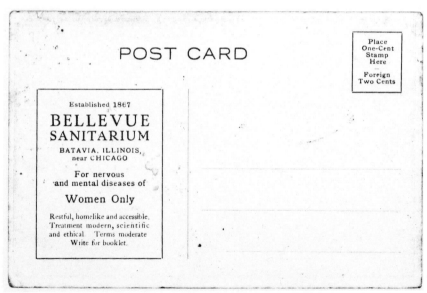

Picture postcard of the Bellevue Sanitarium, printed circa 1908. Mrs. Lincoln was institutionalized here for four months in 1875. From the collection of M. G. Price, Ann Arbor, Michigan. Reprinted by permission.

CHICAGO, *Aug 13* 187~.

Mrs. Myra Bradwell

Madam:—

Dr Patterson encloses to me your note asking for Mrs Edwards' Letter. He had already some days over the letter to me to be transmitted to you and the delay is caused by my accidental neglect or forgetfulness, for which I beg the excuse—

Very respectfully yours
Robert T. Lincoln

Robert T. Lincoln's reply to Myra Bradwell regarding his aunt's (Mrs. Elizabeth Edwards's) letter inviting Mrs. Lincoln to live with her. Courtesy of the Lincoln Museum, Fort Wayne, Indiana, a part of Lincoln National Corporation.

RESTORED.

...ɔm Will Soon Return from Her Brief Visit to the Insane Asylum.

For ᴍer Physicians Pronounce Her as Sane as Those Who Sent Her There.

And She is Only Awaiting Robert's Return from the East to Set Her

Free Again.

How She Talked with a "Times" Correspondent in a Recent Interview.

Her Recollection of Past Events and What She Had to Say of Them.

What Mrs. Myra Bradwell Has Been Doing in Her Behalf.

The public was somewhat shocked a few months since by the announcement that Mrs. Lincoln, the widow of President Lincoln, was insane; and further pained by the announcement of the fact that she had been confined in a private insane asylum at Batavia, in this state, owned and managed by Dr. Patterson. The proceedings before the court were reported with great fidelity, and published in detail in the newspapers of the city. The account of her subsequent departure from the city, and her reluctant parting with her personal liberty, was also given to the world with a painful minuteness. Occasionally some word has come up to the great busy world from this retired spot of earth, concerning the condition of the lady in whom all American people feel a kindly interest. These slight allusions to her were eagerly read, then the active affairs of life went on, and no one thought of the woman who had suffered so much in this world, and whose afternoon of life is filled with such a chilly atmosphere.

Chicago Times article printed August 24, 1875, concerning the institutionalization of Mrs. Lincoln. From the collection of James Gordon, Middleville, Michigan. Reprinted by permission.

NATIONAL WOMAN SUFFRAGE ASSOCIATION.

"Governments derive their just powers from the consent of the governed."—the ballot is consent.

ELIZABETH CADY STANTON, *President,* Johnstown, N.Y.
SUSAN B. ANTHONY, Rochester, N.Y.;
MATILDA JOSLYN GAGE, Fayetteville, N.Y.;
PHOEBE W. COZZENS, St. Louis, Mo.;
REV. OLYMPIA BROWN, Racine, Wis.;
ABIGAIL SCOTT DUNIWAY, Portland, Oregon,
Vice-Presidents at Large.

MAY WRIGHT SEWALL, *Chairman Ex. Com.,*
145 N. New Jersey st., Indianapolis, Ind.
ELLEN H. SHELDON, *Rec. Sec.*
RACHEL G. FOSTER, *Cor. Sec.,* Philadelphia, Pa.
JANE H. SPOFFORD, *Treas.,*
Riggs House, Washington, D. C.

Knapp N.Y. August 7/83

My Dear Mrs Boswell

I wonder if you
cannot send some congrat-
to me this Leonard —. There
is the decision of the
Judge — in the case of Miss
Mary Hall's admission to
the bar in Connecticut— I
hope you will send her all
the amunition you can &
fire at these professional devils !!

Have you a the Judge
a the Glorious Decree? —
Do the practitioners can yet? —
I am here with Mrs
Stanton— hard at work
on vol. III.— History Bost
the end of it before 1886—
claims upon us— but is
a herculean job !!

One of New York
are going to take up
Oliver to rest on
Nov. 9th — under our
own State Constitution —
— Do look out for

Letter to Myra Bradwell, dated August 1881, from Susan B. Anthony. From the collection of James Gordon, Middleville, Michigan. Reprinted by permission.

Women's rights leader Susan B. Anthony at age 36. From volume 1 of Ida Husted Harper's *The Life and Work of Susan B. Anthony* (1899).

7

"Petticoats Instead of Breeches"
Unlocking the Gates of the Legal Profession
to Other Nineteenth-Century Women

In 1879 Myra announced to her readers that within the past ten years there had been twenty-six women admitted to the bars of several states, and that seventeen of those women were currently in active practice.[1] She lamented, however, that "in at least 30 of our 37 States, the laws are such that [a woman] would be refused admission by the Bar, simply on account of her sex." "It is not an exaggeration," she continued, "to say that if some young woman were to apply for admission wearing her ordinary dress, to any justice of the Supreme Court [of New York] for admission to the Bar, she would be almost laughed out of existence by the press." She concluded her column with the Shakespearean suggestion that if women wanted to practice law in certain states, they should disguise themselves as men, because if "she appear[s] in *petticoats instead of breeches* (emphasis added), she [will be] incontinently bundled out of court. Brains and mentality are measured by the formation of the wearing apparel. This will not do!"

And so it was that from its very inception the *Chicago Legal News* dedicated itself to unlocking the gates of the legal profession to other nineteenth-century women. Myra reported in minute detail the travails and occasional successes of all female aspirants to the bar.

She began with entreaties to the nation's burgeoning law schools. In a very early issue of the *News* she berated the University of Chicago Law School for failing to reply to her numerous inquiries as to whether that institution would accept a woman student.[2] In that same column she announced that

129

for the very first time, a law school—Washington University at St. Louis—
had decided that a female applicant was eligible for admission. She beseeched
the University of Chicago to follow suit; it did, less than a year later. In November 1869 Myra victoriously reported that the University of Chicago Law
School "as one of the leading universities in the Northwest, if not the greatest,
most influential and powerful of them all, has opened its doors to all students
without regard to race, sex or color."[3] After noting that the current entering
class included "one single woman, one married woman, and two colored young
men," she remarked, "Truly the world moves! Who would have thought ten
years ago, that women and negroes would be admitted to the law department
of the University of Chicago in 1869, upon an equality with white males?"

It was, indeed, no small feat, and one which was blatantly rejected by
most, but not all of the law schools of the East.[4] In the 1870s two women,
Ellen Martin and M. Fredrika Perry, applied to Harvard Law School and
were promptly rejected. The denial of their applications was accompanied by
the following statement of reason:

> It is not considered practicable to admit young men and young women to
> the law library at the same time, and it is not considered fair to admit [stu-
> dents] to the Law School without giving them privileges to the Library.[5]

Likewise, although Yale was technically one of the first law schools to
admit women, the school promptly changed its policy after permitting only
one woman to matriculate there. In 1885 Alice Jordan entered Yale Law School
and received her degree in due course. However, in 1890 the law school re-
verted to its "for men only" policy, and inserted the following statement in
its catalogue: "It is to be understood that the courses of instruction above
described are open to persons of the male sex only, except where both sexes
are specifically included." In private correspondence the dean of the law school
wrote: "The marked paragraph on page 14 is intended to prevent a repetition
of the Jordan incident."[6]

In California women fared no better than they did in the East. In 1878
Clara Foltz, who had studied law with a local attorney, passed an oral bar
examination and became California's first woman lawyer.[7] After becoming a
member of the bar, Foltz decided that she needed more formal legal education. She thus applied for admission to California's first and only law school,
Hastings College of Law.

In January 1879 Foltz enrolled at Hastings and attended law school for
three days. At that point, she received a letter from the registrar advising
her that the school's directors had "resolved not to admit women to the Law
School."[8] The directors' decision was probably based, at least in part, on

the expressed fear of the school's founder, Judge Clinton Hastings, that the "women would distract the male students by their rustling garments."[9]

Myra probably had reason to foresee the subsequent widespread opposition to women as law students. If so, then she truly did have cause to rejoice when, in 1869, the University of Chicago announced its gender-neutral policy. And it is more than likely that Myra's repeated entreaties to that university were at least partially responsible for the university's willingness to admit women.

One year later, in 1870, Myra reported to her readers that "women are admitted to the Law Department of the Michigan University upon the same terms as men."[10] For the next twenty-four years, until Myra's death, the pages of the *Chicago Legal News* were replete with columns describing the fate, both pro and con, of female applicants to various law schools throughout the country.

It was not the law schools, however, but rather the courts and the legislatures that were the primary targets of Myra's ammunition; for a woman could *study* law without attending law school, but she could not *practice* law (as Myra so well knew) without receiving a license from the court.

Vowing that other prospective women lawyers would not suffer the same indignities that she had borne, Myra began in 1870 (only a few months after the Illinois Supreme Court had denied her application) to wage warfare on the courts and legislatures of all jurisdictions that refused to license women to practice law. Her most protracted battles were with the lawmakers in Illinois, Wisconsin, and Maryland, as well as the federal courts and Congress.

Myra began with her home state Illinois, perhaps because she felt that she could be most influential there, and perhaps also because she was the informal mentor of two young women who would soon be seeking admission to the Illinois bar. One of these, Alta Hulett, was pursuing her studies with a local law firm. The other woman, Ada Kepley, was studying at the University of Chicago where she was a member of the class that had been the first to open its doors to "one single woman, one married woman, and two colored young men." But it was a given that neither Miss Hulett nor Mrs. Kepley would be permitted to practice law in Illinois, for the Illinois Supreme Court would be (and undoubtedly wanted to be) bound by the "for-men-only" precedent that it had enshrined in Myra's case.

Myra began to lay the groundwork for legislative or judicial reversal of that precedent in 1870, a few months before Mrs. Kepley was due to graduate from law school. A *Chicago Legal News* column in April of that year began with the announcement that a female graduate of Washington University Law School had recently obtained a license to practice law in Missouri. Myra continued:

The time will come, and shortly too, when women will not have to obtain legal knowledge and the right to it under such difficulties. Three women, Mrs. Kepley, Miss Stanton, and Mrs. Kilgore, have been pursuing their studies in the law school of Chicago University for some time. One of these ladies [Mrs. Kepley] will soon graduate and under the ruling of the Supreme Court of Illinois in our case, she will have to go to Missouri, Iowa or Wyoming, in order to get a license [which she cannot obtain in Illinois] to follow her chosen profession, notwithstanding the fact that she has spent years of study in one of the best colleges in the land which says she is well qualified to practice law.[11]

Mrs. Kepley was, as predicted, denied a license to practice in Illinois. Myra's announcement of the Illinois Supreme Court's rejection of Mrs. Kepley was entitled: "The Negro Ahead of the Woman."[12] In her opening sentence she exclaimed: "The woman in the race to obtain the legal right to practice law in Illinois has been outdistanced by the Negro." She then claimed to rejoice that a Negro has been admitted to the "legal temple" in Illinois, but questioned why "Mrs. Kepley, equally qualified, had failed to get her license because she is a woman and [has] gone home to watch and wait the magic of events. How long shall we wait?"

Perhaps Myra's intention in announcing that "the woman had been outdistanced by the Negro" was not to appeal to racial sentiments, but merely to demonstrate that her own sex was, in some respects, enslaved to a far greater degree than was the Negro race, which had been freed merely five years earlier. But women had no General Grant and they had no artillery. Myra knew that for the female sex Appomattox would have to be achieved via the pen.

She did, however, have reason to be hopeful, for her writings were widely read and commented upon by other contemporary newspapers and journals. For example, shortly after Myra's article concerning the rejection of Mrs. Kepley, the prestigious *American Law Review* opined:

In Chicago, the best legal newspaper is edited by a woman; and now we have a full account in that newspaper of the attempt of Mrs. Ada H. Kepley to obtain admission to practice at the Illinois bar. . . . If the State [of Illinois] has overcome its prejudices so far as to admit to the equality of the hated black, the time cannot be far distant when women will also find the victory won.[13]

A few months after the Illinois Supreme Court refused to license Mrs. Kepley, an Illinois trial court judge, Judge Decius, admitted her to practice before his court. In commenting on Judge Decius's action, Myra lauded his brave act of defiance, but also lamented the fact that as a practical matter it could only harm Mrs. Kepley. If Mrs. Kepley chose to practice law in Judge

Decius's court, without a license from the Illinois Supreme Court, she could be fined for practicing law without a license.[14]

Mrs. Kepley was ultimately admitted to the practice of law in Illinois. She was not, however, the first woman to be licensed by the Illinois Supreme Court. That "honor" belonged to nineteen-year-old Alta Hulett, another protégée of Myra who had also—the first time around—been denied admission to the bar.

In November 1871 the *Rockford Register* announced with regret that

> the Supreme Court of Illinois has just refused to admit to the Bar Miss Alta Hulett . . . a young lady of superior talents and attainments. The Supreme Court has again, as in the late application of Mrs. Myra Bradwell, the gifted and accomplished editress of the Chicago Legal News, decided against the admission of women. So it seems that there may be brothers but not sisters in law.[15]

Rather than being resigned to the plight of women applicants to the bar, Myra once again expressed her rage and lost little time in informing her readers that:

> Judge Anson S. Miller, who was one of the examining committee, informs us that Miss Hulett was one of five applicants for license, and that she answered questions much more readily than the four gentlemen who were examined with her and have since been admitted to the bar.[16]

She closed that column by intimating that she would soon lobby for legislative change:

> Well, Miss Hulett, wait a little longer. The doors of the legal temple in Illinois will surely be opened for the admission of women. It only remains to be seen whether it will be done by the Supreme Court of the U.S. or the state legislature.[17]

The year was 1871, and women had for the past three consecutive years "struck out" with the Illinois Supreme Court: Myra in 1869, Ada Kepley in 1870, and Alta Hulett in 1871. Myra knew, as did all other interested observers, that further applications to the Illinois court would be futile. There were, however, still two other avenues of redress. One was simply to wait until the United States Supreme Court decided Myra's pending appeal. The nation's highest tribunal had, however, been "sitting on" that case for two years, and a decision did not seem imminent. Moreover, Myra must have known that there was high likelihood that the U.S. Supreme Court would ultimately decide against her, in which case she would still be compelled to resort to the state legislature.

And so, without waiting for the U.S. Supreme Court's decision in *Bradwell* v. *Illinois,* Myra and Alta Hulett drafted and lobbied through the state legislature a statute that secured to all persons freedom in the selection of any "occupation, profession, or employment . . . without regard to sex."[18] Given that statutory mandate, the Illinois Supreme Court had no choice in 1873 but to accept begrudgingly Alta Hulett's second application for admission to the bar, but not without putting her through a double ordeal. First, the court required her to take a second bar examination, even though she had passed her first one with high honors.[19] Second, immediately upon passing her second examination—also with honors—she was rebuked by one of the examining justices: "If you were my daughter, I would disinherit you!"[20]

Noting that "Nothing save a blast from Gabriel's trumpet can dispel these life-long prejudices,"[21] Myra continued to encourage Alta Hulett and to comment publicly upon her every success. For example, a year after Ms. Hulett began to practice law, Myra informed the readers of the *News*:

> Miss Hulett appeared before the court in some complicated bankruptcy matters. It gives us great pleasure to say that Miss Hulett tried these cases with ability which would have been creditable to a man much more her senior. In her argument she comprehended the facts and applied the law to them with a readiness which seemed to astonish the court and members of the bar present.[22]

Unfortunately, Alta Hulett died at the age of twenty-three, only three-and-a-half years after being admitted to the practice of law. In eulogizing her, Myra wrote that Hulett had been *the* rising star of the Chicago bar—a formidable opponent who had not allowed herself to be victimized by her brethren in the profession—and who had thus served as an indomitable role model for other women lawyers:

> And we beg pardon for drawing the contrast—but we know of no young man at the Chicago Bar who has arisen as rapidly to distinction as Miss Hulett. . . . Sometimes members of the Bar, thinking they had an opponent of the gentler sex, would presume upon this, and imagine that a few slurs and a little ungentlemanly conversation would phase their fair opponent and thus dispose of her most easily. But in this way they were sadly disappointed, for she would answer them with a withering sarcasm or a witty repartee.[23]

Regrettably, the early demises of Alta Hulett and another young Chicago woman lawyer, M. Fredrika Perry, who died at age thirty-two, were viewed by some male commentators as evidence of the unfitness of women for the "hard usage and severe mental application incidental to a legal professional career."[24] For example, one Chicago judge wrote:

> Two of the brightest and most promising of our women lawyers, Miss Hulett and Miss Perry, have died, young in years and young in their profession. It may be that they made a mistake in adopting so laborious a profession, one so trying to the nervous and physical system.[25]

Myra, who would not let that conjecture go unchallenged, immediately fired off the following rejoinder:

> In reflecting upon the fact that this Bar has lost two of its lady members recently, the thought was suggested that perhaps the labors and duties of the profession were more than the female constitution could endure; but when we reflect that a number of the male members of the profession have been recently stricken by the relentless hand of death, who were young, strong and vigorous, we find that it will not do to generalize in that way.[26]

Perhaps Myra should have noted that while it was unlikely that the practice of law per se had contributed to the premature deaths of Miss Hulett and Miss Perry, it was at least possible that the obstacles that had been thrown in their course and the consequent humiliation that they had both suffered had played some small part. (Miss Perry, it will be recalled, had been denied admission to Harvard Law School on the grounds that it was not sound policy to admit young men and women to the law library at the same time.) Myra, perhaps wisely, did not raise that argument. Women were by that time moving freely through the gates of the profession in Illinois, and Myra had already turned her attention to other, seemingly more impenetrable jurisdictions, most notably the states of Wisconsin and Maryland, and also the federal government.

Myra's battles with both the federal government and the state of Maryland centered around a female attorney named Belva Lockwood. Mrs. Lockwood's travails coincided, chronologically, with Myra's. It was through the combined efforts of these two remarkably tenacious women that the United States Supreme Court—six years after its rejection of Myra's claim—was forced to open its own doors to Mrs. Lockwood, rendering her the first woman to be admitted to practice before the nation's highest tribunal.

Mrs. Lockwood's saga was long and arduous.[27] It began in 1868 when she applied for admission to the law school at Columbian College (later George Washington University) and was rejected on the grounds that "her presence in classes would distract the young men." She then applied for admission at both Georgetown and Howard, but was rebuffed by both institutions. Because she was married to a minister who was affiliated with a church in the District of Columbia, attendance at an out-of-town law school was simply not a viable option for her.

In 1870 Mrs. Lockwood was accepted for admission by the newly-formed National University Law School. Once enrolled she was not permitted to participate in regular class recitations with the male students, but instead recited separately with the one other female member of the class. At first, the two women were allowed to attend coeducational lectures. But after several of the male students protested, the women were notified that they could no longer attend any lectures but would be permitted to pay fees and continue to be "enrolled" as students at the law school. At graduation the two women were not permitted to appear on stage with the male students, or even to receive their diplomas.

Although the other woman "graduate" simply gave up, "became merged in her husband,"[28] and left the city, the unstoppable Belva Lockwood appealed to the school's highest executive officer (ex officio), President Ulysses S. Grant, "demanding" that he take action in her case. One week later she received her diploma in law.

Her ordeal continuing, Lockwood was then required to take two bar examinations. After she took the first exam, the examining committee refused to issue a report, citing a provision in the District of Columbia Code that restricted bar admission to male applicants. Lockwood immediately instituted a court action in which she sought to have the word "male" removed from the prerequisites contained in the code.

While the court action was pending, Lockwood retook the bar exam. The second examining committee delayed its report while it awaited the court's decision. Finally, the District's highest court "ordered the word 'male' to be stricken out [from the Code], thus opening the way to women to practice law."[29] Mrs. Lockwood was soon thereafter admitted to the bar for the District of Columbia.

A few days after Lockwood was admitted to the bar, Myra invited her to Chicago to deliver a speech on the topic "Woman and Her Relations to the Law." Moved by Lockwood's eloquence, Myra commented, "[Mrs. Lockwood] spoke of the disabilities of woman under . . . law as only one can who has suffered by them."[30] From that day forward, the two women carried on a correspondence; and through the pages of the News, Myra became Mrs. Lockwood's publicity agent.

Mrs. Lockwood faced no further hurdles in gaining admittance to the bar of the District of Columbia or in being allowed to appear before the courts of that jurisdiction. Her battle to be permitted to practice law, however, was far from over. Her next dispute was with the Federal Court of Claims (which is also located in Washington, D.C.) and, soon thereafter, with the United States Supreme Court.

The problem with the Court of Claims surfaced in 1874. One of Lockwood's clients had a $100,000 contract action against the Navy department, and wanted to file a lawsuit. Most contract actions against branches of the federal government were heard in the Court of Claims. In order to pursue her client's case, she moved to be admitted before that court. Chief Justice Drake appeared to be stunned by Mrs. Lockwood's motion for admission, and the following colloquy (reported almost verbatim by Myra in the *Chicago Legal News*) occurred between them:

> Chief Justice Drake: Mistress Lockwood, you are a woman.
>
> Mrs. Lockwood: I plead guilty to the charge of the court.
>
> Justice Drake: Your application is not contemplated by the rules of the court. The rules require that an attorney be a *man* of good moral character.
>
> Mrs. Lockwood: I have carefully examined the law, without finding therein anything disqualifying a practicing attorney from admission on the ground of sex.
>
> Justice Drake: I'll examine the matter and render a decision on Monday.
>
> Mrs. Lockwood: That course will be satisfactory to me, if, meanwhile, I can file papers and proceed to take testimony in the case, as my client is in town, waiting to go on with the claim.
>
> Justice Drake: If the case is pressing, you can appear again tomorrow by which time a decision might be reached.[31]

The following day, Mrs. Lockwood appeared promptly at court, accompanied by her husband and another man. Before calling any other case, Chief Justice Drake addressed Mrs. Lockwood. The following dialogue ensued:

> Justice Drake: I have not yet been able to decide as to the question of your admission, but I will do so as soon as practicable.
>
> Mrs. Lockwood: (advancing to the bench) Will you grant me leave to take testimony?
>
> Justice Drake: The court cannot recognize you in any way as an attorney at law until you have been admitted, but your client can proceed in his own name.

Mrs. Lockwood: *Her* own name!

Justice Drake: *Her* own name, then. If you, Mrs. Lockwood, were the claimant, you would have a right to appear in person; otherwise you are at liberty to act for your client outside the court . . . [as an] attorney, but not to appear before the court for any purpose. There are difficulties in the way of admitting a married lady to practice.[32]

Justice Drake's position was, of course, incongruous but entirely consistent with nineteenth-century social ethos. The justice seemed to think that it was permissible for Mrs. Lockwood, a married woman, to act as an attorney for her client—to give legal advice on a matter pending before the Court of Claims, to negotiate with the attorney for her opponent, etc.—as long as she (Mrs. Lockwood) did not show her face in court. Giving legal advice and negotiating with a client's adversaries do, in fact, constitute the practice of law. If Mrs. Lockwood in her capacity as a married woman (or perhaps merely in her capacity as a woman) were deemed unqualified to practice law, then she would be equally as unqualified to practice "outside the court" as she was to practice in the courtroom itself. But Justice Drake did not seem aware of this paradox; it was obviously Mrs. Lockwood's presence in court, rather than her behind-the-scenes conduct, that he found so unsettling.

Their dialogue continued:

Justice Drake: Mistress Lockwood, you are a married woman! You have a husband have you not?

Mrs. Lockwood: Yes (she indicated the doctor by a graceful wave of the hand; whereupon that gentleman advanced and placed himself beside her).

Justice Drake: These difficulties the court has not yet been able to consider.

Mrs. Lockwood: I care very little about the question, as long as my client's business goes all right; but, would you please inform me what course I should pursue in order to prevent my client's interest suffering by delay.

Justice Drake: This is no part of my duty. But (reluctantly) I think it will be all right if you carry on outside proceedings, and take testimony in your client's name without using the name of an attorney.[33]

Myra was indignant over Justice Drake's treatment of Mrs. Lockwood, but declined lengthy comment pending the justice's final decision in the matter:

We shall speak of this case again after the final decision, but in the meantime we will say we presume Chief Justice Drake never considered marriage such a disability as to prevent a husband from being admitted to the Bar, or taking a seat upon the bench.[34]

Six weeks later, the Court of Claims, speaking through a different judge, Judge Nott, entered a final order denying Mrs. Lockwood's motion to be admitted to the Court of Claims. The rationale behind Judge Nott's decision, judged by the standards of today, was a piece of sophistry but a novel one at that. The judge reasoned that if the court allowed Mrs. Lockwood to practice before it, then it would have to grant that privilege to all qualified women, one of whom might be married to a judge. That hypothetical wife might try a case in her husband's court, using her seductive powers of persuasion to influence and corrupt the administration of justice. Judge Nott's opinion, which Myra reprinted in the *Chicago Legal News,* reads in part as follows:

> This is an application in effect, though not in purpose, to have the law declared to be that the wife of a judge of a United States court may appear at its bar, and being duly qualified, be admitted to the practice of the law before her husband. This has probably not entered the mind of the applicant, but . . . if it be true that there is no law to prevent a woman from acquiring the office of an attorney, it is equally true that there is no law to forbid the wives of the judges and law officers of the government from acquiring the same privilege. . . . [Such] judges [are] liable to be swayed by the most powerful influence known to law or to humanity. Whenever the wife of a judge or attorney general is admitted to practice, she will speedily acquire a very lucrative practice, which may sufficiently piece out her husband's salary, but which will as quickly occasion suspicions of partiality and corruption on the part of [the judiciary].[35]

Immediately after reprinting Judge Nott's opinion, Myra gave equal space to her own extra-judicial dissent, which was based on two grounds. First, even if the wife of a judge were admitted to practice, she and her husband could always refrain, as a matter of discretion, from having her cases tried before him:

> If the wife of a judge should apply, it would be no reason for her rejection that her husband happened to be one of the judges of the court; but it would be a matter of taste after her admission whether she should practice before her husband or not.[36]

In the second part of her editorial dissent, Myra reduced Judge Nott's "wife-of-a-judge" rationale to the absurdity by pointing out that the application of such reasoning would also disqualify all men from practicing law because one such man might be the son of a judge. She noted that

> Judge McClean, one of our ablest and purest judges that ever sat upon the bench of the Supreme Court of the U.S., allowed his son to practice in the Court over which he presided. While we would not favor a wife practicing in her husband's court, or a son in his father's, still we claim it is a matter of taste.[37]

Nevertheless, the Court of Claims had refused to qualify Mrs. Lockwood, and its decision was final. There was no forum to which she could appeal—except Congress. Thus, one month after she was rejected by the Court of Claims, Belva Lockwood petitioned Congress to pass a statute or resolution to the effect that "no woman, otherwise qualified, shall be disbarred from practice before any [federal] court on account of sex or coverture."[38] Lockwood's brief in support of her petition shows the influence of Myra's editorial dissent from the decision of the Court of Claims. Indeed, her rationale was almost identical to the reasoning employed by Myra. Lockwood argued:

> The petitioner in this case has been debarred from practice before the Court of Claims because she is a married woman; or in the words of the court, lest the wife of a judge should practice before him. Notwithstanding this, the son of Judge Peck of said court does practice before him, and there is no law to prevent such practice, or that of any other degree of relationship, so that it be of the male line. A simple rule of court, however, would suffice to do away with any irregularity where the relationship of the parties might seem to influence a partiality in the verdict.[39]

The matter remained buried in Congress for two years. In 1876, however, Belva Lockwood once again emerged in the limelight with Myra Bradwell at her side, giving strong moral and editorial support. In that year, Mrs. Lockwood had the temerity to apply for admission to the United States Supreme Court. As she recalled years later, "those nine gowned judges looked at me in amazement and dismay."[40] They then promptly rejected her application for admission. Chief Justice Waite, writing according to "instructions from the Court," announced the following decision:

> By the uniform practice of the Court, from its organization to the present time, and by the fair construction of its rules, none but men are admitted to practice before it as attorneys and counselors. This is in accordance with immemorial usage in England, the law and practice in all the States until within a recent period; and the Court does not feel called upon to make

a change until such a change is required by statute, or a more extended practice in the highest Courts of the States.[41]

Once again, with impeccable logic, Myra berated the Court, arguing that if the "immemorial usage in England" is the standard governing attorneys who argue before the U.S. Supreme Court, then all attorneys appearing before that Court should be required to wear a gown and wig:

> The practice [of the Supreme Court] has been to admit any attorney in good standing of any of the Supreme courts of the States or the District, on motion, without asking any questions. The same reasoning which the Chief Justice used to exclude Mrs. Lockwood would compel every attorney who appears in the Supreme Court of the U.S. to wear a gown and wig. Women have never been admitted to practice in Westminster Hall, and therefore Mrs. Lockwood is denied the right to practice in the U.S. Supreme Court. *Counselors have never been allowed to practice in Westminster Hall and other superior courts in England unless they wore gowns and wigs, and therefore it follows that they should not be allowed to practice in the Supreme Court of the United States without these necessary articles. We call upon the court to enforce the English rule and practice in this respect.*[42]

Two years after being denied the right to practice before the U.S. Supreme Court, Mrs. Lockwood persuaded a sympathetic congressman to introduce in the House of Representatives a bill that provided for the admission of women to practice in all federal courts, including the U.S. Supreme Court, upon the same terms as men.[43] The bill was a modification of the same bill that had been introduced and defeated four times in the prior four years, ever since Mrs. Lockwood had been refused admission to the Court of Claims.[44] Upon its fifth introduction in the House, the bill was passed by a margin of two to one.[45] But the bill still had to gain approval in the Senate, where it once again faced seemingly insurmountable obstacles. When the proposed law was sent to the Senate Judiciary Committee, that body issued an adverse report, arguing that Congress simply did not have the power to regulate the admission of attorneys to the U.S. Supreme Court and that such a power was vested exclusively in the Court itself.[46] Immediately, Myra realized that the report was a dangerous one because it transcended the issue of women's rights and struck at the very core of the concept of checks and balances between co-equal branches of the federal government. In a lengthy and scathing editorial she wrote:

> The question of the admission of women to the bar sinks into insignificance in comparison with the importance of the other question involved in the refusal to pass the law for the reasons given by the Judiciary Committee, that

Congress has no power to regulate the admission of attorneys to the Supreme Court of the U.S. and that this power is exclusively in the Court, is the most dangerous report that has come from any Committee during the present session in either house of Congress. . . . Let this law be defeated for the reason given by the Committee and should the Supreme Court of the U.S. hereafter wish to defy the power of Congress in matters relating to the court, it would have to look no further than this report of the committee for a precedent. . . . What would be thought of a Supreme Court, where [a statute requiring applicants for admission to the bar be at least twenty-one years old] was in force, if it should knowingly disregard it, and admit a boy of twelve years of age, and send him forth with a license to practice law, saying that the legislature had no power to say who should be admitted to the bar? We say to Congress, and . . . to the legislatures of the States, that the most dangerous power in this government is that which is claimed to exist in the Federal Supreme Court, independent and beyond the power and control of Congress. It is exercised in silence; it moves on, uninterrupted, and is more to be feared than any other.[47]

Whether the Senate Judiciary Committee was persuaded by Myra's logic or by other factors is unclear. That committee, however, did promptly change its rationale. Although it once again reported adversely on the bill, the second time it gave a different reason that constituted an even more serious subterfuge. This time the committee argued that there was no necessity for the passage of the bill because there was no statute that expressly *excluded* women from practicing befdore the federal courts. Therefore, the report rationalized, there was no need for legislation that expressly *included* them.[48]

While the Senate committee's second adverse report may have had logical appeal, as a practical matter it made no sense, for it was the Supreme Court's rejection of Mrs. Lockwood (and, by implication, of all women) that had, in fact, led to both the introduction of the bill and its passage in the House. As Myra noted:

The friends of the measure regard this action of the Senate as an evasion of the issue, because, in point of fact, the courts do not admit women to practice, and the U.S. Supreme Court has refused to entertain any application for admission on behalf of a woman. She is in the same position, therefore, as if expressly excluded by law.[49]

The Senate ultimately rejected both adverse committee reports and passed the bill specifically providing for admission of women to the bar of the U.S. Supreme Court on the same grounds as men.[50] The law was signed by President Hayes in February 1879.

In prophesying the reaction of some members of the Supreme Court to the new law, Myra took a swipe at her old foe, Justice Bradley. Her tone definitely smacked of sweet revenge:

> Judging from the opinions previously expressed by some of the members of [the Supreme Court], it might be in keeping with their feelings to wear crape for a period of thirty days or more, for they evidently consider it in the nature of a calamity when such rights are accorded to women as a class. See opinion of Bradley, J in the Matter of the Application of Myra Bradwell: "the paramount destiny and mission of women are to fulfill the noble and benign office of wife and mother. This is the law of the Creator."
>
> Now it occurs to us that the above has just as little to do in deciding whether women shall be allowed to practice in the courts as for us to insist that each applicant for a position on the Supreme Bench should exceed a certain number of pounds avoirdupois.[51]

Then, in a final lunge:

> The court which has said to woman, "you cannot enter here," must now open its door at her approach when she comes armed with the proper documents."[52]

And so it was that on March 3, 1879, Belva Lockwood, "armed with the proper documents," was admitted to the Supreme Court of the United States "without objection or hesitation, it having been found unnecessary even to argue her motion for admission."[53] Three days later, she applied for admission to the bar of the Court of Claims for the second time. That court, upon learning of her admission to the Supreme Court, promptly admitted her.[54]

Some members of the Supreme Court, however, could not accept the matter gracefully. One justice, for example, quipped that the admission of women to practice before the Supreme Court would necessitate the attachment of a nursery for babies to the courtroom. While the comment might have been made in jest, Myra responded to it seriously, obviously believing that no slur against women attorneys should go unchallenged. She wrote:

> We learned a few days [ago] that some member of this honorable court remarked now that women were admitted to practice in their court, they would find it necessary to have a nursery attached to the court room, so that the babies could be amused while the mothers pleaded their causes.
>
> Now, my noble brothers, let me entreat you to have no unnecessary fears in this regard, for the average lawyer spends only a few days in a year in your sanctified domain. Allowing a lady lawyer to spend an equal amount of time, we think there need be no attachment of this kind on account of the mothers who shall have the honor to appear before you, for the . . . dry

goods houses in our land have not found it necessary to arrange for this emergency, and I am sure that you are willing to admit that women spend more time in shopping than they will in the courts. We will try to be very respectful; if we do not succeed, the power of fining for contempt is yours, but in the meantime don't "man-dam-us" before we have had a hearing.[55]

Although Mrs. Lockwood had reigned triumphant in the District of Columbia courts, the United States Congress, the United States Supreme Court, and also the Court of Claims, her struggle for admission to the bar was not yet over. The legislation mandating that women be licensed on the same terms as men applied only to the federal courts. The courts of the various states were still free, in the absence of legislation such as that which had been enacted in Illinois, to formulate their own policies excluding female attorneys. Thus, when Belva Lockwood attempted to file a lawsuit in the neighboring state of Maryland, she was met with the all-too-familiar rebuff. Mrs. Lockwood described that court's treatment of her in a letter that she wrote to Myra in October 1878:

Dear Mrs. Bradwell,

The fight for the admission of women to the "bar" seems not yet to be over. You began the contest, I intend to complete it. Having recently filed a suit (an ordinary suit at law) in the Prince County Court at Marlborough, Maryland, . . . I was told that I must first be formally admitted. . . . Upon the filing of [a brief in support of admission] and my appearance one week later, Judge Magruder, not in a gentlemanly manner, but in a very offensive and disagreeable way refused the admission, going out of his way to animadvert upon a woman getting out of her sphere, saying she was created as the help mate of man; "that the seas and the rocks and the mountains had their bounds"; and closing by saying "*I pray to God that the time may never come when the State of Maryland will admit women to the Bar* [emphasis added]."

Determined to explain my position, I engaged the court room after the adjournment of the court, for the purpose of addressing the members of the bar, and for this purpose had obtained leave of the Commissioners of the building. The judge ascertaining this, ordered the bailiff not to allow me to speak in the court room. Whereupon the members of the Bar invited me to speak from the court house steps, which I did, addressing about 200 persons, mostly members of the Bar. . . . I enclose to you a report of the . . . *Baltimore Sun*.

Yours truly,

Belva Lockwood[56]

Apparently Judge Magruder felt that Mrs. Lockwood's attempt to appear in his courtroom was akin to an act of prostitution. During the course of the proceeding, he referred to her as "[a] wandering woman."[57]

Myra was enraged by the judge's "shameful" treatment of Mrs. Lockwood, and, as always, was determined to have the last word. In an article in the *News* in which Myra referred to the judge as "Past Century Judge Magruder," she reprinted the full text of Mrs. Lockwood's letter so that "the Bar throughout the United States may judge Past Century's conduct." She opined:

> Whatever may have been his opinion about the propriety of admitting women to practice at the Bar, he had no right to abuse a woman from the Bench, and then to refuse to hear her, adjourn his court, run away, and tell his sheriff that if she attempted to address the Bar in the room to arrest her or put her out. We have known Mrs. Lockwood for many years. She is a worthy woman of a sensitive nature, and feels the rebuffs of judicial tyrants most keenly.[58]

While Myra had previously attacked "for-men-only" judicial opinions on the basis of their irrationality, her assault on Judge Magruder was based on his lack of chivalry. Myra concluded her editorial by contrasting Judge Magruder's "shameful" conduct with the Illinois courts' gallant treatment of the late Alta Hulett:

> The judges of our courts [in Illinois] always treated the lamented Miss Hulett with the greatest courtesy and did all in their power to make her professional life pleasant.[59]

The foregoing editorial seems, at first blush, to manifest a temporary lapse of memory. Certainly Myra had not forgotten that only seven years earlier the Illinois courts had denied Miss Hulett's application for admission, and that it was only by dint of a piece of express legislation, drafted by Miss Hulett and Myra herself, that women had won the right to practice law in Illinois. Even then, one of the Supreme Court justices reprimanded Hulett: "If you were my daughter, I would disinherit you."[60]

It is doubtful, however, that Myra had forgotten. Instead, her contrasting of Judge Magruder's unchivalrous conduct towards Mrs. Lockwood with the Illinois courts' "courteous" treatment of Miss Hulett was probably an appeal to the raw emotions of the members of the bar and judiciary throughout the entire country. At the time of Myra's sentimental editorial, women were still being precluded from practice in at least thirty out of thirty-seven states.[61] Myra was employing every weapon in her verbal arsenal: logic, emotion, repartee, and even *ad hominem* attacks on unsympathetic judges. For example, the *Chicago Legal News*'s numerous accounts of Mrs. Lockwood's continuing battles with the Maryland courts included the following terse report:

> Mrs. Belva Lockwood, the well-known woman lawyer of Washington, has been denied admission to the Bar by a fossilized Bourbon Judge at Westminster, Maryland, notwithstanding she has been admitted to practice in the Supreme Court of the United States.[62]

Mrs. Lockwood's plans, however, were far more grandiose than simply practicing law in the local courts of Maryland.[63] By the time she had been denied admission by the "fossilized Bourbon Judge at Westminster, Maryland," she had already become deeply immersed in national politics, running twice for president of the United States under the banner of the newly formed National Equal Rights Party.[64] Moreover, Myra Bradwell, always looking for the good fight, had already turned her attention elsewhere, this time to the Supreme Court of Wisconsin. The case involved a woman named Lavinia Goodell.

Myra's involvement with Lavinia Goodell began in 1874 when the latter was admitted to practice before the Circuit (trial) Court of Rock County, Wisconsin. Myra, following her standing habit of commenting on the admission of any woman to the practice of law, wrote, rather innocuously:

> Miss Lavinia Goodell, a young lady of good education, fine appearance, and modest bearing has been admitted to the bar. Her father, 85 years old and a celebrated abolitionist, rejoices in his daughter's success.[65]

Several weeks later, the *London Law Times* printed the following caustic response:

> The world has had some experience of the difficulties which may attend the entrance of women into the professions. These have been more particularly illustrated in connection with medicine; as far as we are aware, no English lady yet contemplates the study and practice of law. What may happen if the bold venture should be made may be conjectured from a paragraph which appears in a recent number of the *Chicago Legal News*: "Miss Lavinia Goodell, a young lady of good education, fine appearance, and modest bearing has been admitted to the Bar." The *News* is edited by a lady, and ladies consider another's personal appearance fair matter for observation. It is hardly possible to conceive what demoralization of juries, the Bar, solicitors, and the press would result from young ladies of "fine appearance" entering the ranks of the Bar. We think we can promise, however, that we should not emulate the example of our contemporary of Chicago.[66]

Myra immediately fired off the following retort:

We always supposed it was the duty of juries to decide cases upon the law and the evidence, and not upon personal appearance of the advocate. If we have been mistaken and they are influenced, as stated by our contemporary, as all our juries have been composed of men, does it not show that we need some change in our jury system?[67]

Miss Goodell practiced before the trial court without hindrance for approximately one year. At that point she appealed one of her cases to the Supreme Court of Wisconsin, and filed a motion to be permitted to appear as an attorney before that higher court. Her application, supported and argued by the Assistant Attorney General of the State of Wisconsin,[68] was promptly denied by Wisconsin's Supreme Court. The opinion of Chief Justice Ryan was a classic:

This is the first application for admission of a female to the bar of this court. And it is just matter for congratulation that it is made in favor of a lady whose character raises no personal objection; something perhaps not always to be looked for in women who forsake the ways of their sex for the ways of ours. . . . The law of nature destines and qualifies the female sex for the bearing and nurture of the children of our race and for the custody of the homes of the world and their maintenance in love and honor. And all life-long callings of women, inconsistent with these radical and sacred duties of their sex, as is the profession of law, are *departures from the order of nature; and, when voluntary, treason against it.*[69]

Apparently Chief Justice Ryan believed that Miss Goodell's unmarried status was not voluntary, and hence not treasonous. Indeed, he seemed to believe that it was simply a cruel act of fate that she had remained single, for his opinion continued:

The cruel challenges of life sometimes baffle both sexes, and may leave women free from the peculiar duties of their sex. These may need employment and should be welcomed to any not derogatory to their sex. . . . But it is public policy to provide for the [female] sex, and not for its *superfluous* members; *and not to tempt women from the proper duties of their sex by opening to them duties peculiar to ours.* There are many employments in life not unfit for female character. The profession of the law is surely not one of these.

The peculiar qualities of womanhood, its gentle graces, its quick sensibility, its tender susceptibility, its purity, its delicacy, its emotional impulses, its subordination of hard reason to sympathetic feeling, are surely not qualifications for forensic strife. Nature has tempered woman as little for the juridical conflicts of the court room as for the physical conflicts of the battle field. Womanhood is moulded for gentler and better things.[70]

Justice Ryan concluded his opinion with a *reductio ad absurdum*:

And when counsel was arguing for this lady that the word "person" [in the statute relating to admission of attorneys] necessarily includes females . . . the same construction of the same word would subject woman to prosecution for the paternity of a bastard . . . and to prosecution for rape.[71]

Myra immediately launched a three-pronged attack on Justice Ryan. First, there was her characteristic repartee:

The court says it is not sorry that no statute can be found admitting women to the bar of the state courts, for it does not think it the proper place for the exercise of her peculiar qualities or for the preservation of her purity. . . . If her purity is in danger, it would be better to reconstruct the court and the bar, than to exclude the women.[72]

Second, Myra inserted in the *News* a snippet that hinted that Justice Ryan was a troublesome person and that he was persona non grata to his colleagues. The innuendo reads as follows:

The Supreme Court of Wisconsin—We are pleased to learn that the unpleasantness which has existed between Chief Justice Ryan and his associates on the bench has passed away and that they now recognize and treat each other as gentlemen.[73]

The third prong of Myra's attack was to give Miss Goodell a forum, the *Chicago Legal News,* in which to respond to Justice Ryan's opinion. A large portion of one whole issue of the *News* was devoted to Miss Goodell's critique, much of which was a rejoinder to that part of Justice Ryan's opinion which stated that "it is public policy . . . not to tempt women from the proper duties of their sex by opening to them duties peculiar to ours."

Miss Goodell replied:

His honor, with a humility at once touching and naive, assumes that matrimony is so undesirable a state for woman that, were she allowed freely to earn an honorable and lucrative support in any other manner she would never enter it. The well-being of society requires her to marry and she should therefore be forced to do so by having no other alternative. Possibly this is so, though I confess I am slow to believe it. Yet, granting it, for argument sake, would it not be better to render the lot of a married woman more attractive by according her fuller rights therein, and by effort on the part of husbands to so refine and ennoble themselves as to become more desirable companions than so to lower the standard as to take wives who marry because no other alternative is open to them? . . . His honor gives as a reason why women should not be permitted to practice law, the fact that in their business relations they would meet with so many bad men whose society would be unpleasant and contaminating. And yet, according to this theory, these very women should marry these men; and should even be forced to marry them by being shut out from the higher class of employment, lest possibly they might seek a way of escape. . . . If nature has built up barriers to keep woman out of the legal profession, be assured that she will stay out; but if nature has built no such barriers, in vain shall man build them, for they will certainly be overthrown.[74]

And overthrown they were! In 1877 the Wisconsin legislature, in response to strong lobbying by both Myra and Miss Goodell, enacted a statute providing that "no person shall be denied admission or a license to practice as an attorney in any Court in this State on account of sex."[75] Moreover, newspapers throughout the country viewed the combined lobbying efforts to be so persuasive and successful that they began to refer to Miss Goodell as "Miss *Goodsell.*"[76]

Although Goodell had successfully maneuvered the bill through the legislature, her renewed application for a license to practice before the Wisconsin Supreme Court was not automatically granted. Instead, her old nemesis, Chief Justice Ryan, took the "weighty" matter under advisement. Of course, there was not legitimate basis for his doing so! A legislative mandate is a legislative mandate; a statute cannot be overturned by a court unless it violates the federal or state constitution, and no one was arguing that the new statute authorizing women to practice law was unconstitutional. Thus, the Wisconsin Supreme Court was duty-bound to submit to the legislative will and to grant Miss Goodell's application for admission just as the U.S. Supreme Court had done in Belva Lockwood's case and the Illinois Supreme Court had done in Alta Hulett's case. Nevertheless, Justice Ryan decided that the court had the power to reconsider the matter. Myra never forgave him! She continued to attack him, vituperatively, until his death and even afterwards. In her initial editorial on the matter she wrote:

Under this statute the application of Miss Goodell is now made, and the court takes the "weighty" matter under advisement. It is intimated, however, by some of the Bar that Chief Justice Ryan is disposed to hold that the court is above the law and the legislature, and that it can disregard the law, and say what class of persons shall, and what class of persons shall not, have the right to practice law. If he should so defy the law-making power, let him be impeached and driven from the Bench in the only legal way of getting rid of Judges who usurp powers not belonging to the courts. The only proper way is for the court to admit Miss Goodell and submit to the law-making power as the Supreme Court of the United States did in the case of Mrs. Lockwood.[77]

In a second editorial, Myra once again asked her readers to focus not on the issue of whether women should be admitted to the Bar, but instead on the more significant issue of whether Justice Ryan's "deep rooted prejudices" ought to be allowed to reign supreme over the legislative will, an issue that threatened "the right of every citizen":

We have not yet learned what the Supreme Court of Wisconsin has "advised" as to Miss Goodell's case. If Chief Justice Ryan should rule the court, we have no doubt at all what the decision will be. It will be in accordance with prejudices as deep rooted as the everlasting hills, which nothing but death itself can ever remove. . . . If ever courts can set themselves up as above the law, and substitute their own will in its place, the country is in danger. The question as to who shall or who shall not be admitted to the bar sinks into insignificance compared with the principle now involved in the case. The rights of every citizen of the State is involved, for if Miss Goodell can be stricken down by the Supreme Court of the State in defiance of an express statute of the State, every citizen can, and the will of the Supreme Court is the law of the land; if so, let the legislature be abolished.[78]

Several weeks later Myra reported that the Wisconsin Supreme Court had decided to act in accordance with the mandate of the legislature and to grant Miss Goodell a license to practice law. Once again she reprimanded Chief Justice Ryan: "We think in taking this case under advisement and retaining it so long before deciding it is not creditable to the Court."[79]

Lavinia Goodell died at age forty-one, less than a year after being issued a license by the Wisconsin Supreme Court. Myra, in eulogizing her as "an able woman, a gifted writer and [one who was] possessed by great force of character," intimated that Chief Justice Ryan's hostile treatment of Miss Goodell might have contributed to her early demise: "The long bitter controversy she had with Chief Justice Ryan in relation to her admission will be remembered by our readers."[80]

At the time of Miss Goodell's death, Justice Ryan was terminally ill. Myra, rather shockingly, used the occasion of his illness to continue her public vendetta against him. She wrote:

Chief Justice Ryan of the Supreme Court of Wisconsin is very low at the capital and not expected to recover. He is as able a judge as any on the

Bench, and in legal learning and the application of common law principles to the decision of the cases he has no superior, but the bane of his whole life has been an ungovernable temper, which no amount of cultivation or legal learning could control.[81]

Even death brought Justice Ryan no respite from Myra's vengeance. When he died in 1880, the *Chicago Legal News* carried an obituary written, of course, by Myra. She began by giving the judge's personal history and praising his attributes. She concluded by mentioning his "one failing":

his ungovernable temper, which pained his friends, . . . made him hosts of bitter enemies, . . . [and] was a great annoyance to his associates on the Bench. . . . The young man entering the profession may well admire the talents of Judge Ryan, and the name he left behind him for sterling integrity; but at the same time, remembering his only failing, he should not forget that the first lesson for a lawyer is to control himself.[82]

Myra's repeated public attacks on Justice Ryan during his illness and after his death are certainly manifestations of the darker side of her character. It was with dogged zealotry that she had labored to open the gates of the legal profession to women in all parts of the country. She seemed to believe that any tactic was appropriate if it might possibly serve to unlock yet another door.

Gradually, during the twenty-five years of Myra's crusade, almost every door did become unlocked. Year after year, in state after state, scores of women, if not enthusiastically welcomed, were at least permitted to engage in the practice of law. One of the last domains of male exclusivity removed its gender-based barriers to the legal profession in 1894, a few months after Myra's death. Myra would have been pleased by the announcement, which was written by her daughter, Bessie, the new editor-in-chief of the *Chicago Legal News*:

We are glad to learn that Mrs. [Belva] Lockwood has at last been admitted to the Bar away down in Old Virginia. . . . Mrs. Lockwood is to be congratulated upon the successful [conclusion] of her persistent effort to be admitted to practice in . . . Virginia. . . . All honor also to that sterling old Virginia jurist, Judge Christian, who, as one standing upon the heights, his vision untrammeled by clouds and mists, discerned the passing away of an old era, and having seen, was not afraid to lead the way to the new order of things.[83]

NOTES

1. *CLN* 11 (May 24, 1879): 298, col. 3–4.
2. *CLN* 1 (December 26, 1868): 100, col. 2.
3. *CLN* 2 (November 6, 1869): 44, col. 3–4.
4. One notable exception was the law department of Boston University, where the graduating class of 1881 included a woman, Lelia Robinson. That same year, however, Robinson was refused admission to the Massachusetts bar. *Robinson's Case,* 131 Mass. 376 (1881). In 1882, the state legislature enacted a law permitting women to practice. Robinson immediately took the bar examination, passed, and became a member of the bar.
5. Weisberg, "Barred from the Bar: Women and Legal Education in the U.S. 1870–1890," *Journal of Legal Education* 28: 485–86, fn 8.
6. Robinson, "Women Lawyers in the U.S.," *Green Bag* 2 (1890): 13.
7. For an excellent account of the struggles and triumphs of Clara Foltz, see Barbara Allen Babcock, "Clara Shortridge Foltz: 'First Woman,' " *Arizona Law Review* 30 (1988): 673. See also Susan L. Brandt, Mortimer D. Schwartz, and Patience Milrod, "Clara Shortridge Foltz: Pioneer in the Law," *Hastings Law Journal* 27 (1976): 545.
8. Babcock, "Clara Shortridge Foltz," p. 700.
9. Ibid. One month after receiving the registrar's letter of rejection, Foltz filed suit against the Hastings College of Law. She prevailed in both the trial court and the California Supreme Court. *Foltz* v. *Hoge,* 54 Cal. 28 (1879). In spite of the court decision granting women the right to attend Hastings, Foltz never again sought to enroll at the law school.
More than a century later, on December 3, 1990, the Hastings Law Faculty voted to award Foltz a posthumous Degree of Juris Doctor. The degree was bestowed at the School's 1991 Commencement Exercises. Accepting the degree on behalf of the Foltz family was Foltz's biographer, Professor Barbara Babcock of the Stanford law faculty. See *Hastings Community* (University of California, Hastings College of Law), Summer 1991.
10. *CLN* 2 (August 20, 1870): 377, col. 4.
11. *CLN* 2 (April 3, 1870): 212, col. 3.
12. *CLN* 2 (July 23, 1870): 344, col. 3–4.
13. *American Law Review,* reprinted in *CLN* 3 (October 8, 1870): 13, col. 1.
14. *CLN* 3 (November 19, 1870): 60, col. 2–3.
15. *Rockford Register,* reprinted in *CLN* 4 (November 18, 1871): 37, col. 1–2.
16. Ibid.
17. Ibid.
18. Harvey B. Hurd (comp. and ed.), *The Revised Statutes of the State of Illinois,* 1874 (Springfield: Illinois Journal Co.): 169.
19. *CLN* 5 (June 7, 1873): 438, col. 1. See generally, Alfred Theodore Andreas, *History of Chicago from the Earliest Period to the Present Time* vol. 2 (Chicago: A. T. Andreas, 1884–86).
20. *CLN* 5 (June 14, 1873): 453, col. 4.
21. Ibid.
22. *CLN* 6 (April 18, 1874): 241, col. 4.
23. *CLN* 9 (March 31, 1877): 229, col. 1.
24. Robinson, "Women Lawyers in the United States," *Green Bag* 2 (1890): 13.
25. Quoted in *CLN* 15 (June 30, 1883): 347, col. 4, and 348, col. 1–4.
26. Ibid.
27. See Belva Lockwood, "My Efforts to Become a Lawyer," *Lippincott's Monthly Magazine* (February 1888). See also, Inez Haynes Gilmore, *Angels and Amazons: A Hundred Years of American Women* (Garden City, N.Y.: Doubleday, Doran, and Company, Inc. 1933), p. 1768.

28. Lockwood, "My Efforts to Become a Lawyer," p. 178.

29. Quote is from *CLN* 4 (April 20, 1872): 220, col. 1.

30. *CLN* 4 (May 4, 1872): 236, col. 2–3.

31. *CLN* 6 (April 22, 1874): 233, col. 4. See also Lockwood, "My Efforts to Become a Layer,"
p. 178.

32. Ibid.

33. Ibid.

34. Ibid.

35. *CLN* 6 (May 23, 1874): 277, col. 3.

36. Ibid., p. 281, col. 1.

37. Ibid.

38. *CLN* 6 (June 20, 1874): 315, col. 3–4.

39. Ibid.

40. Lockwood, "My Efforts to Become a Lawyer," p. 178.

41. Charles Warren, *The Supreme Court in United States History,* vol. 2 (Boston: Little,
Brown and Company, 1937), pp. 550–51, fn. 1.

42. *CLN* 9 (February 10, 1877): 169, col. 3.

43. *CLN* 10 (March 2, 1878): 191, col. 3

44. Ibid.

45. Ibid.

46. *CLN* 10 (March 23, 1878): 215, col. 3-4.

47. Ibid.

48. *CLN* 10 (June 23, 1878): 318, col. 4.

49. Ibid.

50. *CLN* 11 (February 15, 1879): 179, col. 2–3.

51. Ibid.

52. Ibid.

53. *CLN* 11 (April 26, 1879): 260, col. 3–4; 261, col. 1–2.

54. Ibid.

55. *CLN* 11 (February 22, 1879): 187, col. 3.

56. *CLN* 11 (November 16, 1878): 69, col. 4.

57. Extract from *Baltimore Sun* (October 17, 1878), reprinted in *CLN* 11 (November 16,
1878): 69, col. 4.

58. *CLN* 11 (November 17, 1878): 69, col. 4.

59. Ibid.

60. *CLN* 5 (June 14, 1873): 453, col. 4.

61. *CLN* 11 (May 24, 1879): 298, col. 3–4.

62. *CLN* 13 (May 14, 1881): 296, col. 4.

63. But see *CLN* 26 (June 23, 1894): 346, col. 1.

64. *Notable American Women, 1607–1950; A Biographical Dictionary* 2 (Cambridge, Mass.:
Belknap Press of Harvard University Press, 1971), p. 414.

65. *CLN* 6 (July 4, 1874): 330, col. 2.

66. Reprinted in *CLN* 7 (August 15, 1874): 377, col. 2.

67. Ibid.

68. See *CLN* 8 (January 1, 1876): 116, col. 1.

69. *In re Goodell,* 30 Wis. 232 (1875).

70. Ibid.

71. Ibid.

72. *CLN* 8 (March 4, 1876): 191, col. 2–3.

73. Reprinted in *CLN* 9 (September 23, 1876): 8, col. 3.

74. *CLN* 8 (March 25, 1876): 215–16 and 222–23.

75. *CLN* 11 (April 26, 1879): 259, col. 1–2. See also article from *Albany Journal,* reprinted in *CLN* 11 (May 24, 1879): 298, col. 3–4.

76. Reported in *Albany Journal,* op. cit.

77. *CLN* 11 (April 26, 1879): 259, col. 1–2.

78. *CLN* 11 (May 3, 1879): 267, col. 4.

79. *CLN* 11 (June 21, 1879): 323, col. 4.

80. *CLN* 12 (April 3, 1880): 249, col. 3.

81. *CLN* 12 (January 31, 1880): 171, col. 3.

82. *CLN* 13 (October 23, 1880): 47, col. 3–4.

83. *CLN* 26 (June 23, 1894): 346, col. 1.

Almost two decades after she was admitted to practice before the United States Supreme Court, Belva Lockwood applied to the Virginia bar but was promptly refused admission. She then petitioned the United States Supreme Court for a writ of mandamus but was unsuccessful. Citing its *Bradwell* decision, the Supreme Court held that each state had complete discretion to determine who was qualified to be admitted to its bar. In *re Lockwood,* 154 U.S. 116 (1893).

In 1894, however, "Mrs. Lockwood [was] at last admitted to the Bar away down in Old Virginia."

8

"May Paddle Her Own Canoe" Opening the Doors of Other Occupations to Nineteenth-Century Women

Women's work and wages, her place in the industrial field—that problem so puzzling to political economists and fraught with such immense consequences to the most interested party—the woman who must work or starve, what does the merit system mean to this class of workers? It means the abolition of sex prejudice.

—Myra Bradwell (1894)[1]

Myra's struggle to gain for women their rightful "place in the industrial field" was not confined to securing for women the right to enter the legal profession. She believed that there was *no* occupation, whether "important" or "menial," from which women should be barred solely on account of either their gender or their marital status.

Myra's fight for the right of women to enter *all* professions and occupations began as a personal one. A few months after she was denied a license to practice law by the Illinois Supreme Court, sixty leading members of the Chicago bar petitioned Illinois Governor John Palmer to have Myra appointed as a notary public for the city of Chicago. Palmer promptly rejected the petition on the ground that Myra was a married woman. He wrote to her:

Being a married woman, you are legally incapable of executing the bond required by this statute, nor could you, if appointed, be held responsible in

155

a common lawsuit to any person who might be damnified by your official neglect of duty, or for any malfeasance in office.[2]

He concluded his rejection with the following lament:

> But I will say that while I do not believe you are eligible to the appointment you seek under the law, there is no one that I would more cheerfully appoint if the matter were within the limits of my official discretion.[3]

The governor's rejection of Myra was based not on the fact that she was a woman, but, instead, that she was a *married* woman who under the law of coverture[4] was incapacitated from entering into contracts, executing bonds, or performing many of the other duties of a notary public. In order to prove that his rationale for rejecting her was a genuine one, he publicly promised to appoint a widow to the position that Myra sought.

Myra, who fervently believed that the principle of coverture was no longer viable and that married women enjoyed the same legal capacities as single women,[5] was disappointed that Palmer had rejected her in favor of an unnamed widow. Never one to suffer silently, she immediately wrote to him:

> Dear Sir,
>   . . . I see by this morning's Tribune that you have promised to appoint a widow [as notary public]. Am I not just as good a woman and just as capable with a husband as I would be without?
>   Now, my dear governor—while many have criticized your course in the matter I have invariably said to them—*that you were a good friend of ours*—and I was sure you acted conscientiously in refusing the application—but that if you would insist in looking through those *old fogey* spectacles—all that could be done was to try to get some legislation to do away with them.
>   Please remember me as your friend.
>
> Myra Bradwell[6]

Myra immediately drafted the desired legislation, but five years elapsed before she was able to secure its enactment.[7] During the interim, however, and even afterwards, she conducted a journalistic vendetta against Governor Palmer. Her most vicious attack was in the form of an anonymous letter to the *Chicago Legal News,* ostensibly written by a member of the state legislature. In it, the "legislator" wrote:

> I have noticed in the *Legal News* and other papers severe criticisms of the acts of our last General Assembly. . . . It must . . . be borne in mind that the legislature was much embarrassed by a crotchety and whimsical governor,

who forced upon it . . .unnecessary matters and diverted and distracted the attention of members; and that he vetoed bills on the most frivolous grounds and was constantly threatening and interfering with members about bills not yet approved by him. . . .

[Signed]

"A Member of the Illinois State Legislature"[8]

The "legislator's" letter was followed by a brief commentary by Myra:

We recognize in the writer of the above one of the ablest members of our General Assembly, and for whose opinions we have the greatest respect, and cheerfully give the communication space. We agree with much that is said in it. That Governor Palmer by his peculiar and unreasonable interference, greatly embarrassed and retarded the action of the General Assembly, there can be no doubt with anyone conversant with the facts.[9]

Governor Palmer was displeased by Myra's charge of "peculiar and unreasonable interference" with the actions of the state legislature. In a letter to the *News* he termed her accusation "unfounded and singularly unjust."[10]

The governor was even more disturbed by the anonymous character assassination that had ostensibly been penned by a state legislator. Palmer requested that Myra furnish him with the name of the "member" so that he [Governor Palmer] could give that lawmaker "an opportunity to specify the bills 'vetoed' on the most frivolous grounds" and the instances in which Palmer had interfered with members of the legislature.[11]

Myra promised to forward Palmer's letter to the "member," but stated that without that man's consent she would not furnish Palmer with his name.[12] Of course, the "member" did not consent. Instead, he wrote:

Who I am is . . . a matter of no importance to Governor Palmer or to the public. . . . Governor Palmer's good or bad conduct as an executive is of little interest [to the public] at present. . . . And the space in your valuable journal can be better used than in publishing epistolary correspondence between his excellency and myself. . . . The public will do him justice as heretofore.

A Member[13]

Myra's treatment of Governor Palmer was, at best, shoddy. How could the governor possibly respond to the "legislator's" charges that he [Palmer] was "crotchety and whimsical," that he had "vetoed bills on the most frivolous grounds," and that he was "constantly threatening and interfering with members [of the legislature]" when he knew neither the identity of his accuser nor the specifics of the accusations that had been levelled against him? In all likelihood, the "member's" letter had been written either by Myra herself or else by her favorite legislator, James Bradwell, who was then a member of the Illinois General Assembly.

In any event it was clear that Myra simply could not forgive Governor Palmer for refusing to appoint her as notary public. Her vindictiveness seemed interminable. Indeed, nineteen years later, when Myra had already achieved a position of preeminence and when scores of other married and single women were serving as notaries public in Illinois, Myra made yet another carping remark about her former foe. The occasion was an interview with the *Chicago Tribune*. During the course of that interview, Myra noted that after being denied admission to the Illinois bar, she had never reapplied for a license to practice law because she had been too busy publishing, editing, and writing the *Chicago Legal News*. Myra then continued:

> However, I have been made an honorary member of the State Bar through the courtesy of ex-Governor Palmer, who, after the denial of my petition to practice law, *refused as Governor to grant my petition for appointment as Notary Public.*[14] (Emphasis added)

There appears to have been no rational justification for Myra's gratuitous swipe at Governor Palmer. Her remark related to an action that the former governor had taken almost two decades earlier, and it was not made in the context of any matter that she was currently discussing with the *Tribune*. The only explanation seems to be that Myra simply could neither forgive nor forget.

While Myra had the capacity to be vindictive, her true forte was and always had been her ability to take constructive action and to effect legislative and/or social change. After Governor Palmer rejected her application for appointment as notary public, Myra drafted and James introduced in the Illinois house of representatives a bill making *all* women, married and single, eligible to hold the office of notary public. The bill met with some opposition, but was finally passed by the house in February 1875.[15] Two months later the bill was passed in the state senate[16] and was soon thereafter signed into law by the governor.

Two years later, the following item appeared in the *Chicago Legal News*:

> Governor Cullom, on Thursday of this week appointed Miss Ida Wood of Jacksonville a notary public. There are now 24 women notaries in Illinois. When Judge Bradwell introduced the bill in the House making them eligible

it was urged as an objection to it that if it became a law there would be no appointments under it as women did not desire office and would not qualify.[17]

It was not only the position of notary public but also other public offices that through the efforts of Myra and James became accessible to Illinois women during the 1870s. For example, in 1873 Myra drafted and James introduced in the state house of representatives a bill rendering women eligible to hold any office in the Illinois public school system.[18] Despite the all-too-familiar objection that "women did not desire [such school] office[s] and would not become candidates and would not qualify if elected,"[19] the bill passed both the state house and senate and was signed by the governor within three weeks after its introduction.[20]

The school law was significant in that it was the first to recognize the right of women to hold an *elective* office even though they were not eligible to *vote* for that office or any other. Indeed, it was not until eighteen years later, in 1891, that women were rendered eligible to vote in Illinois school elections.[21]

Myra realized that the new 1873 law making women eligible to *hold* an elective office was a first and very important step toward the enfranchisement of Illinois women:

> If women hold office, why should they not be allowed to vote? . . . We predict that this is the first in a series of acts which will . . . aid in extending the right of suffrage to women in Illinois.[22]

Although Myra was delighted that women had become eligible to hold offices in the public school system, she cautioned that "no person should be elected . . . to any of these offices simply because she is a woman." Only "the ablest and most experienced [teachers] . . . should be selected."[23] Scoffing at the earlier predictions that very few women would ever choose to run for election, she proudly announced that "only four months after the law was passed, there were thirty-four women candidates in thirty counties of the state for County Superintendent of Schools."[24] She ended her brief report by asking a rhetorical question: "Is there any good reason why this law should not be extended so as to allow women to fill other offices if the people see fit to elect them?"[25]

Although the legislation rendering women eligible for elective school offices had been passed in both houses by overwhelming majorities (101 to 30 in the house and 29 to 6 in the senate[26]), the law was apparently offensive to many men—or at least to many of those who were delegates to the Republican State Convention of 1874. In giving an account of that convention, Myra stated that one of its main purposes was to nominate two persons for statewide offices—state treasurer and state superintendent of schools. After noting that five men had been put in nomination for treasurer, she described the proceedings:

> Eloquent and earnest speeches were made in favor of each candidate [for State Treasurer]. After the nomination of Treasurer when it was known that a woman would be put in nomination for [State Superintendent of Schools], a resolution was passed forbidding any speeches in favor of candidates.[27]

Notwithstanding that resolution, Miss Frances Willard, a nationally renowned educator, prohibitionist, and author, received a plurality of 124 votes on the first ballot, fifteen more than any other candidate. On the second ballot, however, the judge who had proposed Miss Willard's name to the convention withdrew it on the ground that Miss Willard could not possibly secure a majority of the votes.[28] Apparently, the specter of a woman and/or a prohibitionist as the highest ranking school official in the state was too much for some men to bear.

Three years after the sham attempt to nominate Frances Willard, Myra predicted that "either the Democrats or Republicans will elect a woman State Superintendent of [Schools] at the next election."[29] That prophecy, however, was not fulfilled at the "next election" or at any other time during Myra's life.

Although not elected to *statewide* office in the public school system, women soon began serving as superintendents of schools for the various counties in Illinois. Within three years after the enactment of the school law, seventeen women had been elected to such countywide offices.[30] Some of those women served with great distinction; accolades flowed into the offices of the *Chicago Legal News*. For example, an elderly male school teacher wrote to James Bradwell:

> Dear Sir: Knowing that you, as the author of the bill making women eligible to school offices in this State, take a deep interest in the practical workings of the law, it gives me pleasure to be able to say that during my residence here in this county more than twenty years, we have never had so competent a County Superintendent as our present incumbent, Miss West of Galesburg; and this is admitted by nearly, if not all interested, and as proof of her popularity, she has been unanimously nominated for a second term. This is competent evidence that she is very highly appreciated.
>
> M. B. Waldo[31]

In ensuing issues of the *News,* Myra continued to praise the standards of performance set by *all* of the women who either were currently serving or had served as county superintendents of schools. She noted that many of them had been reelected several times. Citing the opinion of the male state superintendent of schools "that the average ability of the women that were elected was higher than that of the men,"[32] Myra concluded that "all of . . . [the female superintendents] have proved faithful and efficient officers, and not a defaulter has been found among them, and this is more than can be said of all their brother superintendents."[33]

Once again, Myra recalled scornfully:

> When Judge Bradwell, in 1873, introduced in the legislature of this state the bill which is now a law, making women eligible to all school offices, the opponents of the measure claimed if passed it would be a dead letter as women would not consent to take office, and if they did, they would only show that they were inefficient; and that if a woman was once elected to a responsible school office, she would never be reelected.[34]

Much to Myra's delight, the opponents of the school law had been proved wrong.

During the 1880s, Illinois women were elected not only to the administrative post of county superintendent of schools, but also to policy-making positions as members of various county boards of education.[35] The grand finale, however, and one which was undoubtedly a source of great anxiety and consternation to many men and women, occurred in 1886. Myra described the event briefly in the *News* under the caption "Woman Beats Her Husband for Trustee":

> Mrs. H. B. Kepley is a graduate of the Union College of Law of this city, and a member of the Effingham, Illinois bar. Her husband is also a well known member of the bar of that place. At a recent school election, Mrs. Kepley ran against her husband for school trustee, and defeated him, receiving a majority of twelve votes.[36]

School offices were the only elective positions that Illinois women had been *statutorily* authorized to hold. In 1870 one brave woman, Amelia Hobbs, ran for another elective position: justice of the peace. Although she won by a majority of twenty-six votes, her election could have been challenged as there was no law rendering women eligible to hold that position. The challenge did not occur. As Myra reported:

> We learn that Mrs. Hobbs' opponent is too gallant to contest her election on the ground that she is a woman. It therefore remains to be seen who will volunteer to stifle the voice of the people and prevent her from performing the duties of the office to which she has been elected.[37]

Surprisingly, no one stepped forward to prevent Mrs. Hobbs from performing the duties of her office. A decade later, however, a disgruntled male resident of Illinois did attempt to prevent another female court official from doing the job to which she had been *appointed*. In the late 1870s an Illinois judge appointed his daughter, Mrs. Helen Schuchardt, to the position of master in chancery. Masters in chancery were assistants to those judges who presided over certain types of courts, called courts of equity. The position was one of great responsibility, as masters in chancery were empowered to take testimony, determine damages, and perform many other judicial functions.

Mrs. Schuchardt performed her duties with distinction. After the death of her father, however, a disapproving Illinois man filed a lawsuit that charged that Mrs. Schuchardt, because she was a woman, could not lawfully hold office.[38] In commenting on the lawsuit, Myra wrote what was, in essence, a brief on behalf of Mrs. Schuchardt[39] that was ultimately relied upon by the Supreme Court of Illinois when that court upheld Mrs. Schuchardt's right to hold the office of master in chancery.

Myra began her "brief" by quoting from the Illinois statute of 1872, which had been drafted by Myra and Alta Hulett.[40] That law provided that "no person shall be precluded or debarred from any occupation, profession or employment, except military, on account of sex," and concluded with the provision "that this act shall not be construed to affect the eligibility of any person to an *elective* [italics mine] office." After quoting from the statute, Myra argued:

> Is not the inference strong that the legislature by not adding the word
> *"appointive"* before the last word in the section, intended that women *should*
> be affected by it and be eligible to all appointed offices.[41]

One month after Myra published her "brief" in the *Chicago Legal News*, the *trial court* rendered an adverse decision in Mrs. Schuchardt's case. In a column captioned "Another Dred Scott Decision," Myra announced that the trial judge, Judge Harker, had held that a woman was not eligible to hold the office of master in chancery.[42] The judge had begun his opinion by noting that none of the eleven masters in chancery in the district where he presided had been "more faithful or attentive to the discharge of his duties [than Mrs. Schuchardt] and none . . . have exhibited higher qualifications to discharge those duties well." He concluded by expressing his hope "that the next session of the legislature will make this office accessible to females."[43] Judge Harker's opinion was not particularly well-reasoned. The Illinois legislature already had, in 1872, enacted the law providing "that no person be precluded or debarred from any occupation, profession or employment, except military, on account of sex."

Responding to Judge Harker's decision, Myra commented:

> Judge Harker is an able, conscientious Judge. So was Judge Taney [the au-
> thor of the Dred Scott decision]. The one held that a colored slave and the
> other a woman Master in Chancery had no rights that anybody was bound
> to respect. Judge Dougherty in the same county held that a woman could
> be a Master in Chancery, Judge Harker that she could not. The one looked
> through judicial glasses dimmed with the dust of a thousand years: the other
> viewed the case through the glasses placed in his hands by a free and enlight-
> ened people.[44]

Pending the appeal of her case, Mrs. Schuchardt continued to perform
her duties as master in chancery. During that period, Myra published frequent editorials about this "most estimable lady . . . [this] capable, deserving
woman . . . [who] has been earning a living for herself and children as Master in Chancery."[45]

After an additional adverse decision by the intermediate appellate court,[46]
Mrs. Schuchardt appealed to the Supreme Court of Illinois. Reversing the
judgments of the two lower courts, the Supreme Court held that "there is nothing in the origin of the office [of Master in Chancery] or in the nature of
the duties to be discharged which renders it impossible that a female should
fill the office."[47]

In reaching its conclusion, the court adopted almost verbatim Myra's "brief,"
which had appeared in the *News* the preceding year. The court reasoned:

> The statute . . . is as follows: that no person shall be precluded or debarred
> from any occupation, profession, or employment except military on account
> of sex, provided that this act shall not be construed to affect the eligibility
> of any person to an elective office. . . . *By implication it may affect, that
> is to say, affect those to be filled by appointment by allowing women as
> well as men to be appointed.*[48]

In discussing the Supreme Court's opinion, Myra did not comment on
the fact that the court had relied heavily on the argument set forth in her
"brief." Instead, she merely applauded the court's reasoning:

> The reasoning of . . . [the Court] is clear and conclusive and must be satis-
> factory to everyone who carefully and candidly examines the statute and the
> opinion.[49]

Moreover, she carefully pointed out to her readers that while the Supreme
Court's opinion involved only the eligibility of a woman to hold the office
of master in chancery:

[The court's] reasoning and the construction placed upon the statute is to the effect that *women are eligible to hold any of the appointive offices in this state.*[50]

In one of her final editorials regarding Mrs. Schuchardt's case, Myra recapitulated the progress made by Illinois women during the previous decade:

One by one the old rules of law which prevented woman from standing side by side upon an equality with man, are being removed by the liberal enactments of the [legislature] and the construction of our courts.[51]

Those "liberal enactments of the [legislature] and the [decisions] of our courts" were all directly traceable to Myra, for it was, after all, Myra who, along with Alta Hulett, had drafted the 1872 statute that provided that "no person shall be precluded or debarred from any occupation, profession or employment, except military, on account of sex." Moreover, it was Myra who drafted (and James who secured the passage of) both the 1873 statute rendering women eligible to hold elective school offices and the 1875 legislation that permitted women to become notaries public. Finally, it was the "brief" authored by Myra in 1880 that became the basis for the Illinois Supreme Court's decision that women could hold the office of master in chancery.

Myra's endeavors to secure occupational and professional freedom for *all* women were not confined to the drafting of statutes and the writing of "briefs." Her chief vehicle for reform was, and always had been, the *Chicago Legal News.* Its pages were studded with accounts of women gaining access to various appointive positions such as postmaster[52] and elective offices such as clerk of the Illinois house of representatives.[53]

The pages of the *News* were also replete with accounts of successes by women in the private sector of the economy. For example, in 1887 she informed her readers that "the largest salary received by any woman in this country for editorial work is paid by *Harper's* [*Bazaar*] to Miss Mary L. Booth. The salary is said to be $8,000 [plus] . . . a percentage of the profits of the publication."[54]

As to those occupations from which women were still excluded, she ran numerous editorial pleas urging that members of her sex be given a chance. One such exhortation read as follows:

Who shall have the credit of being the first man in Illinois to give women a representation on the census board? We hope to be able to give his name before many days.[55]

Some of Myra's pleas for occupational equality for women might strike a modern-day reader as smacking of sex-role stereotyping. For example, in commenting on the fact that no women had been appointed to the first board of directors of the Chicago Library Association, she lamented:

We must raise our voice in favor of 150,000 women of Chicago who are unrepresented on this Board. *There is no public institution that women are better fitted to participate in the management of and would take greater interest in than the Library Associaton.*[56]

On the other hand, she obviously took great pleasure in announcing to her readers that a woman at last had been ruled eligible to hold one of the country's most "masculine" occupations as captain of a Mississippi steamboat. Myra closed an issue of the *News* by quoting from the U.S. secretary of the treasury who had issued that ruling:

It is my opinion that any person, whether male or female, *may paddle his or her own canoe* or control his or her own vessel. . . . There [is no] need to talk pro or con of social status or "woman's rights," so called. Having been put on God's footstool by Him, she has the right to win her bread in any moral decent way which is open to any of his toiling creatures. She chooses to do so as master of a steam vessel. It is an honest calling. If she is fitted for it, *though clothed in skirts rather than breeches,* she has the right to follow it and no man should say her nay.[57] (Emphasis added)

NOTES

1. Bradwell's speech on civil service reform, reprinted posthumously in *CLN* 27 (October 27, 1894): 71–74.
2. *CLN* 2 (January 1, 1870): 109, col. 1.
3. Ibid.
4. Sir William Blackstone, *Commentaries on the Law of England* 1 (Oxford: Clarendon Press, 1765–1769; reprint: New York: Oceana, 1966), pp. 442–45; Norma Basch, *In the Eyes of the Law* (Ithaca, N.Y.: Cornell University Press, 1982); Bradwell's "additional brief to the Illinois Supreme Court," reprinted in *CLN* 2 (February 5, 1870): 145, col. 3.
5. Ibid.
6. Letter from Myra Bradwell to Governor John Palmer dated January 22, 1870 (on file at Illinois State Historical Library).
7. *CLN* 7 (February 13, 1875): 165, col. 3; *CLN* 7 (April 10, 1875): 238, col. 1.
8. *CLN* 4 (August 17, 1872): 424, col. 4.
9. Ibid.
10. *CLN* 4 (August 31, 1872): 455, col. 1.
11. Ibid.
12. Ibid.

13. Ibid.
14. *Chicago Tribune* (May 12, 1889): 26, col. 1–2.
15. *CLN* 7 (February 13, 1875): 165, col. 3.
16. *CLN* 7 (April 10, 1875): 238, col. 1.
17. *CLN* 10 (November 10, 1877): 61, col. 4.
18. *CLN* 5 (March 15, 1873): 296, col. 2.
19. *CLN* 6 (November 15, 1873): 67, col. 1–2.
20. *CLN* 5 (April 5, 1873): 330, col. 2–3.
21. *CLN* 25 (March 11, 1893): 234, col. 1.
22. *CLN* 5 (April 5, 1873): 330, col. 2–3.
23. *CLN* 5 (August 23, 1873): 537, col. 3.
24. *CLN* 6 (November 15, 1873): 67, col. 1–2.
25. Ibid.
26. *CLN* 5 (April 5, 1873): 330, col. 2–3.
27. *CLN* 6 (June 20, 1874): 313, col. 3.
28. Ibid.
29. *CLN* 9 (February 24, 1877): 187, col. 1.
30. Ibid.
31. *CLN* 10 (September 22, 1877): 8, col. 4.
32. *CLN* 12 (December 13, 1879): 118, col. 3–4.
33. Ibid.
34. Ibid.
35. See, e.g., *CLN* 20 (June 2, 1888): 325, col. 4; *CLN* 21 (July 13, 1889): 386, col. 4.
36. *CLN* 18 (May 29, 1886): 315, col. 4.
37. *CLN* 2 (February 12, 1870): 156, col. 4.
38. *CLN* 12 (September 4, 1880): 435, col. 2–3.
39. Ibid.
40. Harvey B. Hurd (comp. and ed.), *The Revised Statutes of the State of Illinois, 1874* (Springfield: Illinois Journal Company, 1874).
41. Ibid.
42. *CLN* 13 (October 2, 1880): 21, col. 4.
43. Ibid.
44. Ibid.
45. *CLN* 13 (May 21, 1881): 298, col. 3–4; see also *CLN* 13 (November 20, 1880): 82, col. 4.
46. *CLN* 13 (June 25, 1881): 340, col. 2.
47. *Schuchardt* v. *People,* 99 Ill. 501 (1881).
48. Ibid.
49. *CLN* 13 (August 27, 1881): 411, col. 1–2.
50. Ibid.
51. *CLN* 13 (June 25, 1881): 340, col. 2.
52. *CLN* 12 (November 15, 1879): 80, col. 4.
53. *CLN* 6 (April 4, 1874): 225, col. 4.
54. *CLN* 19 (May 21, 1887): 297, col. 4.
55. *CLN* 12 (February 21, 1880): 200, col. 4.
56. *CLN* 4 (April 13, 1872): 212, col. 2.
57. *CLN* 16 (February 9, 1884): 182, col. 3–4.

9

"Uncaging Eve"
Bradwell's Contribution to the
Woman Suffrage Movement

One thing we do claim—that woman has the right to think and act as an individual—believing if the great Father had intended it to be otherwise, he would have placed Eve in a cage and given Adam the key.

—Myra Bradwell (1868)[1]

The Prologue to this biography began with the lament that "[while] the names of many of her female contemporaries are known to all, . . . Myra Bradwell has, sadly, been consigned to obscurity." In no area has Myra been more widely or unjustifiably ignored than in the recorded history of the woman suffrage movement. When one focuses on Myra's writings and contemporaneous accounts of her activities during that period, it is clear that she was one of the Midwest's preeminent suffragists. Yet when one reads the standard histories of the movement, Myra's name is seldom mentioned except in the context of the protracted litigation in which she attempted to establish her right to practice law. Discussions of her numerous efforts on behalf of the movement to enfranchise her sex are virtually nonexistent.

Why, one might ask, should historians have ignored Myra Bradwell as a suffragist when her contributions to the movement were so substantial? A possible clue can be found in the recently discovered letters written to Myra by the nation's premiere suffragist, Susan B. Anthony. Those letters, coupled with other historical data, indicate that Anthony often harbored negative feelings towards Myra. And when Anthony, the first and most important historian of woman suffrage, was angry or hostile towards other women in the movement, she often dealt with those women by simply ignoring them in the first three volumes of the *History of Woman Suffrage*, of which she was the primary author.[2] Because those three volumes provided the major factual foundation for most subsequent histories of the first half-century of the movement,[3] when a suffragist's contributions were ignored or downplayed by Anthony, they were usually unknown to those historians who followed. That appears to have been the fate of Myra Bradwell.

Myra's efforts on behalf of the movement were substantial, and her writings voluminous. Because her readership was widespread and included many of the nation's elite—judges, lawyers, and prominent businessmen—one can speculate that her influence, particularly on that stratum of the male population, was significant.

The history of the woman suffrage movement has been recounted in numerous sources,[4] and will here be summarized very briefly. The inception of the organized woman's movement in the United States is generally set at 1848 when a woman's rights convention was held in Seneca Falls, New York. Out of that convention came the Seneca Falls Declaration in which the participants stated their goals of equal social and legal rights for women. The declaration closed with a series of twelve resolutions, the ninth of which read: "Resolved, that it is the duty of women of this country to secure to themselves their sacred right to the elective franchise."

The franchise resolution gained great momentum during the ensuing thirteen years. Prosuffrage pamphlets and articles proliferated, and woman's rights conventions were held in several eastern states. The last pre–Civil War woman's rights convention was held in Albany in 1861; but during the four years of the war, all such activities came to a halt. At the war's end, with the emancipation and enfranchisement of the slaves, the question once again emerged as to whether women should be included in the electorate. Some leaders of the woman's suffrage movement believed, perhaps somewhat naively, that the expansion of the franchise to include black males would in all likelihood encompass white and black women as well.

The first hint that something was amiss came in the summer of 1866 when the Fourteenth Amendment to the Constitution of the United States was introduced into Congress. The second section of that amendment reduced the number of representatives apportioned to those states that denied black males the right to vote. Many woman's rights leaders were appalled by the wording of that provision:

> Representatives shall be apportioned among the several states according to their respective numbers . . . of persons in each state. . . . But when the right to vote at any election . . . is denied to any of the *male* inhabitants of such

state, or in any way abridged, the basis of proportion therein shall be reduced, in the proportion which the number of such *male* citizens shall bear
to the whole number of *male* citizens twenty-one years of age in such state.
(Emphasis added)

The Fourteenth Amendment's threefold use of the word "male" seemed
to carry a strong implication that women were not to be included in the franchise. The amendment was ratified in July 1868. Six months later, woman's
suffrage advocates were dealt yet another blow when the Radical Republicans, seeking to further ensure the enfranchisement of the newly emancipated
slaves, introduced into Congress a Fifteenth Amendment, which read: "The
right of citizens of the United States to vote shall not be denied or abridged
by the United States or any State on account of race, color, or previous condition of servitude."

Again, many suffragists were indignant—among them Susan B. Anthony
and Elizabeth Cady Stanton. Believing that it would have been so easy to
include "sex" in the list of conditions that could not disqualify a citizen from
voting, Miss Anthony and Mrs. Stanton pledged that they would work for
the defeat of the Fifteenth Amendment. Their writings in their newly-launched
publication, *The Revolution,* became increasingly polemical and strident. Mrs.
Stanton wrote derogatorily about the enfranchisement of "Sambo," and Miss
Anthony vowed that she would "cut off this right arm of mine before I will
ever work for or demand the ballot for the Negro and not the woman."[5]

On the other hand, many leaders of the woman's movement, while saddened by the exclusion of women from the voting rights protections of the
Fourteenth and Fifteenth Amendments, nevertheless favored the passage of
those two provisions. They simply did not begrudge black men the right to
vote, even though they sought to secure that right for women as well. "I will
be thankful in my soul if anybody can get out of this terrible pit," proclaimed
the leader of this moderate faction, Lucy Stone.[6]

The rift between the suffragists who opposed the Fifteenth Amendment
and those who favored it continued to deepen until finally, during the summer of 1869, Lucy Stone wrote a letter to many of her friends, urging a break
with the radical Anthony–Stanton camp of the movement:

I think we need two national associations for woman suffrage [she wrote]
so that those who do not oppose the Fifteenth Amendment nor take the
tone of *The Revolution* may yet have an organization with which they can
work in harmony. There are . . . distinctly two parties to the woman movement. . . . Each organization will attract those who naturally belong to it,
and there will be harmonious work.[7]

She concluded her letter by asking the recipients to sign a "call" to a woman suffrage convention to be held in Cleveland in November 1869, "to unite those who cannot use the methods which Mrs. Stanton and Susan use."

Neither Susan nor Mrs. Stanton was invited to the convention, but copies of the "call" fell into their hands. Susan was distraught when she saw some of the signatures. One of those that disturbed her most was that of her good friend, Myra Bradwell.[8]

Susan B. Anthony had some reason for her belief that Myra was loyal to her faction, and would not support the Fifteenth Amendment unless women were also included within its aegis. Myra's early writings, while not nearly as polemical as those of Anthony and Stanton, did decry the fact that blacks could vote while women could not. For example, in a column in one of the early issues of the *Legal News,* Myra wrote:

> A woman may be a citizen of the U.S., be subject to the laws, own property and be compelled to pay taxes to support a government she has no voice in administering, or vote in electing its officers. In many of the states of the union, negroes can vote, women can not. Is not a woman as good as a negro? Shall it be said that we accord to the negro a voice in this government that we deny to women?[9]

Moreover, shortly after the ratification of the Fourteenth Amendment, which reduced the number of representatives apportioned to those states that denied blacks the right to vote, Myra expressed chagrin over the fact that women were not given similar treatment, at least within the state of Illinois. After pointing out that under the Illinois constitution state senators and representatives were to be apportioned among the several counties according to the number of all inhabitants, male and female, she questioned why females should be counted for purposes of apportioning the number of representatives and yet be given no voice in the choice of those representatives:

> If all the females had been removed from Cook County before the last apportionment, instead of two senators and seven representatives, they would be entitled to only one senator and three and one half representatives. Is there any good reason for refusing the females of Cook County any voice or vote in the selection of three and one half representatives and one senator sent to Springfield by the representation of the female inhabitants of Cook County?[10]

While Myra may have agreed with the Anthony-Stanton faction on some issues, she had sufficient political acumen to realize that if she wanted to persuade her predominantly male readership—judges and lawyers who would, in turn, have great influence over the final resolution of the woman suffrage question—it was important for her to join forces with the moderates. And so it was that Myra not only signed the "call" to the convention of anti-Anthony forces, but also served as corresponding secretary of that convention.[11] James Bradwell acted as temporary chairman.

Although the purpose of the Cleveland convention was to form an organization of moderates, known as the American Woman Suffrage Association, and to sever ties with Susan B. Anthony's radical National Woman Suffrage Association, Myra and James made many attempts to appease Miss Anthony. The first of these came at the Cleveland convention, which Anthony attended even though she had not been invited. James saw her in the audience and immediately moved that she be allowed to sit on the platform with the other notables.[12] Although his motion met with some resistance, he persisted until it finally carried. Susan B. Anthony was then permitted not only to sit on the platform but also to give an impassioned speech in which she urged the newly-formed American Woman Suffrage Association to petition Congress to initiate a Woman Suffrage Amendment to the Constitution:

> I hope [Anthony said] that the work of this association, if it be organized, will be to go in strong array up to the Capital at Washington to demand a Sixteenth Amendment to the Constitution. The question of the admission of women to the ballot would not then be left to the mass of voters in every State, but would be submitted by Congress to the several legislatures of the States for ratification and . . . be decided by the most intelligent portion of the people. If the question is left to the vote of the rank and file, it will be put off for years.[13]

Those attending the convention rejected Anthony's plea. Instead of pledging themselves to seek a federal constitutional amendment, they decided to work for the franchise on a state-by-state basis. Myra agreed with the convention's approach, but only because she believed that it would more quickly yield the desired result—at least in some states. Yet she also felt that Anthony's push for a federal constitutional amendment had much to commend it. In an attempt at conciliation, Myra paid the following tribute to Miss Anthony:

> Miss Anthony is terribly in earnest in this suffrage question. We fully agree with her that the great battle ground in the first instance should be Congress. . . . She is now fifty and the best years of her life have been devoted solely to the cause of woman. She has never turned aside from this object but has always been in the field, defending her principles against all assaults with an ability which has not only won the admiration of her friends but the respect of her enemies.[14]

While both Myra and James became leaders of the moderate camp, they did attempt to placate Susan B. Anthony and her followers. But what Myra gave with one hand, she took away with the other. For example, from the outset, Myra's espoused position was that the franchise would be obtained by "devoted wives and mothers" and not by strident unmarried women, for whom Susan B. Anthony served as an obvious unnamed prototype. In one such editorial Myra wrote:

> You ask us, how shall this great privilege [suffrage] be obtained for women? We will tell you. Not by the class who term man "a tyrant"—but by the sensible and devoted mothers, wives and daughters of the state uniting together: we mean those who have the respect and love of their fathers, husbands and brothers, and asking of them that they give women the right to vote.
>
> If this class of women ask it, it will not be two years before women will be allowed to vote in the State of Illinois.[15]

The above editorial seems to be a by-product of Myra's embracement of the ethos of "true womanhood." She, along with many other nineteenth-century feminists, believed that it was only the "true woman" who could obtain the franchise and who would in turn purify the political process.

The "devoted-wife-and-mother" theme was one that permeated many of Myra's writings on behalf of the cause of suffrage. Whenever a prominent member of the movement also happened to be a "wife and mother," Myra would comment, indeed dwell on the fact in order to illustrate the principle that these dual roles (political and domestic) were not inconsistent. Thus, in paying tribute to the eminent suffragist Mary Livermore, Myra devoted as much space to Livermore's domestic accomplishments as she did to Livermore's substantial contributions to the cause of gender equality.[16]

Of course, Myra, too, was a devoted wife and mother, a fact to which she alluded whenever given the opportunity. In an interview with the *Chicago Tribune,* she once exclaimed, "I often wish all those excellent folk who . . . picture me as a fanatic destroyer of *domesticity and the sweetness of true womanhood* [emphasis added] could see my two daughters and our home life."[17]

Myra's reiteration of the "devoted-wife-and-mother" theme seems even more understandable when one considers the chief argument that was being made by the antisuffrage forces of the day: that giving women the right to vote would create a society of Amazons constantly pitted in an adversarial relationship with the men in their lives and undermining the harmony of the home. The following speech by Senator George Williams of Oregon was typical:

Sir, it has been said that "the hand that rocked the cradle ruled the world," and there is truth as well as beauty in that expression. Women in this country, by their elevated social position, can exercise more influence upon public affairs than they could coerce by the use of the ballot. When God married our first parents in the garden according to that ordinance they were made "bone of one bone and flesh of one flesh"; and the whole theory of government and society proceeds upon the assumption that their interests are one, that their relations are so intimate and tender that whatever is for the benefit of the one is for the benefit of the other. . . . The woman who undertakes to put her sex in an adversary position to man, who undertakes by the use of some independent political power to contend and fight against man, displays a spirit which would, if able, convert all the now harmonious elements of society into a state of war, and make every home a hell on earth.[18]

Myra's response to the "enfranchised-woman-as-Amazon" argument was two-fold. First was the previously discussed rejoinder, complete with illustrative examples such as Mary Livermore and Myra herself, that suffragists could and did live in domestic harmony with their husbands and children. Her second form of riposte was the use of her sardonic wit to portray male opponents of suffrage as uncouth louts:

We cannot see any valid reason against extending the right of suffrage to women.

A few days since we were in a crowded streetcar—obliged to stand—yet scarcely able to assume an upright position on account of crushing and crowding; with a gentleman (!!) by our side who expectorated at least a gill every five minutes—somewhere from three to five more of the lovers of the weed puffing upon the front platform—with a current of air bringing volumes of smoke through the car—when we heard a remark like this: "My wife shall never vote—the idea of her making herself ridiculous by crowding up to the polls on election day!"—we felt like asking the gentleman if his wife ever rode in street cars or attended matinees. Another says: "I would not allow my wife to vote!" The very expression that this man used, shows that he regarded the poor being who was unfortunate enough to be selected as the companion of his life, more as his cringing slave than his wife.[19]

Thus, the two verbal weapons that Myra used against opponents of suffrage were those of reasoning by example and derisive ridicule. Myra's contributions to the movement, however, were not limited to her writings; she was also a woman of action.

Early in 1869, along with Mary Livermore and a few others, Myra organized the Midwest's first woman suffrage convention, which was held in Chicago. Appended to the "call" to that convention were the endorsements of every single judge in Cook County, Illinois, as well as those of many leading members of the Bar, endorsements that Myra had secured singlehandedly.[20] Myra served as one of the vice presidents of the convention and reported on its sessions in the columns of the *Legal News*. In one editorial, after reporting on the convention's resolution regarding the enfranchisement of women, Myra concluded:

> Not enough people are willing to stand up and say "We believe it right to give the ballot to woman"—about the same number that some time ago were willing to admit that a colored man had the God-given right to be free. . . . But the time will come when the opposition to this suffrage movement will melt away before the glorious sunlight of truth and right, as did the old arguments in favor of slavery. Methinks human nature will be about the same then as now—the love of a mother for her darling child will not be lessened nor the respect and esteem for the noble one who walks by her side, as her protector and her guide.[21]

At the conclusion of the Chicago convention, the Illinois State Suffrage Association was formed and a committee was appointed to visit Springfield to lobby for a change in the laws relating to women. Although Myra was a member of that six-person committee and did in fact accompany them on their pilgrimage to Springfield, she was well aware of the fact that the legislature did not have the power to enfranchise women and that suffrage could be accomplished only through amendment to the state constitution:

> We are asked what are the necessary steps to take in order to make this change in the law?
> The legislature, by a mere act, have no power to give a woman the right to vote. It can be done only by an amendment to our state constitution. The people by . . . the constitution, have limited the right to vote to the "male citizen above twenty-one years."
> We shall have a constitutional convention some time during the coming year to amend the old or to make a new constitution.
> Let the word male before the word citizen in this section of the present constitution be dropped and the work is done—woman would have the right to vote in Illinois.
> When the convention is called, let the women who are in favor of this change see that the delegate for the district in which they reside is pledged not to confine the right to vote to the male citizen.[22]

And so it was that Myra turned her energies to the seeking of a suffrage amendment to the state constitution of Illinois. Her forum was a state constitutional convention held in late 1869 and early 1870. The specific issue was whether a proposed amendment for woman suffrage should be submitted by referendum to a vote of the male electorate. This was only the second time in American history that the question of woman suffrage had come up for a political test. The first such occurrence had taken place in Kansas in 1867. In that state the proposal, actually submitted to the voters, would have taken the word "male" out of the requirements for eligibility to vote. The proposition was defeated, receiving only nine thousand votes out of a total of thirty thousand.

But in Illinois, unlike Kansas, the question was never even submitted to the electorate. The Illinois convention debate was heated and protracted. Several members of the convention gave eloquent speeches in favor of suffrage; the opponents were equally vocal and seemed to be better organized. Indeed, 1,380 women of Peoria actually submitted a prayer that the Illinois constitution not be amended so as to enfranchise women.[23]

Initially the members of the convention agreed that the question of a suffrage amendment should be submitted to the male voters by way of referendum, but then a rather startling development occurred. As Susan B. Anthony later recalled:

> The strange inconsistency of the opponents of woman suffrage was perhaps never more fully illustrated than by the following occurrence: While the patriotic and earnest women of Illinois were quietly acting upon the advice of their representatives, and relying upon their "quiet, moral influence" to secure a just recognition of their rights in the constitutional convention, a conservative woman of Michigan, who, afraid that the women of Illinois were about to lose their womanliness by asking for the right to have their opinions counted, deserted her home in the Peninsular State, went to Springfield, secured the hall of the convention and gave two lectures against woman suffrage. A meeting was called at the close of the second lecture, and in a resolution moved by a member of the convention, *as Mrs. Bradwell pertinently says, "the people of the State were told that one woman had proved herself competent and well qualified to enlighten the constitutional convention upon the evils of suffrage."* Such was the effect of this self-appointed obtruder from another State that the members of the convention, without giving a woman of their own State opportunity for reply, not only struck out the clause submitting the question to the people . . . but actually incorporated in the body of the constitution a clause which would not allow a woman to hold any office or public position in the State. *Through the efforts of such staunch friends as [James] Bradwell . . . and others, this latter clause was stricken out.*[24] (Emphasis added)

Myra, who had been instrumental in securing the initial decision of the convention, i.e., to submit the question to the male voters, expressed dismay over the fact that one vocal female opponent of suffrage had been able to persuade the convention members to reverse their decision, thereby preventing the issue from ever reaching the electorate. At the close of the convention she wrote:

> The course of the convention upon the question of woman suffrage has been anything but manly and straightforward. . . . Mrs. Dr. Wheaton of Kalamazoo, Michigan, delivered two lectures against woman suffrage in the hall of the convention. . . . A meeting was called and in a resolution, the people of the State were told that they regarded Mrs. Wheaton as competent and well qualified to enlighten them upon the evils of suffrage. . . . They then struck the clause submitting the question [of suffrage] to the voters. . . . When the question [of suffrage] is being discussed throughout the length and breadth of the land, the Constitutional Convention of Illinois, influenced by a single woman, reconsidered their former action, and refused to allow the people the privilege of saying whether they wished to extend the exercise of the right of suffrage to women or not, the Convention has manifested great distrust in the ability and wisdom of the people to govern themselves.[25]

The irrationality of the workings of the Illinois constitutional convention was manifested in another of its products: the accidental insertion of a new constitutional clause that gave any foreign-born man *or woman* naturalized prior to January 1870 the right to vote. The inclusion of foreign-born women was clearly a mistake on the part of the drafters, and a carefully guarded one at that. But Myra, ever vigilant, brought it to the attention of her readers under the misleading headline, "Woman Suffrage Adopted in Illinois." Her report, which ended with subtle humor but certainly not good cheer, read in part:

> Illinois has the honor of being the first State in the Union to adopt woman suffrage. It is true she allows this right to be exercised only by foreign born women who were naturalized in this State before the first day of January last. Under [this section] of the new Constitution, this class of women can vote. There are some women in the State who have been naturalized, but the number is not large. . . . We therefore have woman suffrage in Illinois, but in homeopathic doses.[26]

Bitter over the inconsistent and arbitrary actions of the delegates to the constitutional convention, Myra refused to devote any further effort to seeking a suffrage amendment to the state constitution. She did, however, remain active in the suffrage movement, serving as an officer of the American Woman Suffrage Association and for many years as a member of the executive committee of the Illinois State Suffrage Association.[27] She reported frequently on the activities of the latter organization. For example, when the Illinois group held its first convention, a report in the *Chicago Legal News,* captioned "Illinois Woman's Suffrage Convention largest in the West," read as follows:

> The two day Illinois Woman's Suffrage Convention held in Chicago was the largest meeting of the advocates of woman suffrage ever held in the West, with more than three thousand people in attendance. Many members of the bar, leading clergymen, college professors, physicians, and other prominent citizens attended. A vote upon the question of woman suffrage was taken, and its advocates were surprised to find that less than one hundred of three thousand voted against it.[28]

Myra's expression of surprise at the outcome of the vote was probably disingenuous. It is unlikely, particularly in 1871, that many foes of the movement would have bothered to attend a "meeting of the advocates of woman suffrage."

Although she continued to attend state suffrage meetings and conventions, Myra knew that with the defeat of the suffrage amendment to the state constitution there was little likelihood that the women of Illinois would be fully enfranchised in the near future. Thus, she turned her energies to the reporting of suffrage victories in other states, territories, and countries.

The first victory for woman suffrage in America took place in the territory of Wyoming. The text of this historic law, enacted in 1869, read:

> That every woman of the age of twenty one years, residing in the Territory, may, at every election to be holden [sic] under the laws thereof, cast her vote; and her rights to the elective franchise, and to hold office, shall be the same under the elective laws of the Territory, as those of the [male] electors.[29]

There is considerable historical debate as to which individuals and what forces served as the stimuli for this law. Edward M. Lee, an emigrant from Connecticut, claimed to have drafted the bill, which was passed by the diminutive Wyoming legislature by a vote of six to two (with one abstention) in the senate and six to four (with one abstention) in the lower house. The territorial governor, John A. Campbell, who had first expressed opposition to the measure, signed it after many days of indecision.

In commenting on this momentous piece of legislation, Myra wrote: "To all well educated, ambitious females, who have no legal ties to bind them, we would say, emigrate to Wyoming."[30] But she admonished them to

> Engage in no business unless you understand it thoroughly, and under no circumstances take any office unless you are able to perform its duties with credit to yourself and honor to the Territory.[31]

Myra envisioned Wyoming as an experimental laboratory where women would prove their competence as voters and office holders, thereby serving as role models who would provide the impetus for the granting of the franchise in other states and territories. Others, foes of suffrage, predicted disaster, prophesying that women would descend upon Wyoming election sites in Amazonian hordes, and that a virtual battle of the sexes would take place at every polling place. As for women as officeholders, visions of incompetence abounded.

Fortunately for the advocates of suffrage, the Wyoming elections of 1870 and 1871 went smoothly. An account by a minister, who had recently emigrated from Vermont, portrayed the following beneficent scene:

> I saw the rough mountaineers maintaining the most respectful decorum whenever the women approached the polls, and heard the timely warning of one of the leading canvassers as he silenced an incipient quarrel with uplifted finger, saying "Hist! Be quiet! A woman is coming!" And I was compelled to allow that in this new country, supposed at that time to be infested by hordes of cut-throats, gamblers and abandoned characters, I had witnessed a more quiet election than it had been my fortune to see in the quiet towns of Vermont. I saw ladies attended by their husbands, brothers, or sweethearts, ride to the place of voting, and alight in the midst of a silent crowd, and pass through an open space to the polls, depositing their votes with no more exposure to insult or injury than they would expect on visiting a grocery store or meat market. Indeed, they were much safer here, every man of their party was pledged to shield them, while every member of the other party feared the influence of any signs of disrespect.[32]

Thus, the prophecy of the moderate suffragists had become a reality in Wyoming. Granting the ballot to women had actually purified the political process.

The initial test of woman as holder of public office in Wyoming also bode well for the advocates of suffrage. The first woman officeholder, Esther Morris, often referred to as "the mother of woman suffrage in Wyoming," was appointed to serve as justice of the peace in South Pass City. Although she rendered more than forty decisions during her eight months in office, she was not once reversed by a higher court.

Indeed, the Wyoming suffrage experiment proved so successful that Governor Campbell, who had originally opposed the measure and had signed it only reluctantly, publicly stated in 1874 that the effect of woman suffrage in Wyoming had been extremely beneficial, and that after four years of practical trial, "no one wishes to abolish it."

Myra was quick to seize upon Governor Campbell's statement. After reprinting it in the *Chicago Legal News,* she analyzed its significance as two-fold. First,

> [Governor Campbell's statement] removes from the proposition to enfranchise the women of America the stigma under which it has heretofore labored of being an untried hypothesis or a dream. The success of the first experiment, we are informed by those who have occasion to know, is an accomplished fact.[33]

Second, the governor's statement was even more remarkable because of the fact that he had originally opposed suffrage. Commenting on this phenomenon, Myra concluded: "The most surprising feature of the matter is the revolution that it seems to have accomplished in the minds of those who have witnessed its working."[34]

Wyoming's neighbor, the territory of Utah, enacted a suffrage law in 1870; but during the following decade, no other state or territory granted full suffrage to women. Suffrage referenda were held in several states, but they merely resulted in a series of defeats.

During the 1870s, however, advocates of the franchise were achieving some gains. These were in the form of "partial" or "limited" suffrage. That is, in some localities women were permitted to vote on certain questions, most often school matters. Some jurisdictions also allowed them to vote on taxes and bond issues, and a few granted woman suffrage in all municipal elections.

Limited suffrage was in some ways a positive step towards achieving the full franchise. It did, however, have its disadvantages, the major one being that in some elections a large majority of women did not vote. This phenomenon furnished antisuffrage forces with the argument that it would be a futile gesture to extend the full franchise to women when they were simply not interested in voting. This, of course, was not true; in Wyoming and Utah, where full suffrage had been granted, women came to the polls in large numbers. Some historians have attributed this difference to the fact that where women enjoyed the full vote, the major parties had a political stake in ensuring that they received fair treatment. In contrast, when women were voting on very limited matters, they often encountered serious obstacles. The political parties had little incentive to protect those with such limited political power. Historian Eleanor Flexner cites the New York State school board elections of 1880 as an example of the impediments faced by partially enfranchised women:

> In the New York state school board elections of 1880, such deterrents ran the full gamut: outright denial of the right to vote (in defiance of the law); threats of reprisal—clerical, anonymous, even husbandly; crowded or unsuitable polling premises, uncouth behavior by loiterers and even election offi-

cials (some of whom puffed smoke in the women's faces), and actual cases of stone-throwing. Small wonder that the turnout of women varied from one locality to another and did little to strengthen their case for the full vote.[35]

The issue of partial enfranchisement was the basis for a further rift in the suffrage movement. The militant forces, led by Susan B. Anthony, were vehemently opposed to partial suffrage for two reasons. First, they believed that the scant turnout of women voters in some localities would simply be another weapon in the antisuffrage arsenal. The radicals were, indeed, correct on that point. Second, they pointed to the fact that, when given a limited vote, many women tended to align themselves with a political party, and thereafter would follow the party line not only on the substantive question at hand (e.g., school board elections) but also on the issue of suffrage itself. Indeed, in many instances, partially enfranchised women actually capitulated to the insistence of party leaders that measures for full suffrage be omitted from their party's platform.

On the other hand, the moderates in the movement—Myra among them —continued to press for limited suffrage even though they were well aware of its pitfalls. They believed that a partial loaf was better than none, and that limited access to the ballot was simply one of many strategies that would lead, eventually, to full enfranchisement.

Myra must have searched long and hard to find a jurisdiction where limited suffrage was "working." When she finally did editorialize on the subject, she drew her example not from the states or territories, but from England, where women were permitted to vote in municipal elections:

> One of the strongest and most effective arguments urged against allowing women to exercise the right of [limited] suffrage was that women did not wish to vote and would not exercise the right if all legal obstacles were removed. This was not only the strongest argument, but it was the most difficult to answer, as the friends of woman suffrage could point to no facts or statistics to refute the assertion. We are pleased to be able to say that the experience of the last three years in England has effectually answered this argument and demonstrated beyond all question that women in general not only wish to vote, but give them the opportunity and they will exercise the right.
>
> The *London Examiner* reports the results in municipal elections where women have the privilege of voting. Out of every 1000 women on the register, 516 went to the polls compared to 564 out of every 1000 men.
>
> Making allowances for the reluctance of old spinsters to change their habits, and the more frequent illness of the sex, it is manifest that women, if they had the opportunity would exercise the franchise as freely as men.

This is an end, therefore, of the argument that women would not vote if they had the power.[36]

One can speculate that Susan B. Anthony was probably offended by Myra's references to "old spinsters" and other such derisive terms. Moreover, Susan had been deeply disturbed by Myra's joining forces with Lucy Stone's moderate American Woman Suffrage Association and her concomitant support of the Fourteenth and Fifteenth Amendments. Myra's endorsement of partial suffrage must have been a matter of further contention. But Susan needed Myra in some respects more than she needed any other woman who was active in the movement. Susan realized that Myra was an extremely influential legal journalist whose weekly newspaper reached an audience of men—lawyers, judges, and prominent businessmen—some of whom would never be influenced by Susan and her followers. Indeed, many of Myra's admirers in the legal community had openly expressed contempt for Susan's *The Revolution* and other radical suffragist publications.[37] Myra's columns in the *Chicago Legal News* had made suffrage respectable.

That Susan was well aware of the potential impact of Myra's writings is reflected in one of the few public tributes that Susan paid to Myra:

On Saturday, October 3, 1868, a genuine sensation was produced by the appearance of the *Chicago Legal News,* edited by Mrs. Myra Bradwell. At this day it is impossible to realize with what supreme astonishment this journal was received. Neither can we estimate its influence upon the subsequent legislation of the State. Looking through its files we find that no opportunity was lost for exposing all law unjust to woman or for noting each indication of progress throughout the world. . . .

When we realize that one of the Supreme Judges soon after [the launching of the *Legal News*] . . . assured Mrs. Bradwell that she was editing a paper that no lawyer could afford to do without, we shall understand how important a part this journal has played in the courts.[38]

And so it was that Susan wrote to Myra, requesting Myra's legal, journalistic, and financial support for a number of her pet projects. This author has discovered six letters written by Susan to Myra. At least some, perhaps all, of those letters went unanswered. Twice Susan rebuked Myra for not responding to her. Also, it seems that Myra gave Susan much less support than Susan requested, and that Susan retaliated by making only scant mention of Myra in her monumental *History of Woman Suffrage.*

What little support Myra did give to Susan arose in connection with Susan's being criminally prosecuted and convicted for voting in a federal election. In 1871 and 1872 approximately one hundred fifty women attempted to vote in ten states and the District of Columbia. A few of those women were actually successful in having their ballots counted. None of them received much publicity until Susan B. Anthony led a group of sixteen women in Rochester, New York, first in registering to vote and then in casting their ballots in the presidential election of 1872.

Susan had planned her strategy very carefully. Using her powers of persuasion, she convinced the election inspectors to register her group, promising that she would defray their costs if any legal measures were taken against them. Having been duly registered, the women actually cast their ballots, knowing full well that "illegal voters" could be subjected to a maximum prison sentence of three years and a fine as high as five hundred dollars.

The wide publicity given to the "illegal" voting of Susan and her followers caused a great deal of embarrassment to President Grant's Republican administration. Thus, the federal government decided to make both a literal and figurative "federal case" out of the matter. Early in 1873, Susan B. Anthony was criminally indicted in a federal district court in Rochester. The indictment charged that she had "knowingly, wrongfully, and unlawfully" voted in a federal election. Susan's defense, which she carried to the people in a series of speeches delivered in fifty postal districts, was that she had believed that the Fourteenth Amendment to the Constitution guaranteed her right to vote, that she had cast her ballot in good faith, and that she therefore lacked the necessary criminal intent that was requisite (she argued) for a criminal conviction.

Susan had in fact violated the New York voting law, which had explicitly limited the franchise to members of the male sex. However, she had not been indicted by the state of New York, but instead by the federal government, and it is doubtful that she had violated any federal law. As Myra was quick to point out to her readers:

> Miss Anthony was arrested under a federal statute known as the Enforcement Act which provides that "all citizens . . . shall be allowed to vote . . . without distinction of race, color, or previous condition of servitude, any law . . . of any state . . . to the contrary notwithstanding." The law was enacted to protect Negroes and has nothing to do with sex.[39]

In spite of the fact that Susan had probably not run afoul of any federal law, the federal prosecutor and the presiding judge took great pains to ensure that a verdict of guilty would be forthcoming. Although a jury trial in criminal cases is mandated by the federal constitution, the court, in effect, denied Susan that right by directing the jury to return a verdict of guilty. The neophyte Republican judge, Ward Hunt, was apparently appalled by what Susan had done and/or he was desirous of producing the results sought by the Republican administration. At the close of the trial, he orally instructed the jury that "there is no question for the jury; the jury should be directed to find a verdict of guilty." When Susan's lawyer, former Appeals Court Judge Henry R. Selden, objected to the judge's instruction, Judge Hunt read to the jury the following written instruction that he had prepared before the trial had even begun:

> The question is wholly a question of law, and I have decided as a question of law, in the first place, that under the Fourteenth Amendment, which Miss Anthony claims protects her, she was not protected in a right to vote. And I have decided also that her belief and the advice which she took does not protect her in the act which she committed. If I am right in this, the result on your part must be a verdict of guilty, and I therefore direct that you find a verdict of guilty.[40]

The jury promptly returned a verdict of guilty, and Susan was sentenced to a fine of $100 plus court costs. That was an extremely lenient sentence, but Susan immediately vowed that she would never pay a dollar of it, and she never did.

Judge Hunt could have committed Susan to prison until she paid the fine, a well-accepted procedure in the nineteenth century, but he did not. Some historians have concluded that Judge Hunt refrained from committing Susan because he wanted to deprive her of the opportunity to take her case directly to the Supreme Court on a writ of habeas corpus. Myra viewed the matter differently. Judge Hunt, Myra believed, must have felt that the specter of Susan B. Anthony's incarceration would have been too much for the public to bear. In her first report on Anthony's trial, Myra wrote:

> [We wish to comment on] the opinion of the U.S. Circuit Court, delivered by Hunt, J., directing the jury in the case of Miss Anthony to return a verdict of guilty and sentencing her to pay a fine of $100 for illegal voting. It was not claimed that Miss Anthony had not resided in the place long enough, or was not of sufficient age, or had not the required amount of intelligence to entitle her to vote, but the prosecution rested the case solely upon the fact that Miss Anthony was a woman and that it was a criminal offense for a woman to exercise the right of suffrage. The time will soon come when the recollection of such decisions will be as distasteful to American people as the Dred Scott decision now is. Judge Hunt evidently felt this when he omitted to make the usual order that the prisoner be committed [to prison] until the fine was paid.[41]

The above column appeared in the *Chicago Legal News* four days after Susan's trial, when Myra had not yet had an opportunity to read Judge Hunt's opinion. After Susan mailed her a copy of that opinion, Myra published it in the *News* along with a scathing editorial in which she denounced Judge Hunt for violating Susan's constitutional right to be tried by a jury:

> [Reprinted above is] the opinion of the U.S. Circuit Court, delivered by Hunt, J. in Miss Anthony's case, directing the jury to find her guilty of illegal voting, and sentencing her to pay a fine of $100 and costs. . . . We regard his action in directing the jury in a criminal case to find a verdict of guilty, as a violation of the Constitution which provides that "the trial for all crimes except in cases of impeachment shall be by jury." A trial can hardly be said to be by jury if a judge has the power to direct them to find the defendant guilty and thereby take from them the consideration of the guilt or innocence of the prisoner. Miss Anthony was in reality tried by Judge Hunt and not by a jury of her peers. . . . Hundreds of illegal votes are polled by *men* in New York every year, but we have yet to learn that the federal authorities have followed them with the earnestness they have Miss Anthony. Was Judge Hunt fearful if he simply stated the law to the jury and allowed them to draw their own conclusions, that they would acquit Miss Anthony?[42]

Myra had neglected to send Susan a copy of her first editorial regarding her case. She did, however, send her a copy of the second one; and Susan responded by return mail. Her letter to Myra, dated July 30, 1873, reads as follows:

> My dear Mrs. Bradwell:
>
> Your full freighted Legal News of the 19th is just here—Many thanks for it and its good words. The Albany Law Journal takes the *States' Rights Side* and justified Judge Hunt. I am ashamed that you were not compelled to *credit me* with handing you Judge Hunt's opinion—and lest you may not get my counsel's argument for my new trial—I now clip and enclose it in this—Please mark—his name is *Selden* not *Sheldon—Selden*—and he is just a splendid man. I wish President Grant had the sense and the honesty to put such a man—such a judge in the chair of the Chief Justice—What a spectacle will be either Conklin or Howe! To what shall we not go?—Hunt is small and pettifogging and pitiable in his partisanship actions.
>
> What are we going to do or say next? *I shall vote* again in November *if I can*—my ballot into the box—I have refused, wholly, to pay either fine or costs—and now wait to see if Uncle Sam will take his pay out of me by *imprisonment* for debt! Eh!
>
> How I would love to talk of our Constitutional position and work for the future.
>
> I wish you would send me your *June number* that I may see what you say of Judge Hunt on my *legal* right to vote—Can you give me a copy of the Supreme Court's decision of your case? Also a copy of Matt Carpenter's

argument—Do you know that I can't help but feel that if you had such a man as Judge Selden argue your case before the U.S. Court—it would have weight with them—Carpenter's argument was such a school boy *pettifogging speech*—a *special pleading*—wholly without *basic principle*—but still the courts are so entirely controlled by prejudice and precedent we have nothing to hope from them but *endorsement of dead men's actions*—

Now that Mrs. Jones is gone, I'm hearing nothing from you Chicagoans—any more than if you were all dead and buried or *burned up*—

With best love to yourself and *respectful consideration* for your Husband—I am Sincerely yours

Susan B. Anthony[43]

Susan was certainly grateful that Myra had taken Susan's "side" in her "illegal voting" case. It appears that the *Chicago Legal News* was the only legal periodical that had done so. Beneath Susan's expression of gratitude, however, one senses a state of pique at several points in the letter. Most pronounced is Susan's scolding of Myra: "I am ashamed that you were not compelled to *credit me* [emphasis in original] with handing you Judge Hunt's opinion." Why should that have mattered to Susan? Was her expression of irritation over such a petty matter symptomatic of a deeper hostility, or was Susan simply an egomaniac? The answer is probably both. There is evidence in the letter itself, and in other letters that Susan wrote to Myra, that Susan was upset that Myra had given her such limited support. Three months earlier, Susan had written to Myra urging her to "come down to [a] meeting and see our trial through the following week here in Rochester."[44] Not only did Myra not attend Susan's trial, it is fairly clear that she did not even write a reply to Susan's request. In Susan's letter of July 30, she complained of "hearing nothing from you Chicagoans—any more than if you were all dead and buried or *burned up*," an extremely insensitive remark in light of the fact that the massive fire two years earlier had left so many Chicagoans "dead and buried [and] *burned up*."

Moreover, in the same letter Susan expressed displeasure that Myra had retained Matt Carpenter to represent her before the U.S. Supreme Court. She stated that "Carpenter's argument was such a school boy *pettifogging speech* —a *special pleading*—wholly without a *basic principle*." Carpenter, it will be recalled, had argued in Myra's case that in the absence of a woman's suffrage amendment women had no constitutional right to vote, the very constitutional right that Susan was asserting as the basis for her defense at her own trial. Susan must have been displeased not only with Carpenter but with Myra as well, for if Myra had not wanted Carpenter to make the "no Constitutional right to vote" argument, he would not have made it. It must have infuriated Susan that Myra had thus undermined Susan's defense, indeed, the very cause to which Susan had devoted her life.

During the next two decades, Myra continued to give editorial kudos to "moderate" suffragists—Mary Livermore, Lucy Stone, Catherine V. Waite,[45] and others—but made no further mention of Susan B. Anthony, except in one brief column in 1874 when Myra wrote:

> We have no doubt if Miss Anthony were publishing *The Revolution* now, she would devote an occasional Article to Judge Hunt, who while on the federal bench violated the Constitution of the U.S. more to convict her of illegal voting [by depriving her of her right to trial by jury] than she did in voting, for he had sworn to support it—she did not.[46]

While Myra made no further editorial mention of Susan, Susan continued to write to Myra. In four of the letters that this author discovered, Susan solicited Myra's aid as a writer, speaker, and/or financier. In the first of these letters, written in July 1876, Susan requested that Myra contribute a biographical sketch as well as a picture of herself for Susan's forthcoming *History of Woman Suffrage.* She also asked for Myra's financial help in launching the volumes. Susan's letter, dated July 16, 1876, reads in pertinent part as follows:

> My dear Mrs. Bradwell:
>
> . . . Mrs. Stanton and myself are going to devote the summer to writing or gathering up the history of our Woman's Rights Movement—Will you give me a fuller account of yourself and work and decision for the history —If you will furnish your picture with your biographical sketch—It shall go into the history—Or if you will contribute the sum necessary to meet the extra cost—I have not yet decided exactly the style of picture—nor do I know the expense—But will you help us financially to get out the first edition? If so how much? We shall need $2000—probably—several women have already pledged 1 and 2, and if need be $500—to get this started.
>
> Kind regards to the judge and as ever yours sincerely,
>
> Susan B. Anthony[47]

Myra did send the picture of herself; it appears in volume 2 of Susan's *History.* It is unclear whether Myra also sent the requested "fuller account of [herself] and work and [court] decision." Either she did not send them (doubtful, because Myra enjoyed publicizing her accomplishments whenever possible), or she did send them and they were simply ignored by Susan. Nowhere in the *History* does there appear a full or even partial account of Myra and her work. Volume 2 simply contains a picture of Myra together with an account of the proceedings in *Bradwell* v. *Illinois,* reprinted verbatim from the *Chicago Legal News.* Volume 3 of the *History* devotes two paragraphs to the founding of the *Chicago Legal News* and one sentence plus three footnotes listing Myra, along with several others, as an officer of the Illinois State Suffrage Association.

Oddly, Susan ends her discussion of the formation of the Illinois State Suffrage Association with the following:

> Immediately after this enthusiastic [Chicago] convention, the Illinois State Suffrage Association was formed, [and] a committee appointed to visit Springfield and request the legislature to so "change the laws that the earnings of a married woman may be secured to her own use; that married women may have the same right to their own property that married men have; and that the mother may have an equal right with the father to the custody of the children." The need of such a committee existed in that year of 1869, and they seemed to have wrought effective service, since on March 24, the married woman's earnings act was approved. . . .
>
> Mrs. Livermore, Mrs. Stanton, Judge Waite, Judge and Mrs. Bradwell, had an enthusiastic meeting in the Opera House, Springfield, most of the members of the legislature being present.[48]

Nowhere in her account does Susan mention that it was Myra who drafted all three of the aforementioned laws: the married woman's earning's act, one of the married woman's property statutes, and the law giving mothers equal rights with fathers to the custody of their children.[49] Nowhere does Susan mention that Myra not only drafted these laws, but also was the person primarily responsible for their passage through both her lobbying efforts and her frequent editorials in the *Legal News.* These omissions, coupled with the scant mention of Myra in relation to the suffrage movement, seem significant. Susan must have been well aware of the role that Myra had played. Indeed, after completing a draft of the chapter relating to the woman's rights movement in Illinois, Susan wrote to Myra asking her to read that chapter and "then write out any important facts which we have not [included]" and "suggest . . . any errors or omissions."

Susan's letter to Myra, dated June 22, 1881, reads as follows:

My Dear Mrs. Bradwell,

How did you like the first print of your engraving? I thought it fine! . . . I send you our Senate Committee report for a 16th Amendment [the Woman Suffrage Amendment[50]]. Am working to get the House Committee to report too, before this session closes. Please, do you and Judge read up what we have in Volume II—the minute you get it—and then write out any important facts that we have not—and give to Mrs. Herbert to go into Illinois chapter—By the way—do you, too, read her the Chapter carefully—and suggest to her any errors or omissions—I know she will accept them kindly and gladly, and I must have the Illinois chapter to supplement—all we have not.

What you do to help us in our Nebraska work?

Loving yours,

Susan B. Anthony

p.s. How about your precious Bessie? Is she Graduated? What branch of the world's work does she choose for hers? Same to her and the Judge. S.B.A.[51]

It is highly likely that Myra did send Susan the requested material, including accounts of her own contributions to the Illinois suffrage movement and her role as draftsman of and chief lobbyist for the Illinois laws granting women rights to their property, earnings, and children. Modesty was not one of Myra's virtues. In a frequently appearing *Chicago Legal News* column captioned "Ourselves," she constantly reminded her readers of her law reform activities, particularly those that had culminated in legislative change. Certainly, if she was willing to have her accomplishments featured in her own newspaper, she would have been willing to have them included in Susan's monumental *History of Woman Suffrage*. One can conclude (based, of course, on very incomplete evidence) that Susan deliberately refrained from focusing on Myra's accomplishments in much the same way that Susan had chosen to downplay the contributions of Lucy Stone and other "moderates" in the movement.[52]

Why, one might ask, would Susan request "a full account of Myra's work" and also Myra's supplement to the Illinois chapter, and then refrain from including a "full account" or even an adequate partial account of Myra's contributions? The answer seems to be that Susan was ambivalent towards Myra, and that as the years passed, her negative feelings began to outweigh the positive. In addition to the aforementioned ideological schism between Susan and Myra, together with Matt Carpenter's (ergo Myra's) "women have no Constitutional right to vote" argument in the U.S. Supreme Court, and Myra's scant mention of Susan in the pages of the *Chicago Legal News,* there was the matter of money. While Susan repeatedly requested Myra's financial assistance, there is no indication that Myra ever made a monetary contribution to Susan's *History* or to any of Susan's other projects, although as one of the wealthiest women in the movement, Myra certainly could have afforded to do so.

Susan's final letter to Myra (or, at least, the final one which has been preserved) reiterates the themes found in the previous correspondence: Susan's expression of disappointment that Myra has not answered her letters, coupled with a plea for Myra's support, professional, social, and above all, financial. The occasion was a convention marking the fortieth anniversary of the woman suffrage movement, an event that Susan dubbed "this great jubilee that marks the close of our first forty years of shrieking to get out of the Wilderness of Disenfranchisement." Five weeks prior to that convention, on February 14, 1888, Susan wrote:

My dear Mrs. Bradwell

I wrote you a long time ago—asking you or your Brave Bessie to make a 10 minute speech on "women as Lawyers"—in the session devoted to the Professions—but as no reply came—we have to ask Mrs. Dittenbender of Nebraska who is in the city—But there is still room for you—if you will only come—You surely must all be coming to this great jubilee that marks the close of our first forty years of shrieking to get out of the Wilderness of Disenfranchisement!

But whether you can come or not—you surely will not fail to help us along financially—will you—it is a mammoth undertaking—this of bringing together the women of all lines of work to better themselves and the world— But if each one will give a little lift we shall tug through splendidly—Hoping to see you there.

Very sincerely yours

Susan B. Anthony

p.s. And then my dear Mrs. Bradwell—you are one of our Honorary and honored Vice Presidents—so you belong to the family and the Host of this feast of future things and ought to be here to help entertain the guests![53]

There is no indication that Myra attended the convention, made a financial contribution, or even bothered to answer Susan's letter. There may have been no further contact between the two.

Myra did, however, continue to work for the enfranchisement of her sex. Instead of joining forces with Susan's cadres who were working for the passage of a suffrage amendment to the federal constitution, Myra devoted the last years of her life to the cause of partial suffrage in Illinois, more specifically to the granting of the ballot to women in school elections. There was no question, in the 1890s, that women could run as candidates for and be elected to hold offices in the Illinois public school system. That issue had been settled in 1873 when the Illinois legislature passed a law making women eligible to hold elective school positions,[54] a statute that had been drafted by

Myra and introduced in the legislature by James.[55] But while women were eligible to *hold* school offices, and were in fact *elected* to such positions, only men could *vote* for them. Myra recognized the irony in this state of affairs, but she also realized that a law authorizing women to *hold* any public office was an important step on the road leading to the enfranchisement of women. In commenting on the 1873 law, Myra noted:

> If women *hold* office, why should they not be allowed to vote? . . . We predict that this is the first of a series of acts which will at no very distant day aid in extending the right of suffrage to women in Illinois."[56]

But alas, the day was in fact distant. There was an eighteen-year hiatus between the passage of the law entitling women to hold school offices and the law that permitted women to vote for such office. During that interim, Myra frequently editorialized on behalf of "school suffrage" for women, pointing out that by 1890, nineteen states had already granted women the right to vote in school elections.[57] In 1891 Illinois became the twentieth to do so when its legislature passed the following law:

> Any woman of the age of twenty-one years and upwards . . . [shall be entitled to vote at] any election held for the purpose of choosing any officer or schools in the school district of which she shall at the time have been for thirty days a resident.[58]

The law was immediately contested in the courts. The occasion for that challenge was a school board election held in April 1892 in Mt. Vernon, Illinois. Four persons—two men and two women—were candidates for two vacant positions. There were 883 voters, 590 males and 293 females, each of whom was entitled to cast two votes. The ballots of the male voters were placed in one ballot box; the ballots of the female voters in another. The results of the election were that the two female candidates won by large margins, but if the ballots of only the male voters had been counted, then the male candidates would have been victorious. The male candidates brought suit in county court, alleging that the 293 "female votes" were invalid, and since they (the male candidates) had won a majority of the "male votes," they, and not the female candidates, had been duly elected to office. The county court agreed with the challengers, and held that the statute granting women the right to vote in school elections was in conflict with the Illinois constitution, which restricted the right to vote to "male citizens of the United States." Therefore, concluded the court,

Upon the foregoing facts . . . at said election there were only 590 legal votes cast, that [the two male candidates] . . . received 299 and . . . 358 of said legal votes, and that [the female candidates] received only 224 and 225 of said legal votes; that the [male candidates] . . . received a majority of all the legal votes cast at said election and were duly elected to said offices.[59]

The female candidates appealed, and the decision was promptly reversed by the Illinois Supreme Court, which held:

We are of the opinion that the women who voted at the election in question . . . were entitled to vote at that election, and that their ballots were properly counted in favor of the defendants [the female candidates].

It follows that the defendants were legally elected to the offices of members of the board of education . . . in Mt. Vernon township and that the judgment of the county court deciding the contest in favor of the [male candidates] is erroneous.

If the language of the act [granting women the right to vote in school elections] and the words of the constitution thus incorporated therein [restricting voting eligibility to male citizens] are construed literally, they would seem to indicate that it was the legislative intention to confer upon women the right to vote in any . . . [school election], *provided such women were males.*[60] (Emphasis added)

In order to avoid such an absurd result, the court concluded that since the office at stake, i.e., member of the board of education, was not a position created by the Illinois constitution, it followed that the matter of eligibility to vote for such an official was also not governed by the state constitution. Thus, the constitutional provision limiting eligibility to "male citizens" was irrelevant:

Hence it would seem that the legislature would have complete power over the matter; that the legislature might provide for the election or appointment of school district officers as it should choose, when it should choose, in the manner it should choose, *and by whom it should choose.*[61] (Emphasis added)

Myra had cause to rejoice, for this was the first time in Illinois history that the state supreme court had decided a woman's rights case in favor of women. Indeed, it had been twenty-four years earlier that the same court had refused to admit Myra to the practice of law solely because she was female. As one reads her report of the Illinois court's "school suffrage" decision, one can almost feel her gloat:

The Supreme Court's opinion in this case reverses the decision of the court below, turns the men out of the board of education and puts women in the board who had been elected by the votes of women. The victorious women are Martha E. Plummer and Mary M. Moss of Mt. Vernon. The county Court marched them out of the office to which they had been elected, but the Supreme Court marched them in again. . . . We have no doubt women will find no difficulty now in voting for such school officers as they are entitled to, under this opinion.[62]

Myra was correct. After the state supreme court had given female voters its imprimatur, Illinois women faced no further difficulties in voting at school elections.

Later that year, a few months before her death, Myra Bradwell voted for her first and last time, casting a ballot in the Chicago school board election of 1893. It must have given her great pleasure to exercise the right—albeit on a limited basis—for which she had campaigned so ardently for a quarter of a century.

NOTES

1. *CLN* 1 (November 7, 1868): 45, col. 1.

2. *The History of Woman Suffrage* was published in six volumes. The first three volumes are considered to be the most important because they contain a wealth of original material reprinted in full. They were compiled by Susan B. Anthony along with Elizabeth Cady Stanton and Mathilda Gage. Volume 4 was edited by Anthony along with Ida Husted Harper, and volumes 5 and 6 were edited by Harper alone.

For an indication that Anthony had a propensity to ignore the contributions of those who disagreed with her, see Eleanor Flexner, *Century of Struggle: The Woman's Rights Movement in the United States,* (Cambridge, Mass.: Belknap Press of Harvard University Press, 1959): p. 360, n. 19: "It should be borne in mind that the generally useful *History of Woman Suffrage* is highly inadequate in its treatment of Lucy Stone, owing to longstanding disagreements among the leaders of the movement."

3. See Flexner, *Century of Struggle,* in her bibliographical summary at p. 349:

The greatest debt of all scholars in the history of American women is of course to the indomitable trio: Elizabeth Cady Stanton, Susan B. Anthony, and Mathilda Gage, who compiled the first three volumes of that monumental six volume series, *The History of the Woman Suffrage Movement.*

4. See, e.g., Eleanor Flexner, *Century of Struggle: The Woman's Rights Movement in the United States* (Cambridge, Mass.: Belknap Press of Harvard University Press, 1959); Elizabeth Cady Stanton, *History of Woman Suffrage* (New York: Arno Press, 1896); Ida Husted Harper, *The Life and Work of Susan B. Anthony* (Indianapolis, Kansas City: the Bowmen-Merrill Company 1898–1908); Alma Lutz, *Susan B. Anthony: Rebel, Crusader, Humanitarian* (Boston: Beacon Press, 1959); Carrie Chapman Catt, *Woman Suffrage and Politics* (New York: C. Scribner's Son, 1923);

Andrew Sinclair, *The Better Half: the Emancipation of the American Woman* (New York: Harper and Row, 1965); Aileen S. Kraditor, *The Ideas of the Woman Suffrage Movement 1890–1920* (New York: Columbia University Press, 1965).

5. Flexner, *Century of Struggle*, p. 147.
6. Ibid., p. 148.
7. Quoted in Lutz, *Susan B. Anthony*, p. 169.
8. Ibid., p. 170.
9. *CLN* 1 (October 31, 1868): 37, col. 3.
10. *CLN* 1 (November 28, 1868): 68, col. 2.
11. Edward T. James and Janet Wilson James, eds., *Notable American Women, 1607–1950: A Biographical Dictionary* 1 (Cambridge, Mass.: Belknap Press of Harvard University Press, 1971): p. 223 (entry on Myra Bradwell).
12. Lutz, p. 172.
13. Ibid.
14. Quoted in Harper, *The Life and Work of Susan B. Anthony*, vol. 1, p. 364.
15. *CLN* 1 (November 7, 1868): 45, col. 1.
16. *CLN* 16 (January 26, 1884): 166, col. 1–2.
17. *Chicago Tribune*, (May 12, 1889): 26, col. 1–2. For a fuller version of this quote, see chapter 2, text accompanying footnote 24.
18. Quoted in Flexner, *Century of Struggle*, p. 151.
19. *CLN* 1 (November 7, 1868): 45, col. 1–2.
20. Edward T. James and Janet Wilson James, *Notable American Women, 1607–1950*, p. 224.
21. *CLN* 1 (February 27, 1869): 172, col. 2.
22. *CLN* 1 (November 7, 1868): 45, col. 1–2.
23. Anthony, et al., *History of Woman Suffrage*, vol. 3, p. 571.
24. Ibid., pp. 570–71.
25. *CLN* 2 (May 14, 1870): 260, col. 2–3.
26. *CLN* 2 (May 28, 1870): 280, col. 3.
27. James, *Notable American Women, 1607–1950*, p. 224.
28. *CLN* 3 (February 11, 1871): 157, col. 4.
29. Anthony, et al., vol. 3, p. 727.
30. *CLN* 2 (December 25, 1869): 100, col. 3.
31. Ibid.
32. Flexner, *Century of Struggle*, p. 164.
33. *CLN* 6 (January 17, 1874): 189, col. 2.
34. Ibid.
35. Flexner, *Century of Struggle*, p. 180.
36. *CLN* 4 (July 6, 1872): 328, col. 4.
37. See, e.g., article in *Western Jurist* reprinted in *CLN* 1 (May 15, 1869): 274, col, 4; editorial in *Central Law Journal*, reprinted in *CLN* 6 (January 31, 1874): 154, col. 3.
38. Anthony et al., vol. 3, pp. 562–63.
39. *CLN* 5 (June 14, 1873): 449, col. 1.
40. Proceedings in the trial of Susan B. Anthony (Rochester, 1874), pp. 87–88, quoted in Flexner, *Century of Struggle*, p. 170.
41. *CLN* 5 (June 21, 1873): 466, col. 1.
42. *CLN* 5 (July 19, 1873): 498, col. 1–2.
43. Letter from Susan B. Anthony to Myra Bradwell dated July 30, 1873.
44. Letter from Susan B. Anthony to Myra Bradwell dated April 18, 1873.
45. *CLN* 18 (June 12, 1886): 331, col. 3.

46. *CLN* 7 (November 28, 1874): 77, col. 1–2.

47. Letter from Susan B. Anthony to Myra Bradwell dated July 16, 1876.

48. Anthony et al., vol. 3, pp. 569–70.

49. For a discussion of these and other laws that Myra drafted, see chapter 10, *infra.*

50. The Woman Suffrage Amendment, which eventually became the Nineteenth Amendment, was added to the Constitution in 1920.

51. Letter from Susan B. Anthony to Myra Bradwell dated June 22, 1882.

52. See footnote 2.

53. Letter from Susan B. Anthony to Myra Bradwell dated February 14, 1888.

54. *CLN* 5 (April 5, 1873): 330, col. 2–3.

55. Ibid.

56. Ibid.

57. *CLN* 22 (July 19, 1890): 383, col. 3. See also Flexner, *Century of Struggle,* p. 179.

58. *CLN* 25 (March 11, 1893): 234, col. 1.

59. Ibid. (*Yost* v. *Plummer* [Jefferson County Court], reprinted in part).

60. Ibid. (*Plummer* v. *Yost,* Supreme Court of Illinois [1893], reprinted in part).

61. Ibid.

62. *CLN* 25 (March 11, 1893): 234, col. 1.

10

"Unfastening Well the House Door" The Reform of Other Laws Relating to Women

The writer of a hundred years hence will read with as much surprise the laws of the present day, in regard to the rights of women, as we do the laws of a hundred years ago upon the same subject.

We copy from the Gentoo Code, published in 1775, the following laws relating to a woman: "If a man goes on a journey, his wife shall not divert herself by plays, nor shall see any public show, nor shall laugh, nor shall dress herself in jewels and fine clothes, nor shall see dancing nor hear music, nor shall sit in the window, nor shall ride out, nor shall behold anything choice and rare; *but shall fasten well the house door,* and remain private, and shall not blacken her eyes with eye powder, and shall not view her face in a mirror; and shall never exercise herself in any such agreeable employment during the absence of her husband."

—Myra Bradwell (1869)[1]

Disenfranchisement was not the only legal encumbrance faced by nineteenth-century women, but because they were unable to vote, they were seemingly powerless to secure the removal of the many other handicaps imposed on them by law. Without access to the ballot, certainly without recourse to the bullet, women had virtually one weapon in their arsenal: the written and spoken word. It is generally conceded that it was the words of Myra Bradwell that had the most striking impact in improving the legal status of nineteenth-century women in Illinois and in many other states as well. Indeed, twenty years after

Myra's death, the Illinois Equal Suffrage Association compiled in a single volume a list of all "Laws in Illinois Affecting Women and Children." The preface to that compilation was dedicated to Myra Bradwell and reads as follows:

> The object of the compiler has been to place in the hands of the women of the State in a form convenient for use a volume in which may be found the laws which govern their lives, property, and the conditions under which they and their children must labor.
>
> . . . There is one woman to whom our thoughts invariably turn whenever we think of the laws of Illinois affecting women; a woman who through her unswerving loyalty to the cause of women's rights made it possible for women to enter the legal profession in Illinois, who in her defense of the weak and oppressed framed laws which were passed by the legislature of this State and which gave the impetus to legislation for women not only in Illinois but throughout the United States. *This woman was Myra Bradwell.*[2] (Emphasis added)

While it is true that Myra, along with Alta Hulett, was responsible for the legislation that enabled women to enter the legal profession in Illinois, that law, and others dealing with women's occupation choices, affected the lives of only an infinitesimal number of nineteenth-century women. In contrast, two other laws that Myra drafted and lobbied through the Illinois legislature had a potential impact on virtually every married woman within the state of Illinois. One of those statutes gave women equal rights to the custody of their children. The other allowed married women to keep their own earnings.

By the common law of both England and the United States, fathers had a right to the custody of their legitimate minor children that was virtually absolute.[3] In cases of marital separation or divorce, it was almost impossible for the mother to obtain custody of her children. Cases of the most extreme sort occurred in which mothers were unable to wrest custody of their children from their fathers, even when those fathers were manifestly unfit. Moreover, even when a father abandoned his child and contributed nothing to that child's support, the father could later claim custody and thus be entitled to the services and earnings of that child.

In one such case,[4] a husband and wife were divorced in New Jersey in 1860, and the wife with their three minor children to Connecticut. During the ensuing six years, the father did not furnish any support for the children, nor did he visit them or ask for their custody. When the oldest son reached his thirteenth birthday and was thus capable of providing services and earnings for the father, the father employed two men to kidnap the child. While riding in the carriage of his kidnappers, the son saw a friend of his mother and "called to [that friend] repeatedly to save him." In spite of the friend's efforts to retrieve the boy, the boy was delivered to his father. A lawsuit ensued, and the Supreme Court of Connecticut held that the father had the absolute right of "resuming and continuing the custody and control of the child whenever he thought proper to attempt it. " The court conceded that "the father had regained the possession [of the son] by stratagem" but concluded that "that fact is entirely immaterial. " The court reasoned:

> That the father is entitled to the custody and control of his minor children, even to the exclusion of the mother, is elementary law. . . . It is not claimed that there was any agreement or contract between the father and the mother, by force of which the custody and control was transferred. . . . And if such contract was shown, . . . such a contract would not be recognized as a lawful one. It is not in the power of the father to divest himself by contract, even with the mother, of the custody of the children. . . .
>
> It is further claimed that inasmuch as the father knew where the children were and permitted them to remain undisturbed for several years with the mother, he abandoned them and lost his legal right of control over them. But a right which the law gives [to the father] . . . cannot be lost, dedicated or abandoned.[5]

The Illinois child custody law went even one step further than the Connecticut law. Not only did a father have virtually absolute rights to the custody of his minor children, but also he could, if he chose, actually "dispose" of that custody to another person without the mother's consent. The father could do this during his lifetime by simply "deeding" his child to another in much the same way that he would convey a parcel of real estate. Or, upon the father's death, he could "dispose" of the child's custody through his last will and testament. The pertinent Illinois statute read:

> Every father of sound mind and memory, of a child . . . , under the age of 21 years and unmarried, may by his deed or last will duly executed dispose of the custody . . . of such child during his minority, or for any less time, to any person or persons.[6]

In an early edition of the *News*, Myra labelled the statute a "Law Made By Man For Man." She then discussed a recent case that had arisen under that law:

> In February last one Charles McCarthy died in this city, leaving a widow and a child under three years of age. The deceased, by his will, made during his last sickness appointed his mother and brother *guardians* of his child during its minority, divesting his widow, the mother of the child, of all right to its custody and giving the full custody of the child and its property to the guardians named in the will.[7]

After stating that she would "make no comments upon this particular case," Myra continued the column by commenting both on the case and on the "disgraceful" law under which it had arisen:

> This law has the sanction of years, and the respectability of age to commend it; but is it contrary to the spirit of the present civilization, opposed to the moral sentiments of humanity and repugnant to maternal instincts and affection?
>
> To allow a father, under the authority of law, by a last will and testament, executed in the very face of death, to take his child from the custody of its own mother and give it to a stranger until it shall become a man or woman, is in our opinion legalizing child stealing.[8]

Myra concluded her column by lamenting that the law had been enacted and had remained on the books only because of the disenfranchised status of women:

> Could mothers vote would such a law ever have disgraced our statute book? They, we think, would have placed the mothers' right to the custody of the child equal to that of the father's.[9]

Myra's concern over the shabby treatment accorded to mothers under the child custody law appeared to be boundless. Indeed, it provided the impetus for one of the only occasions upon which she publicly criticized a judicial opinion written by her husband, James, during his tenure as a probate court judge. The case involved a husband who had deserted his wife and had taken their minor child with him. The husband subsequently remarried. After he died, the child's natural mother brought suit seeking custody of the child. The child's stepmother also asked for custody. Apparently believing that almost any male custodian was preferable to the two females who were most closely bonded to the child, Judge Bradwell refused to grant custody to either the natural mother or the stepmother. Instead, he appointed the natural mother's male attorney as guardian for the child, but allowed "both of the mothers to visit the child at all reasonable hours, so long as they conducted themselves with propriety and did not try to take the child away."[10] In an editorial criticism of James's opinion, Myra termed the decision "unfortunate" and stated that she was of the opinion that the natural mother was the "natural guardian" of the child, and upon the death of the father was entitled to custody of that child.

Reacting to both the Illinois statute that allowed the father to "dispose" of the custody of his child without the mother's consent, and also to James's judicial opinion declaring that upon the father's death both the surviving natural mother and the stepmother were unfit guardians for the child, Myra drafted the following bill:

> Neither parent shall dispose of the custody of a minor child without the consent of the other; and in all cases the surviving parent, being a fit and competent person, shall be entitled to the guardianship of his or her minor child.[11]

For the next two years Myra lobbied vigorously for the enactment of the bill. Finally, in April 1871, she proudly announced to her readers that the bill had passed in the Illinois state senate.[12] A few months later the bill was approved by the state's lower house and signed into law by the governor.

The new Child Custody Law was Myra's second legislative victory. The first had occurred two years earlier when Myra had drafted and secured the enactment of a law permitting married women to keep their own earnings.

The law governing the property and earnings of married women during the early and mid-nineteenth century was based on the basic "principle of common law by which the husband and wife are regarded as one person and *her* [emphasis added] legal existence and authority in a degree lost or suspended during the continuance of the matrimonial union."[13] Deducible from *that* principle was another one: that the property and earnings of the wife belonged to her husband. The common law, as succinctly stated by a nineteenth-century Connecticut judge, was that:

> The husband by marriage acquires . . . an absolute right to his wife's [real estate] and may dispose of [it]. . . . He acquires an absolute [right] in her . . . personal [property]. . . . As to the property of the wife accruing during . . . [marriage] the same rule is applicable.[14]

As historian Lawrence Friedman has noted, "essentially husband and wife were one flesh; but the man was owner of that flesh."[15] Or, as historian Norma Basch has stated, "the law created an equation in which one plus one equaled one by erasing the female one."[16]

Agitation to allow married women to retain their own property and earnings began in the 1830s, and led to the enactment of the New York Married Women's Property Act of 1848.[17] During the ensuing decade, many New England states followed New York's example. The reform then spread westward, in spite of some judicial declarations that laws permitting married women to retain their own property went too far "towards clothing one class of females with strange and manly attributes."[18]

In 1861 the Illinois legislature followed suit and enacted a statute which allowed the *property* of a wife to remain during marriage "as her sole and separate property, . . . free from the control and interference of her husband

and exempt from execution of his debts."[19] However, in 1864 the Illinois Supreme Court ruled that the Act of 1861 did not extend to the *wages* of married women, that those *earnings* belonged to the husband and could be taken to pay as his debts.[20] Myra was deeply disturbed by that judicially imposed exception to the married women's property law. During the first five months of publication of the *Chicago Legal News,* she wrote six editorials advocating a change in the law.[21] Her proposed amendment allowed a married woman to retain her own earnings as well as her other types of property. Such a law was necessary, Myra claimed, in order "to protect wife and children in the case of a drunken or spendthrift husband." The case, which "added impetus to her zeal," involved the following "monstrous injustice."

> A drunkard who owed a saloon keeper for his whiskey, had a wife who earned her own living as a scrub woman and the saloon keeper garnisheed the people who owed *her* and levied on *her* earnings to pay her husband's bill.[22]

The case of the drunkard and the scrubwoman inspired Myra to write the following melodramatic editorial:

> The law relating to women has received much attention in England within a few years and in many respects, is in advance of our own. We hope that the legislature of Illinois will, this winter, so amend the law in regard to a married woman's earnings that she may have the benefit of them herself. A man at our elbow says, "Mrs. Bradwell, why repeat this again?" We will tell you why. It is now four years since the [Illinois] Supreme Court decided that the [Married Women's Property] Act did not extend to the *earnings* of a married woman, and that they belonged to the husband and might be taken to pay his debts. Rich, shoddy creditors of the husband have ever since been taking to pay *his* debts the money earned by the honest toil of the wife, for the purpose of supporting her ragged, starving children, which a drunken or unfortunate husband failed to provide for, and the law still remains the same, notwithstanding the fact that two legislatures have met since this solemn declaration of the highest tribunal in our state.[23]

A few weeks later Myra announced that the cause of married women's earnings had been dealt yet a further blow. The Illinois Supreme Court had just held that it was not only *earnings* of married women that belonged to their husbands, but also the *property purchased with those earnings.*[24]

Once again Myra implored the state legislature to amend the Married Women's Property Act so that a married woman would be entitled to retain her own earnings. Realizing that the current [1868–69] legislative session was within ten days of adjournment, Myra decided to take matters into her own hands, *literally.* As she later explained to her readers:

We found, within ten days of the end of the [current legislative] session that there was no general bill before the legislature upon the subject of [married women's] property rights that could or ought to pass.

The editress of this paper wrote a bill for an act giving to a married woman her own earnings and the right to sue for the same in her own name.[25]

After describing how she had hand-carried her bill to Springfield and lobbied it through both houses of the legislature, she concluded the column by proclaiming victory:

These bills have passed both houses of the general assembly and only await the signature of our noble, honest, and ever watchful governor Palmer to become law.[26]

Soon thereafter, she announced that the bill had been signed into law by the governor.[27]

A few years later Myra took great pleasure in informing her readers that a federal court in Illinois had given a very broad and liberal interpretation to the statute that she had drafted. That court had held, among other things, that a married woman not only had the legal right to control her own earnings but also had the legal power to enter into binding contracts and other business relationships without the consent of her husband.[28]

Myra firmly believed, however, that since married women had been accorded the same financial, contractual, and occupational *rights* as men, equality demanded that those women also be charged with the same *responsibilities*. She thus endorsed a bill that provided that the expenses of the family, and of the education of the children, should be "chargeable upon the property of both the husband and wife."[29]

Two months later, after the "equal liability" law had been enacted by the Illinois legislature, Myra reiterated her position:

The Illinois law upon the property rights of husband and wife is greatly in advance of any of her sister states. The husband and wife stand upon an equality before the law. Under the old system the wife could be worth her thousands and bid defiance to suits at law. Now she must pay her debts and if able, help support the family and educate the children.[30]

Because Myra believed in true equality of the sexes, she was also vehemently opposed to property laws that were designed to protect women from their own folly or ignorance, or from undue pressure by their husbands. One such law, in existence in many states during the nineteenth century, required that when a husband and wife conveyed real estate to a third party, the wife had to acknowledge, out of the presence of her husband, that she had executed the deed without compulsion or fear of her husband. If the wife did not make the requisite acknowledgement, she retained dower rights (property rights after the husband's death) in the land that had been conveyed.

In 1872 Illinois repealed its version of that law and passed a statute requiring, instead, only the wife's signature on the deed that conveyed the property. The wife's "acknowledgement," out of the presence of her husband, was no longer necessary. In announcing the new law to her readers, Myra stated that it was cause for rejoicing:

> We rejoice that our legislature, at its last session, placed man and woman, single or married, on an equality in this respect; . . . A married woman will now feel that she is person capable of thinking and acting. We always thought the old statute was humiliating and an insult to the intelligence of every wife and the integrity of every husband, who had to acknowledge a deed under its provisions.[31]

It was not with respect to their children or property, however, that mid-nineteenth-century women suffered the most devastating disability. It was, instead, with respect to their personal liberty. In Illinois, and other states as well, a married woman could be declared insane at the request of her husband and confined to an insane asylum without a judicial hearing.

The pertinent Illinois statute provided:

> Married women and infants, who, in the judgment of the medical superintendent [of the Illinois State Hospital for the Insane] are evidently insane or distracted, may be entered or detained in the hospital *on the request of the husband* of the woman or the guardian of the infant, *without the evidence of insanity required in other cases.*[32] (Emphasis added)

The Illinois law, passed in 1851, had both legal and medical underpinnings. The legal basis for the statute was the principal of coverture,[33] under which the very being or legal existence of a married woman was suspended during her marriage and incorporated into that of her husband. A husband's request for the commitment of his wife was, therefore, in the eyes of the law no different from his voluntary commitment of himself to an "insane asylum."

The medical basis for the statute permitting a married woman to be "detained in the hospital [for the insane] on the request of her husband . . . without [any] evidence of insanity" was the belief, widely held by mid-nineteenth-century doctors, that many women were inherently insane during the various stages of the female reproductive cycle: onset of menstruation, pregnancy, childbirth, lactation, and menopause. For example, in his *Treatise on Insanity in its Medical Relations*, one medical expert wrote as follows:

The beginning of menstruation and its cessation constitute critical periods in the life of the female, and exert a great influence upon her health and mortality.

The first discharge is accompanied, ordinarily, by a variety of abnormal circumstances, such as headache, fever, *nervous derangement,* pain in the loins and uterus, etc., *and even the subsequent returns are often thus attended.* . . . The profound change induced in the female organism by the condition of pregnancy could scarcely leave the mind untouched, and we find, in fact that *mental disturbance going far beyond eccentric "longings"* of women in this state is not an infrequent occurrence. This may exhibit itself mainly as regards the emotions, the subjects becoming irascible, suspicious, jealous or the victims of profound melancholy; or the intellect may be involved, and *delusions become characteristic features of the disorder.* Again, they may manifest the most unreasonable hatred of certain persons, and may make serious attempts to injure or destroy them. . . . Most authors upon the subject of insanity have noticed the relationship between the menopause and the initiation of symptoms of *mental derangement.* Generally the melancholic type prevails, and a tendency to suicide is not uncommon; but quite often there are various forms of *emotional disturbance* or of perversion of the appetite which are sources of great distress to friends and relatives.[34] (Emphasis added)

A secondary cause of female insanity, this expert believed, was the "cramming of the mind" with intellectual material, which would often have a deleterious effect on the nervous system:

. . . the cramming of the mind at school with subjects such as civil engineering and integral calculus, and other mathematical studies, which it grasps with difficulty, influence materially the nervous system primarily and secondarily the generative organs. These, again, react upon the brain, and hysteria, hypochondria, and other forms of *quasi insanity* are produced, to say nothing of neuralgia, spinal irritation, epilepsy, and a dozen other diseases as bad or worse.[35] (Emphasis added)

Other nineteenth-century medical experts agreed.[36]

Given this three-part rationale—a married woman's nonexistence in the eyes of the law, her reproductive biology, and nervous strain caused by "cramming of the mind" with intellectual subjects—it is no wonder that (as Myra wrote many years later): "We know of scores of married women who were taken under this [Illinois statute] and without trial were incarcerated in this insane hospital for years."[37]

One of those "scores of married women" with whose case Myra was well-acquainted was Elizabeth Parsons Ware Packard, a clergyman's wife from Illinois.[38] Packard's "insanity," which became a nineteenth-century cause célèbre, took the form of disagreeing with her husband about the existence of original sin. In her adult Sunday school class Packard not only spoke out against the concept of original sin but also advanced a theory of the acceptability by God of all religions. When her husband asked her to stop expressing these ideas, she refused, stating that she was obliged to follow the dictates of her conscience. On June 18, 1860, he forcibly removed her from her home and from her six children. After a conversation with the superintendent of the Jacksonville State Hospital for the Insane, Dr. Packard had Mrs. Packard "detained" in the hospital, without any evidence of insanity other than his own words. Her "detainment" lasted for three years.

Packard never doubted her own sanity and believed that her husband had had her incarcerated because she posed a threat to the church and to his position in it:

> In other words, instead of calling me by the obsolete title of heretic, he modernized his phrase by substituting insanity instead of heresy as the crime for which I am now sentenced to endless imprisonment in one of our Modern Inquisitions.[39]

Packard had little knowledge of insane asylums, but after being committed to Jacksonville she stayed alert and aware of her surroundings and even managed to keep a secret journal that chronicled her three-year incarceration. One of the first things she noticed was a large group of women at Jacksonville who, Packard believed, were not insane but who had been incarcerated in order to render them compliant with the dictates of their husbands:

> It was a matter of great surprise to me to find so many in the Seventh Wards, who, like myself, had never shown any insanity while there, and these were almost uniformly married women, who were put there either by strategy or by force. None of these unfortunate sane prisoners had had any trial or any chance for self-defense. . . . Another fact I noticed was that [the superintendent] invariably kept these wives until they begged to be sent home. This led me to suspect that there was a secret understanding between the husband and the doctor; that the *subjection* of the wife was the cure the husband was seeking to effect under the specious plea of insanity. . . . Time and time again have I seen these defenseless women sent home only to be sent back again and again, for the sole purpose of making them the unresisting willing slaves of their cruel husbands.[40]

Packard was imprisoned in Jacksonville Insane Asylum for three years before her husband permitted her to be released. However, he had no intention of allowing her any lasting freedom. Instead, he placed her under a "house arrest" while he made plans to move the family to Massachusetts and to commit her for life in the Northhampton Insane Asylum in that state.

Being placed under "house arrest" proved to be the event that gave Packard her freedom. Until that point she had labored under the fact that

> No father, brother, son or friend, or even our Governor himself has the power to protect the personal liberty of any married woman in this state. . . . There is no protection of my personal liberty under the American flag so long as Mr. Packard lives.[41]

It was illegal, however, to detain anyone in a house against his or her will; thus Mrs. Packard's neighbors were able to obtain a writ forcing Mr. Packard to come to court and show reason for her detention. At trial, Mrs. Packard was judged sane.

Packard's husband immediately packed up the children and the family's belongings and moved to Massachusetts. Much of the furniture was stored with a neighbor. Packard attempted to recover her lost possessions but found she had no legal right to do so. She later wrote:

> Under these painful circumstances I found that Mr. Packard had only been telling me the simple truth when he said that: "For twenty years I have given you a home to live in—and also allowed you the privilege of taking care of *my own* children in it—to me alone are you indebted for these privileges —as by law you have no rights to my home, my property, or my children while I live!"[42] (Emphasis added)

Estranged from her family and outraged by the lack of legal protection for married women generally and particularly by the ability of husbands to commit their wives without a legal hearing, Packard began lobbying for a change in the Illinois laws. As a result of her efforts, two "Personal Liberty" laws were passed by the Illinois legislature. Both statutes, one enacted in 1865, the other in 1867, provided for a jury trial for *any* person "with reference to whom [insanity] proceedings may be instituted."[43]

Elizabeth Packard was thus responsible for the *passage* of the two laws prohibiting men from institutionalizing their wives without a jury trial and order of a court. But the fact that those laws *remained* on the statute books was due, in large measure, to the efforts of Myra Bradwell.

In an issue of the *Chicago Legal News*,[44] which was published only one year after the passage of the second Personal Liberty Law, Myra reminded her readers of the "Law of 1851 [which had] allowed married women to be detained in the Illinois Hospital for the Insane at the request of their husbands without a sanity hearing." Myra wrote:

This section was passed upon the supposition that a married woman had not the same right to liberty that her husband had. That if she and her neighbors thought that her husband was insane, before the doors of the insane hospitals could lawfully close upon him, it was necessary that a jury of his peers should be called and sworn, and a verdict of insanity obtained. But turn the tables. Let the husband think the wife insane, or wish to get rid of her, and all he had to do was to seize and bind her, take her to the insane asylum in this condition, which would make a sane woman with any heart appear insane, see the "medical superintendent" and convince his "judgment" that this poor, sorrowful, frightened wife was evidently insane, and she was received as an inmate and the husband returned home. We know of scores of married women who were taken under this section, and, without any trial were "incarcerated" in this insane hospital for years.[45]

In closing, Myra noted that the many abuses of the law of 1851 had led to the two recently enacted statutes requiring sanity trials for married women and children.

The purpose of Myra's discussion of the 1851 insanity law was neither to fill pages nor to assure her readers that such abuses could never again occur. On the contrary, Myra was deeply concerned about new legislative attempts to reinstate the 1851 law in slightly different garb. The new bill, which was introduced in the Illinois legislature shortly after the legal reforms of 1865 and 1867, was known as the "Private Madhouse" bill. The title was a misnomer in that it had nothing to do with private (as opposed to public) madhouses. Instead, it provided for *private* commitments (i.e., commitments not authorized by a court) to *state* insane asylums. The chief difference between the new bill and the 1851 law under which Elizabeth Packard had been incarcerated was that the new bill applied to *all persons* (not just married women and minors) and authorized their commitment to insane asylums upon the certificate of two doctors without a court hearing.

During the first two decades of the *Legal News*'s existence, the "Private Madhouse" bill was introduced in the Illinois legislature in many different forms. The fact that it was never enacted was probably due in large measure to twenty years of campaigning by Myra. In one editorial she wrote:

The private mad-house bill now pending in the house of representatives at Springfield is one of the most dangerous bills to personal liberty ever introduced in this State. Pass it, and the weak and poor will be in the hands of the rich and powerful. No person should be liable to be seized in the name of the law and taken to a mad house without a verdict of a jury.[46]

In another column she explained:

The bill now before the General Assembly of this State which proposes to allow persons to be locked up in insane asylums upon the certificate of two physicians without a jury trial, if enacted into a law will be the means of consigning hundreds of sane people to insane asylums in this State and when once there it is no easy matter to get out if the keeper of the insane asylum is disposed to retain his patient. There is a certain amount of security in having a jury stand between a person and imprisonment or an insane asylum.[47]

She then once again reminded her readers of the law of 1851 under which Elizabeth Packard had been incarcerated:

We had a law once in this State that allowed persons to be imprisoned upon the certificates of doctors and did not require them to be brought before the court before they were committed, and the consequence was a great many people were sent to the insane asylums who were as sane as the person that sent them and much more worthy. We could name a large number of persons who were unjustly incarcerated in insane asylums under the old law but will not do so out of respect to the feelings of their friends.[48]

She continued the column by noting that the legislative nullification of the 1851 law had resulted in her husband James's performance of the Herculean task of conducting eighty-four sanity trials in a single day, as a result of which "12 [persons] were found to be sane and released from custody."[49]

She concluded with the observation—perhaps somewhat commonplace today—that the line between sanity and insanity was an illusive one, and that the more persons (including a jury) who intervened in the process, the less likelihood of a miscarriage of justice:

The fact was upon the passage of [the present] law in many places in the state, the keepers discharged patients who had been confined in the insane departments for a long time, and let them go, knowing that they would never be declared insane by a jury. It is not safe to allow only the certificate of two physicians to consign a person to a mad house. The doctors may be ever so honest and ever so careful, but in insane cases they are very liable to be mistaken. In four out of five of the murder trials, where the plea of insanity is interposed, about as many doctors will swear the prisoner to be sane as will swear him to be insane.[50]

In her final editorial on the subject she admonished:

Any amendment to our laws which allows a person to be committed to an insane asylum without the verdict of a jury will be dangerous to personal liberty. When our laws allowed persons to be placed in asylums without the verdict of a jury upon the certificate of physicians and did not require the person alleged to be insane to be present at a trial, hundreds of people were kept in insane asylums and poor houses as insane, who were sane. The verdict of a jury is the safeguard that has kept many unfortunate sane persons out of the mad house. When the present law was passed, requiring the verdict of a jury, scores of persons were found in the State confined as insane persons, who had never been so declared by a jury so and were set at liberty as sane.[51]

The "Private Madhouse" bill was never enacted by the Illinois legislature. One can speculate that this defeat was due, at least in part, to the efforts of Myra. Through her persistent editorializing on the subject, she had awakened her readership—which included virtually every member of the Illinois legislature—to the plight of the many nineteenth-century women who had been committed as "mad" on the simple "say-sos" of their husbands.

Myra was well aware of the major role that she had played in enabling nineteenth-century women to gain control over their children, their earnings, and, above all, their personal liberty. Shortly before her death, in a column entitled, "Summary of Changes during 25 years of Publication of the *Chicago Legal News*," she concluded by noting, with her characteristic lack of modesty:

[When the *News* began publication] . . . the earnings of the wife of a drunken and worthless, insolvent husband, could be taken from her and her starving children under a garnishee sued out by the grasping creditors of the husband. . . . We rejoice that so many occupations and professions have been opened to women *and take pleasure in the thought that we have aided to the extent of our ability to bring about these results,* and hope to live to see the day when the liberty of pursuit shall be triumphant, not only in Illinois but in every State in the Union, and every man and woman shall stand on an equality before the law."[52] (Emphasis added)

NOTES

1. *CLN* 1 (January 9, 1869): 117, col. 3.
2. "Laws of Illinois Affecting Women and Children," reprinted from *The Revised Statutes of the State of Illinois* (Smith–Hurd: 1923–1935), Harvey B. Hurd, contributor (Chicago: Chicago Legal News, 1874–1921).
3. Joseph W. Madden, *Persons and Domestic Relations* (St. Paul, Minnesota: West Publishing Company, 1931): p. 369.
4. *Johnson v. Terry,* 34 Conn. 259 (1867).
5. Ibid.
6. *Illinois Revised Statutes,* chapter 47, sec. 17, quoted in *CLN* 1 (April 10, 1869): 220, col. 2.
7. *CLN* 1 (April 10, 1869): 220, col. 2.
8. Ibid.

9. Ibid.

10. *CLN* 1 (October 31, 1868): 37, col. 4.

11. *CLN* 3 (April 29, 1871): 243, col. 4.

12. Ibid.

13. Kent, *Commentaries,* vol. 2 (2d ed. 1832): p. 129. See also discussion of "coverture" in chapter 1.

14. *Griswold* v. *Penniman,* 2 Conn. 564 (1818).

15. Lawrence Friedman, *A History of American Law* (New York: Simon and Schuster, 1973), p. 184.

16. Norma Basch, *In the Eyes of the Law: Women, Marriage and Property in Nineteenth Century New York* (Ithaca, N.Y.: Cornell University Press, 1982), p. 17.

17. For a full account of the history of the New York Married Woman's Property Laws, see Basch, *In the Eyes of the Law.*

18. See e.g., J. Crawford, in *Norval* v. *Rice,* 2 Wis. 22, 33 (1853).

19. *CLN* 1 (October 17, 1868): 22, col. 1.

20. *CLN* 1 (October 31, 1868): 37, col. 3-4.

21. *CLN* 1 (October 17, 1868): 22, col. 1; *CLN* 1 (October 31, 1868): 37, col. 3-4; *CLN* 1 (November 14, 1868): 53, col. 3; *CLN* 1 (November 21, 1868): 60, col. 4; *CLN* 1 (February 27, 1869): 172, col. 1-2; *CLN* 1 (March 13, 1869): 188, col. 2.

22. *CLN* 26 (February 17, 1894): 200-202.

23. *CLN* 1 (October 31, 1868): 37, col. 3-4.

24. *CLN* 1 (November 21, 1868): 60, col. 4.

25. Ibid.

26. Ibid.

27. *CLN* 1 (March 27, 1869): 212, col. 1.

28. *CLN* 5 (February 1, 1873): 222, col. 1.

29. *CLN* 6 (January 31, 1874): 153, col. 4; 154, col. 1-2.

30. *CLN* 6 (April 4, 1874): 225, col. 2-3.

31. *CLN* 4 (July 13, 1872): 344, col. 1-2.

32. The statute is reprinted in Elizabeth Parsons Ware Packard, *Modern Persecution or Insane Asylums Unveiled as Demonstrated by the Report of the Investigating Committee of the Legislature of Illinois,* Volumes 1 and 2 (Hartford, Conn.: Case, Lakewood and Brainard, 1875), Volume 1, p. 54.

33. See chapter 1.

34. William A. Hammond, *Treatise on Insanity in its Medical Relations* (New York: D. Appleton and Company, 1883): p. 114.

35. Ibid., p. 105.

36. See, e.g., T. W. Fisher, *Plain Talk About Insanity: Its Causes, Forms, Symptoms and the Treatment of Mental Disease, with Remarks on Hospitals and Asylums, and the Medico-Legal Aspect of Insanity* (Boston: Alexander Moore, 1872), pp. 23-24.

37. *CLN* 1 (November 21, 1868): 60, col. 1-2.

38. The following account of Mrs. Packard's confinement is taken from Packard, *Modern Persecution,* Volumes 1 and 2.

39. Packard, Vol. 1, p. 95.

40. Ibid., pp. 99-100.

41. Ibid., p. 353.

42. Ibid., Vol. 2, p. 72.

43. Ibid., Vol. 2, pp. 210-211.

44. *CLN* 1 (November 21, 1868): 60, col. 1-2.

45. Ibid.

46. *CLN* 11 (May 24, 1879): 291, col. 4.
47. *CLN* 11 (May 3, 1879): 267, col. 3–4.
48. Ibid.
49. Ibid.
50. Ibid.
51. *CLN* 17 (February 28, 1885): 212, col. 4.
52. *CLN* 25 (September 3, 1892): 5, col. 1–2.

Epilogue

In commemorating Justice Thurgood's Marshall's retirement from the United States Supreme Court, columnist Anthony Lewis recently wrote:

> Thurgood Marshall stands for the possibility of change by law. He gave those without power, white as well as black, reason to hope that the system could care for them. In a country still riven by antagonism of race and economic inequality, that is not a small thing.[1]

And so it was with Myra Bradwell, who, a century ago, pioneered the possibility, as well as the reality, of change in the political, social, and legal status of women.

One need only recall that in denying Myra the right to practice law in 1869, the Illinois Supreme Court buttressed its decision by speculating that if it opened the doors of the legal profession to women, then "every civil office in this state may be filled by women—that it . . . [would follow] that women should be made governors and sheriffs."[2] Today, not only have many females been "made governors and sheriffs," but also six women are sitting in the United States Senate and an additional forty-seven are serving in the House of Representatives.[3]

Moreover, Myra's tortuous legal saga continues to have an impact on our contemporary legal system. In 1982, more than a century after the Supreme Court's exclusion of Myra from the practice of law, Justice Sandra Day O'Connor —also a "first"—used Myra's case to demonstrate the absurdity of governmental interference with career choices merely because of the gender of the applicant. That case involved a man named Joe Hogan,[4] who wished to gain admission to a University of Mississippi nursing program that was open only to women. In striking down Mississippi's "for-women-only" policy, Justice O'Connor decried sex-role stereotyping by recalling Myra's struggle:

> History provides numerous example[s] of legislative attempts to exclude women from particular areas simply because the legislators believed women were less able than men to perform a particular function. In 1872 [sic] *this court remained unmoved by Myra Bradwell's argument that the Fourteenth Amendment prohibited a State from classifying her as unfit to practice law simply because she was a female. . . .*[5] (Emphasis added)

In 1989 *Time* magazine opened its "Law" section with the following:

> What brass! *When she had the nerve to try to become a practicing attorney, Myra Bradwell was rebuked by no less a body than the U.S. Supreme Court.* "The natural and proper timidity and delicacy which belongs to the female sex evidently unfits it for many of the occupations of civil life," wrote Justice Joseph Bradley in an 1873 opinion. A century later, the unseemly became ordinary as women, riding a new wave of feminism, swept through the nation's law schools. In the U.S. today, more than 40% of law students and 20% of lawyers are women. As their numbers have swelled, so has their influence."[6] (Emphasis added)

Both Justice O'Connor's opinion in the *Hogan* case and the article in *Time* are evidence of the fact that Myra Bradwell's indomitable spirit is still alive, grinning at us like the disembodied smile of a Cheshire cat.

NOTES

1. Anthony Lewis, "Mr. Justice Marshall," *New York Times* (July 1, 1991): A-11, col. 1–3.
2. *In re Bradwell,* 55 Ill. 535 (1869).
3. *Facts on File* 52, no. 2711 (November 5, 1992): 825, 835.
4. *Mississippi University for Women* v. *Hogan,* 458 U.S. 718 (1982).
5. Ibid.
6. *Time* (April 17, 1989): 51.

Index